KB055023

한국 인권문제

시민적 · 정치적 권리 국제규약 인권보고서 1

한국 인권문제

시민적 · 정치적 권리 국제규약 인권보고서 1

한국학술정보

| 머리말

　일제 강점기 독립운동과 병행되었던 한국의 인권운동은 해방이 되었음에도 큰 결실을 보지 못했다. 1950년대 반공을 앞세운 이승만 정부와 한국전쟁, 역시 경제발전과 반공을 내세우다 유신 체제에 이르렀던 박정희 정권, 쿠데타로 집권한 1980년대 전두환 정권까지, 한국의 인권은 이를 보장해야 할 국가와 정부에 의해 도리어 억압받고 침해되었다. 이런 배경상 근대 한국의 인권운동은 반독재, 민주화운동과 결을 같이했고, 대체로 국외에 본부를 둔 인권 단체나 정치로부터 상대적으로 자유로운 종교 단체에 의해 주도되곤 했다. 이는 1980년 5·18광주민주화운동을 계기로 보다 근적인 변혁을 요구하는 형태로 조직화되었고, 그 활동 영역도 정치를 넘어 노동자, 농민, 빈민 등으로 확대되었다. 이들이 없었다면 한국은 1987년 군부 독재 종식하고 절차적 민주주의를 도입할 수 없었을 것이다. 민주화 이후에도 수많은 어려움이 있었지만, 한국의 인권운동은 점차 전문적이고 독립된 운동으로 분화되며 더 많은 이들의 참여를 이끌어냈고, 지금까지 많은 결실을 맺을 수 있었다.

　본 총서는 1980년대 중반부터 1990년대 초반까지, 외교부에서 작성하여 30여 년간 유지했던 한국 인권문제와 관련한 국내외 자료를 담고 있다. 6월 항쟁이 일어나고 민주화 선언이 이뤄지는 등 한국 인권운동에 많은 변화가 있었던 시기다. 당시 인권문제와 관련한 국내외 사안들, 각종 사건에 대한 미국과 우방국, 유엔의 반응, 최초의 한국 인권보고서 제출과 아동의 권리에 관한 협약 과정, 유엔인권위원회 활동, 기타 민주화 관련 자료 등 총 18권으로 구성되었다. 전체 분량은 약 9천여 쪽에 이른다.

2024년 3월

한국학술정보(주)

┃ 일러두기

· 본 총서에 실린 자료는 2022년 4월과 2023년 4월에 각각 공개한 외교문서 4,827권, 76만 여 쪽 가운데 일부를 발췌한 것이다.

· 각 권의 제목과 순서는 공개된 원본을 최대한 반영하였으나, 주제에 따라 일부는 적절히 변경하였다.

· 원본 자료는 A4 판형에 맞게 축소하거나 원본 비율을 유지한 채 A4 페이지 안에 삽입 하였다. 또한 현재 시점에선 공개되지 않아 '공란'이란 표기만 있는 페이지 역시 그대로 실었다.

· 외교부가 공개한 문서 각 권의 첫 페이지에는 '정리 보존 문서 목록'이란 이름으로 기록물 종류, 일자, 명칭, 간단한 내용 등의 정보가 수록되어 있으며, 이를 기준으로 0001번부터 번호가 매겨져 있다. 이는 삭제하지 않고 총서에 그대로 수록하였다.

· 보고서 내용에 관한 더 자세한 정보가 필요하다면, 외교부가 온라인상에 제공하는 『대한 민국 외교사료요약집』 1991년과 1992년 자료를 참조할 수 있다.

| 차례

정 리 보 존 문 서 목 록

기록물종류	일반공문서철	등록번호	2020020015	등록일자	2020-02-04
분류번호	734.23	국가코드		보존기간	영구
명 칭	시민적.정치적 권리에 관한 국제규약(B규약) 한국 최초 인권보고서 제출 및 심의, 1991-92. 전5권				
생 산 과	국제연합2과	생산년도	1991~1992	담당그룹	
권 차 명	V.1 1991.1-6월				
내용목차	＊ 아국 인권보고서 작성 검토 - 각부처 작성(11개 관련부처), 법무부 종합, 외무부 번역 - 1990.7월 우리나라가 국제인권규약(A/B) 에 가입함에 따라 B규약 가입국은 1년 이내 최초 보고서를 제출하도록 규정				

0001

國際人權規約報告書　作成計劃

1991. 1.

法　務　部

0002

1. 目　的

○ 規約 가입에 따른 人權狀況報告書 제출의무의 이행

- A規約（生存．福祉權） ： ９２．６．３０한
- B規約（自由．參政權） ： ９１．７． ９한

○ B規約 報告書 작성, 제출

2. 基本方針

가. 記述方法

○ 法秩序 확립과 人權伸張을 위한 정부의 확고한 意志와 努力을 이해할 수 있도록 記述

○ 外國人의 시각에서 보더라도 우리의 人權實狀을 올바르게 파악하여 정부의 입장에 共感할 수 있도록 설득력 있는 論理 전개

나. 作成時期

○ 人權保障意志를 대외적으로 홍보하기 위해 기한내 제출이 중요하므로 關係部處간 긴밀한 협의하에 조속 추진

（단, 國家保安法 등 主要 人權關聯法令의 改正日程과도 연계검토 필요）

○ 별첨 ： 각 국가별 人權規約報告書 제출시점별 분류

＊報告書 제출시한을 이행한 국가는 그리 많지 않음.

1

3. 收錄內容

　가. 一般的　事項

　　　ο 當事國내에서　　B規約상　權利가　보장되는　일반적　法律
　　　　體系에　대한　설명을　記述

　　　　　－　規約상　權利의　憲法　등에의　規定여부
　　　　　－　規約　條項과　國內法과의　관계
　　　　　－　人權問題의　관할부처
　　　　　－　人權侵害를　주장하는　個人이　취할　수　있는　措置
　　　　　－　規約상의　諸規定　履行保障을　위한　국가의　措置

　나. 個別的　事項

　　　ο 人權規約의　각　조항（２７개조항）에　관련된　사항을　記述

　　　　　－　개별적　權利의　시행에　따른　司法. 行政的　措置
　　　　　－　法令, 慣行으로　취해지고　있는　制限措置
　　　　　－　人權伸張을　위하여　취한　措置에　관한　사항

　다. 기　타

　　　ο 人權保障에　관한　關聯法令條項　등（영문본）　첨부

2

4. 報告書 작성 관계부처 協議會 설치

　가. "人權擁護政策協議會"에서 基本政策 결정

　　　❉ 人權擁護政策協議會

　　　－ 司正首席, 行政首席, 政策調査補佐官, 外交安保補佐官,
　　　　總理 行調室長, 法務·內務·外務·公報處 次官,
　　　　安企部 特補

　　　　人權規約報告書 작성에 따른 기본방향 수립, 報告書
　　　　내용 확정

　나. "報告書 작성 實務會議"에서 報告書 내용 심의

　　　－ 기히 운영중인 "人權問題實務協議會"를 적절히 운용

　　　－ 參席範圍 : 青瓦台　　法律秘書官, 政策調査秘書官,
　　　　　　　　　　　　　　　外交安保秘書官
　　　　　　　　　總理室　　外交安保審議官
　　　　　　　　　外務部　　國際機構條約局長, 國際聯合課長
　　　　　　　　　法務部　　人權課長
　　　　　　　　　公報處　　公報政策室 第2企劃官,
　　　　　　　　　　　　　　　海外公報官 企劃部長
　　　　　　　　　治安本部　搜査部長
　　　　　　　　　教育部　　教職局長
　　　　　　　　　勞動部　　勞政局長
　　　　　　　　　安企部　　第3特補室

3

－ 任　　務 : 편집방향, 요강 등 政策的 事項 결정 및
　　　　　　　報告書 내용 심의,　　人權擁護政策協議會에
　　　　　　　보고

다. "人權規約報告書 작성 작업반"에서 報告書 작성

－ 法務部 人權課 주관하에 유관부처 實務課長級 중심의
　作業班 편성, 운영 (기히 설치된 "關係部處 人權擔當官
　會議"를 적절히 운용)

－ 委員 : 外務部 國際聯合課長, 法務部 人權課長및 檢事,
　　　　　統一院, 公報處, 治安本部, 國防部, 敎育部, 文化
　　　　　部, 勞動部, 法制處의 擔當課長

－ 任　務 : 人權規約 내용중 소관부처 해당사항에 관한
　　　　　　資料蒐集 및 執筆, 報告書에 첨부될 所管法令
　　　　　　영문본의 정비 등

－ 運營 : 수시 會議開催, 問題点 등 협의

라. 推進日程 (기한내 제출을 전제로 함)

ㅇ 報告書 작성에 관한 협의 : 1월중

ㅇ 報告書 작성 : 1－3월 (유관부처)

－ 각 部處別 作成資料를 3월말까지 法務部 人權課로
　송부

－ 法務部에서 취합, 5월초순 外務部 송부

4

0006

ㅇ 報告書 영문번역 : 5-6월중순 (外務部)

ㅇ 最終檢討 및 提出 : 6-7월초

5. 參考資料

첨부1) 日本의 人權規約報告書 작성결과

첨부2) 各國의 人權規約報告書 제출시기

5

0007

(별첨 1)

```
┌─────────────────────────────────────────────┐
│        日本의  國際人權規約  報告書  作成經過          │
└─────────────────────────────────────────────┘
```

1. 確認經緯

   ○ 日本에 연수 또는 派遣勤務중인 檢事 등에 의뢰하여 확인
   ○ 日辯連의 人權심포지엄 기록 책자

2. 日本의 가입경과

   ○ 77년 署名, 78년 批准 (A，B規約)
   ○ B規約 選擇條項，選擇議政書는 미가입

3. 人權報告書 제출 (B規約)

   ○ 1차 ─ 1980. 10.
   ○ 2차 ─ 1987. 12.

4. 作成經過 (2차 報告書)

   ○ 法務省 각 室·局별로 해당부분의 草案을 작성하여 官房
     秘書課에서 취합 ─〉 外務省

   ○ 外務省에 파견된 檢事 2명 (海外駐在 法務官 요원은 아님)
     이 전담하여 最終案 작성 ─〉 關係部處會議를 거쳐 확정

   ○ UN人權理事會 축조심의시 (1988. 7. 20~23) 10
     명의 外交官，檢事가 出席·答辯

7

0008

Status of the Submission of Initial Report

by States Parties under Article 40

of the International Convenant on Civil and Political Rights

as of 15 November 1990.

State Party	Date of entry into force	Date of Submission
o Afghanistan	24 April 1983	2 April 1984
Algeria	12 December 1989	-
Argentina	8 November 1986	11 April 1989
o Australia	13 November 1980	11 November 1981
Austria	10 December 1978	10 April 1981
Barbados	23 March 1976	24 October 1978
Belgium	21 July 1983	15 December 1987
Bolivia	12 November 1982	26 October 1988
Bulgaria	23 March 1976	27 June 1978
Burundi	9 August 1990	-
Byelorussian Soviet Socialist Republic	23 March 1976	9 June 1978
Cameroon	27 September 1984	11 August 1988
Canada	19 August 1976	18 April 1979
Central African Republic	8 August 1981	28 October 1987

0009

8

State Party	Date of entry into force	Date of Submission
Chile	23 March 1976	5 August 1977
Colombia	23 March 1976	14 November 1979
Congo	5 January 1984	12 February 1986
Costa Rica	23 March 1976	14 August 1979
o Cyprus	23 March 1976	23 March 1977
Czechoslovakia	23 March 1976	17 June 1977
Democratic People's Republic of Korea	14 December 1981	1) 23 October 1983 2) 2 April 1984
Democratic Yemen	9 May 1987	13 January 1989
o Denmark	23 March 1976	21 March 1977
Dominican Republic	4 April 1978	18 July 1984
Ecuador	23 March 1976	31 March 1977
Egypt	14 April 1982	8 March 1984
El Salvador	29 February 1980	2 June 1983
Equatorial Guinea	25 December 1987	not yet received
Finland	23 March 1976	6 April 1977
France	4 February 1981	3 May 1982
Gabon	21 April 1983	not yet received
Gambia	22 June 1979	3 June 1984
German Democratic Republic	23 March 1976	28 June 1977
Germany, Federal Republic of	23 March 1976	25 November 1977

0010

State Party	Date of entry into force	Date of Submission
Guinea	24 April 1978	19 August 1980
Guyana	15 May 1977	20 March 1981
Hungary	23 March 1976	16 May 1977
Iceland	22 November 1979	31 March 1981
India	10 July 1979	4 July 1983
Iran(Islamic Republic of)	23 March 1976	21 April 1982
Iraq	23 March 1976	5 June 1979
Ireland	8 March 1990	-
Italy	15 December 1978	26 February 1980
Jamaica	23 March 1976	12 September 1980
Japan	21 September 1979	24 October 1980
Jordan	23 March 1976	7 July 1981
Kenya	23 March 1976	15 August 1979
Lebanon	23 March 1976	6 April 1983
o Libyan Arab Jamahiriya	23 March 1976	4 March 1977
Luxembourg	18 November 1983	1 July 1985
Madagascar	23 March 1976	16 July 1977
Mali	23 March 1976	14 August 1979
Malta	13 December 1990	-
o Mauritius	23 March 1976	24 January 1977
o Mexico	23 June 1981	19 March 1982

State Party	Date of entry into force	Date of Submission
Mongolia	23 March 1976	20 December 1978
Morocco	3 August 1979	9 February 1981
Netherlands	11 March 1979	11 February 1981
New Zealand	28 March 1979	11 January 1982
Nicaragua	12 June 1980	12 March 1982
Niger	7 June 1986	not yet received
o Norway	23 March 1976	22 March 1977
Panama	8 June 1977	20 July 1984
o Peru	28 July 1978	2 July 1979
Philippines	23 January 1987	22 March 1988
Poland	18 June 1977	23 March 1979
Portugal	15 September 1978	29 September 1980
Republic of Korea	10 July 1990	-
Romania	23 March 1976	29 July 1978
Rwanda	23 March 1976	20 January 1981
Saint Vincent and the Grenadines	9 February 1982	31 December 1989
San Marino	18 January 1986	14 September 1988
Senegal	13 May 1978	8 August 1979
Somalia	24 April 1990	-
Spain	27 July 1977	1 September 1978
Sri Lanka	11 September 1980	23 March 1983

11

0012

State Party	Date of entry into force	Date of Submission
Sudan	18 June 1986	not yet received
Suriname	28 March 1977	1 May 1979
o Sweden	23 March 1976	21 March 1977
Syrian Arab Republic	23 March 1976	28 June 1977
Togo	24 August 1984	22 September 1988
Trinidad and Tobago	21 March 1979	23 March 1984
Tunisia	23 March 1976	30 March 1977
Ukrainian Soviet Socialist Republic	23 March 1976	31 August 1978
Union of Soviet Socialist Republics	23 March 1976	30 January 1978
o United Kingdom of Great Britain and Northern Ireland	20 August 1976	18 August 1977
United Republic of Tanzania	11 September 1976	20 August 1979
Uruguay	23 March 1976	29 January 1982
Venezuela	10 August 1978	5 November 1979
Viet Nam	24 December 1982	7 July 1989
Yugoslavia	23 March 1976	28 February 1978
Zaire	1 February 1977	4 February 1987
Zambia	10 July 1984	24 June 1987

12

인권규약 제40조에 의한 규약당사국 보고서 작성지침

1. PART I : 일반적 사항

O 본 부분에서는 규약당사국 내에서 시민적, 정치적 권리가 보호되도록
   보장하는 일반적 법률체계에 대한 설명을 기술함
   특히 하기내용을 포함해야 함

   a) 규약에서 언급되고 있는 개개의 권리들이 헌법에서 또는 별도의
      "권리장전 (Bill of Right)"에서 보호받도록 규정되어 있는지
      여부와 또한 동 권리의 침해시에 대비하여 헌법 또는 권리장전에
      여하한 규정이 기술되어 있는지 그 내용

   b) 인권규약의 규정들이 재판소, 사법기관, 행정기관에 의해 직접
      원용되고 강행될 수 있는지 또는 규약이 관계기관에 의하여 집행
      되기 위하여는 국내법 또는 행정규정으로서의 전환 과정을 거쳐야
      하는지 여부

   c) 인권문제의 관할부처 (사법, 행정, 기타기관 등)는 어떠한 기관이
      있는가?

   d) 인권침해를 주장하는 개인이 취할 수 있는 조치는?

   e) 인권규약의 제규정의 이행보장을 위해 국가가 취한 조치는?

0014

2. PART II : 인권규약 I. II. III 의 각 조항에 관련된 사항

○ 본 부분에는 인권규약의 각 조항과 관련하여 기술하여야 함

    a) 각각의 권리와 관련, 시행되고 있는 사법적, 행정적 또는 기타 조치들

    b) 인권에 대하여 법령 또는 관행으로서 취해지고 있는 제한조치 (한시적인 조치 포함)

    c) 국가의 관할하에 있는 개인의 권리 향유에 영향을 미치는 요인 또는 문제점 등

    d) 인권신장을 위하여 취해진 조치에 관한 사항

*. 보고서에는 관련 법령 등의 사본이 첨부되어야 함.
관련법령 등을 첨부하지 않을 경우에는 동 관련 법령을 참조치 않아도 이해될 수 있도록 보고서가 상세히 작성되어야 함

*. 인권이사회는 규약당사국의 최근 인권상황의 검토를 위하여 규약 제40조 (1) (b)의 규정에 따라 추가보고서 제출을 요청할 수 있음

0015

국제인권규약보고서 B규약 내용 작성에 따른 소관부처

규 약 규 정	국 내 법 규 정	소 관 부 처
전문 각국의 기본권 존중과 준수를 촉진시킬 의무	헌법전문 (자유민주적 기본질서 확립) 헌법 제10조 (국가의 기본권 보장의무) 헌법 제10-39조 (기본권 규정)	법무부 (법무심의관실)
제1조 자결권 및 자원처분권		법무부 (국제법무심의관실)
제2조 1. 어떠한 종류의 차별도 없는 권리의 평등한 행사보장	헌법 제11조 (평등권) 헌법 제20조 (종교의 자유) 헌법 제31조, 교육법 제9조 (교육의 기회균등) 교육법 제5조 후단 (국.공립학교 종교교육 금지) 헌법 제24조 (선거권)	법무부 (법무심의관실) 내무부,교육부, 노동부,문화부

1

0016

규 약 규 정	국 내 법 규 정	소 관 부 처
	국가공무원법 제35조 (평등의 원칙)	
	가사소송법 제1조 (남녀평등)	
	헌법 제36조 1항 (혼인과 양성의 평등)	
	근로기준법 제5조 (균등처우)	
	지방자치법 제6조 (공공시설의 이용에 있어서의 평등)	
	노동조합법 제11조, 선원법 제32조 (근로관계에 있어서의 평등)	
2. 규약상 권리보장을 위한 각국의 입법의무	헌법 제10조 및 기본권 관련 규정(국가의 기본권 보장의무)	법무부 (법무심의관실)
3. 규약상 권리와 자유침해시 구제	헌법 제29조 (공무원의 불법 행위에 대한 배상) 국가배상법 제2조, 행정소송법 제1조 (국가,공공단체의 배상 또는 보상책임)	법무부 (송무심의관실)

2

0017

규 약 규 정	국 내 법 규 정	소 관 부 처
제3조 남녀평등권의 확보	헌법 제11조 (평등권) 헌법 제24조, 제25조 (선거권, 공무담임권) 헌법 제31조(교육의 기회균등) 헌법 제36조 1항(혼인과 양성 의 평등) 민법 제777조 (친족의 범위) 민법 제809조 (동성혼 등의 금지) 민법 제778조 내지 제799조 (호주제도) 민법 제773조 (계모자 관계) 민법 제774조 (혼인외 출생자 와 그 친계) 민법 제909조 (친권의 행사) 국적법 제2조 제1항 (부계 혈통주의) 국적법 제3조 제1호 (처의 국적취득) 국적법 제6조 제2호 (배우자의 귀화요건)	법무부 (법무심의관실, 법무과) 교육부, 노동부

규 약 규 정	국 내 법 규 정	소 관 부 처
	가사소송법 제1조(남녀평등) 근로기준법 제5조(균등처우) 노동조합법 제11조, 선원법 제 32조(근로관계에 있어서의 평등)	
제4조 1. 비상사태시의 인권제한	헌법 제77조(계엄) 헌법 제37조 2항(국가안보와 기본권제한) 헌법 제27조(군법회의) 헌법 제109조(재판공개의 예외) 계엄법 제7-10조(계엄사령관의 권한) 헌법 제77조(대통령의 계엄선포 및 국회의 계엄해제요구) 헌법 제10조(국가의 기본권 보장 의무)	법무부 (법무심의관실, 검찰국), 국방부, 문화부
2. 규약 제6조(자의적 사형 금지), 제7조(고문의 금지), 제8조(노예제도 금지), 제11조(계약이행 불능으로 인한 구금금지 제15조(형벌 불소급의 원칙), 제16조(법률상	헌법 제37조 2항(기본권 제한의 한계) 형법 제87조, 제92조, 제250조, 국가보안법 제4조(내란,외환, 살인 등 중대한 범죄에 한하여 사형), 헌법 제12조 2항 (고문의 금지), 형사소송법 제309조	

4

규 약 규 정	국 내 법 규 정	소 관 부 처
인격 인정), 제18조 사상,양심,종교의 자유에 대한 어떠한 위반도 불가	(강제 등 자백의 증거능력) 헌법 제13조(형벌불소급, 일사부재리, 소급입법의 제한) 형법 제1조(형벌불소급의 원칙) 헌법 제12조 1항 (형의 선고에 의하지 않는 강제노역 금지) 헌법 제11조 (국민의 평등 및 특수계급제도 부인) 헌법 제19조, 제20조 (양심. 종교의 자유) 헌법 제11조 1항 (종교로 인한 차별대우 금지)	
3. 타체약당사국에 대한 비상조치 즉시 통보의무		
제5조 1. 규약의 부당해석의 금지 2. 규약에 인정되지 아니한 이유로 인한 기본권의 경시 금지	헌법 제37조 1항 (헌법에 열거되지 아니한 이유로 인한 국민의 자유와 권리의 경시금지)	법무부 (법무심의관실)
제6조 1. 생명권 및 자의적 사형 금지	형법 제87조, 제92조, 제250조, 국가보안법 제4조 (내란,외환,	법무부 (법무심의관실, 검찰국,교정국 보호국)

5

규 약 규 정	국 내 법 규 정	소 관 부 처
	살인 등 중대범죄에 한하여 사형)	
2. 중대한 범죄에 대하여 권한있는 법원의 최종 판결에 의해서만 사형 집행	헌법 제27조 (법률에 정한 법관 에 의해서 재판을 받을 권리) 헌법 제13조, 형법 제1조 (형법 의 불소급 적용)	
3. 집단학살 금지		
4. 사형수의 사면 또는 감형 청구권	헌법 제79조, 사면법 제2,3,5,8조 형사소송법 제326조 (대통령의 사면권), 제465조 1항 (사형집행 명령의 시기), 제428조 (재심과 집행정지)	
5. 18세 미만 연소자에 대 한 사형선고금지 및 임산부의 사형집행금지	소년법 제59조(18세미만 소년은 사형집행 대신 15년 징역), 형사소송법 제469조 (임산부의 사형집행 정지)	
6. 사형제도 폐지의 지연을 위한 원용금지		
제7조 고문의 금지 및 동의 없는 의학적 실험 금지	헌법 제12조 2항, 형법 제125조, 형사소송법 제309조 (고문의 금지)	법무부 (검찰국) 내무부

6

0021

규 약 규 정	국 내 법 규 정	소 관 부 처
제8조		법무부
1. 및 2. 노예제도 금지	헌법 제11조 1항 및 2항 (국민의 평등 및 특수 계급제도 부인)	(법무심의관실, 검찰국,보호국)
2. 강제노동 금지	헌법 제12조 1항, 형법 제70조, 사회보호법 제7조 (형의 선고 없는 강제노역 금지)	
제9조		법무부
1. 신체의 자유, 자의적인 체포.억류금지	헌법 제12조, 형사소송법 제70, 73,201,206,207,211,212조 (신체의 자유, 구속의 사유, 영장의 발부, 구속, 긴급구속, 현행범의 체포)	(검찰국)
	보안관찰법상의 보안관찰처분	내무부 국가안전기획부
2. 체포사실 및 혐의사실 통보	형사소송법 제72조 (구금과 범죄 사실의 고지)	
3. 신속한 재판, 미결수의 구금억제	헌법 제27조 (신속히 재판을 받을 권리) 형사소송법 제92,202,203조 (구속기간의 제한) 헌법 제12조 7항 (부당한 장기 구속시 진술의 증거능력 제한)	

7

0022

규 약 규 정	국 내 법 규 정	소 관 부 처
4. 구속적부심사	헌법 제12조 6항, 형사소송법 제214조의 2(구속적부심사)	
5. 형사보상	헌법 제28조, 형사소송법 제325조, 형사보상법	
제10조		법무부
1. 인신구속자에 대한 인도 적 대우	헌법 제12조, 형사소송법 제30, 72,87,88,90조 (죄형법정주의 및 변호인의 조력)	(검찰국,교정국 보호국)
	헌법 제12조 7항 (부당한 장기 구속시 진술의 증거능력 제한), 형사소송법 제72,266조 (구금과 범죄사실의 고지)	내무부
	형사소송법 제33,283,438조 (국선변호인 제도)	
	헌법 제27조 (재판 청구권 및 형사피고인의 무죄 추정)	
	행형법 제46조 2항9호(감식제도)	
2. 미결수와 기결수의 격리 수용	행형법 제2,3조 (미결수 및 만 20세 미만의 분리수용)	
3. 수감제도의 취지 및 미성년자에 대한 특별 대우	행형법 제1,31-34조 (수형자의 교정교화, 사회복귀)	
	행형법 제2,3조, 소년법 제1조, 소년원법 제1,8,23조(미성년의	

8

0023

규 약 규 정	국 내 법 규 정	소 관 부 처
	분리수용, 소년의 건전한 육성, 소년의 교육 및 직업보도)	
제11조 계약상 채무이행불능 의 경우 구금금지		법무부 (법무심의관실)
제12조		법무부
1. 거주이전의 자유	헌법 제14조 (거주이전의 자유)	(법무심의관실,
2. 자유출국	헌법 제14조 (거주이전의 자유)	출입국관리국) 국방부
3. 법률로 국가안보, 공공 질서, 공중보건, 공공 도덕 또는 타인의 권리, 자유보호를 위한 상기 1-2항 권리제한 가능	헌법 제37조 2항 (기본권의 제한 과 그 한계) 계엄법 제9조 1항 (거주이전의 자유의 제한) 출입국관리법 제4조(출국금지)	
4. 자국입국 권리의 자의적 박탈금지	헌법 제14조 (거주이전의 자유)	
제13조 법률에 의해서만 합법적 거주 외국인 의 추방 가능 추방된 외국인은 당국에 대리인을 통하여 이의 제기 가능	출입국관리법 제6장 (강제퇴거) 출입국관리법 제57조 (강제퇴거 에 대한 이의신청)	법무부 (출입국관리국)

9

규 약 규 정	국 내 법 규 정	소 관 부 처
제14조		법무부
1. 재판의 평등 법률에 의해서 설치된 독립.공평한 법원의 재판을 받을 권리	헌법 제11조 1항 (평등권) 헌법 제27조 (재판을 받을 권리) 헌법 제101조 3항, 104조, 법원조직법 제37조, 헌법 제105-106조, 헌법 제103조 등 (법관의 자격, 법관의 양심에 따른 재판을 받을 권리)	(법무심의관실, 검찰국,보호국)
공공질서 등을 이유로한 공개재판의 예외	헌법 제109조 (안전보장, 안녕질서, 또는 선량한 풍속을 해할 우려가 있을 경우 재판 비공개), 법원조직법 제57조 1항 단서 (재판의 비공개)	
2. 형사피고인의 무죄추정	헌법 제27조 4항, 형사소송법 제275조 2항 (형사피고인은 유죄의 판결이 확정될 때까지 무죄로 추정)	
3. 형사상 혐의를 판결함에 있어서 최소한도 다음의 보장을 받을 권리		
(a) 자신의 혐의에 관하여 즉시 상세하게 통보 받을 권리	형사소송법 제72, 266조 (구금과 범죄사실의 고지)	
(b) 자신의 변호준비를 위하여 충분한 시간과	헌법 제12조 4항 (변호인의 조력을 받을 권리)	

10

0025

규 약 규 정	국 내 법 규 정	소 관 부 처
편의를 갖는 것 또는 변호인과 연락을 취할 수 있는 권리	형사소송법 제34조 (피고인, 피의자와의 접견,교통,수진)	
(c) 신속한 재판을 받을 권리	헌법 제27조 3항 (신속한 재판을 받을 권리) 헌법 제12조 7항 (부당한 장기 구속의 경우 진술의 증거능력 제한)	
(d) 직접 출석하여 재판을 받고 자신이 선임한 변호인의 법적조력을 봉하여 자신을 변호하며, 비용부담능력이 없을 경우에도 변호인의 조력을 받을 권리	형사소송법 제30조 1항 (피고인 또는 피의자의 변호인 선임) 형사소송법 제276조 (피고인의 출석권) 형사소송법 제286조 (피고인의 진술권) 헌법 제12조 4항, 형사소송법 제33조 5항 (국선변호인)	
(e) 자신에게 불리한 증인 신문 및 유리한 증인 신문	형사소송법 제161조의 2, 162조, 163조, 164조 (증인신문의 방식, 개별신문과 대질, 당사자의 참여권, 신문권, 신문의 청구)	
(f) 법원에서 사용되는 언어를 이해하지 못할 경우 봉역의 무료조력	형사소송법 제180조, 법원조직법 제62조 2항 (봉역사용)	

11

0026

규 약 규 정	국 내 법 규 정	소 관 부 처
(g) 자기에게 불리한 진술 또는 유죄의 자백의 강요금지	형법 제12조 2항 (불리한 진술의 강요금지) 형사소송법 제310조, 289조	
4. 미성년자의 경우 그 판결절차상 연령 등 고려	소년법	
5. 상 소 권	헌법 제110조 제4항, 군사법원법 제534조, 형사소송법 제3편 (상소)	국방부
6. 새로운 사실입증으로 판결이 무죄로 변경되었을 때 보상을 받을 권리	헌법 제28조, 형사보상법 제1조 2항 (형사보상)	
7. 일사부재리의 원칙	헌법 제13조 1항, 형법 제7조, 형사소송법 제326, 327, 329조 (일사부재리의 원칙)	
제15조 1. 형벌불소급, 죄형법정주의	헌법 제13조 (형벌불소급의 원칙), 헌법 제12조 1항, 형법 제1조 (죄형법정주의)	법무부 (검찰국)
범죄인에게 경한 형벌 규정 적용	형법 제1조 2항(경한 법의 적용)	

12

0027

규 약 규 정	국 내 법 규 정	소 관 부 처
제16조 법앞에서 인간으로 서 인정받을 권리	헌법 제10조 (인간의 존엄과 가치)	법무부 (법무심의관실)

제17조
 1. 사생활, 가족, 가정,
   통신에 대한 자의적
   또는 불법적 간섭배제와
   명예에 대한 불법적
   침해 배제
	헌법 제10조 (행복추구권, 국가
	의 기본권 보장의무)
	헌법 제17조 (사생활의 비밀과
	침해방지)
	헌법 제18조 (통신의 비밀보장)
	헌법 제36조 1항 (혼인과 가족
	생활)
		법무부
		(법무심의관실,
		검찰국),
		공보처

2. 모든 사람은 상기 간섭
   또는 침해로부터 법의
   보호를 받을 권리
	헌법 제10조 (국가의 기본권
	보장의무)
	형법 제307-312조 (명예에 관한
	죄)
	형법 제316-318조 (비밀침해의
	죄)
	형법 제319-322조 (주거침입의
	죄)	

제18조 1. 사상·양심 및 종교의 자유	헌법 제19조 (양심의 자유) 헌법 제20조 (종교의 자유)	법무부 (법무심의관실) 문화부,교육부

13

규 약 규 정	국 내 법 규 정	소 관 부 처
2. 어떤 종교나 신념을 보유, 채택할 자유	상 동	
3. 상기 1-2항 자유는 공공 안전과 질서 등을 위하 여 필요불가결한 경우에 만 법률에 의한 제한 가능	헌법 제37조 2항 (기본권의 제한 및 그 한계)	
4. 부모의 자녀교육권	민법 제913조 (친권자의 자에 대한 보호, 교양의 권리, 의무) 교육법 제5조 2항	
제19조 1. 자기의견을 가질 권리	헌법 제21조 1항 (언론.출판의 자유)	법무부 (법무심의관실) 공보처,문화부 국방부
2. 표현의 자유	정기간행물의등록에관한법률 제 9조 1호, 공연법 제14조의 2, 영화법 제12조	
3. 상기 2항 권리의 행사제 한은 타인의 권리 또는 신용의 존중과 국가안보 등을 위하여 필요한 경 우에 법률에 의해서만 제한가능	헌법 제21조 4항 (언론.출판의 자유의 한계, 언론.출판에 의한 피해 보상) 헌법 제37조(기본권의 제한및 그 한계) 헌법 제77조 3항(비상계엄선포시 언론.출판의 자유 제한)	

규 약 규 정	국 내 법 규 정	소 관 부 처
제20조 1. 전쟁선전 금지 2. 차별, 적대, 폭력조장의 적개심 고취를 법률로 금지	헌법전문(평화애호의 전통) 헌법 제5조 1항(침략적 전쟁의 부인)	법무부 (법무심의관실)
제21조 평화적 집회권 인정 단, 국가안보 등 이유로 필요불사결 한 경우에만 법률로 제한 가능 제22조 1. 노조의 결성, 가입을 포함한 결사의 자유	헌법 제21조 1항(집회.결사의 자유), 집회 및 시위에 관한 법률 헌법 제37조 (기본권의 제한 및 그 한계) 출입국관리법 제16조 2항 헌법 제21조 1항 (집회.결사의 자유) 헌법 제33조 1항 (근로자의 단결권, 단체교섭권, 단체행동권) 노동조합법 권, 단체교섭권, 단체행동권) 노동조합법	법무부 (법무심의관실, 검찰국,출입국 관리국), 내무부 국방부 법무부(검찰국) 내무부,국방부, 노동부,교육부

15

0030

규 약 규 정	국 내 법 규 정	소 관 부 처
2. 국가안보 등을 위하여 필요한 경우에 법률에 의한 1항권리 제한 가능	헌법 제33조 2항 (공무원에 대한 노동3권 제한), 33조 3항 (주요 방위산업체 종사자에 대한 단체 행동권 제한), 제37조, 국가공무원법 제66조, 사립학교법 제55조 헌법 제77조 3항 (비상계엄선포시 집회.결사의 자유에 대한 특별조치), 계엄법	
3. ILO협약 당사국에 의한 규약의 불리한 해석 적용 불가		
제23조 1. 가정의 사회적. 국가적 보호	헌법 제36조 1항 (혼인과 가족 생활) 헌법 제10조 (행복추구권)	법무부 (법무심의관실) 보건사회부 정무제2장관실
2. 혼인적령 남녀의 결혼과 가정을 기초로 한 권리 인정	헌법 제36조 1항 (혼인과 가족 생활)	
3. 혼인은 당사자의 자유롭고 완전한 동의하에 성립	헌법 제36조 (혼인은 개인의 존엄과 양성의 평등에 기초) 민법 제800조 (성년에 달한 자는 자유로 약혼)	

규 약 규 정	국 내 법 규 정	소 관 부 처
4. 혼인중과 이혼시 양배우자의 동등한 권리와 책임의 평등을 확보하기 위한 적절한 조치를 취할 의무	헌법 제11조 1항 (평등권) 헌법 제36조 1항 (혼인과 양성의 평등)	
이혼시 자녀보호를 위한 필요한 조치	민법 제837조 1-2항 (이혼시 부모의 자녀양육 책임)	
제24조 1. 어린이에 대한 각종 차별금지, 미성년자로서 보호받을 권리	헌법 제32조 5항 (소년의 근로에 대한 특별보호), 근로기준법, 아동복지법 등	법무부 (법무심의관실, 법무과) 노동부, 보사부 교육부
2. 모든 어린이는 출생즉시 등록되고 이름을 가짐	호적법	
3. 모든 어린이의 국적취득	국적법	
제25조 차별과 비합리적인 제한없이 다음 권리 향유		법무부 (법무심의관실) 내무부
(a) 직접 또는 자유선출한 대표자를 통하여 정치에 참여	헌법의 참정권 규정 (제24조, 25조, 67조, 41조 등)	

17

0032

규 약 규 정	국 내 법 규 정	소 관 부 서
(b) 보통·평등선거 및 자유·비밀투표권에 의한 투표 및 이에 의한 피선	상 동	
(c) 공무취임권	헌법 제25조 (공무담임권)	
제26조 모든 사람은 법앞에 평등, 차별금지 및 이의 법률적 보장	헌법 제11조 1항 (평등권)	법무부 (법무심의관실) 노동부, 교육부
제27조 종족적·종교적·언어적 소수민족의 문화 종교, 언어 사용권 인정	헌법 제11조 1항 (평등권)	법무부 (법무심의관실) 문화부

발 신 전 보

분류번호	보존기간

번   호 : WGV-OO31   910108 1715 CG 종별 :

수   신 : 주   제네바   ~~박사. 송영촥~~//////   (김종훈 서기관님)
(유연과 송영환 배)

발   신 : 장   관

제   목 :   업   연

　　　　법무부에서 업무 참고자료로 번역.출판코자 한다 하는 바, 일본의
인권규약 B규약 2차보고서(85년) 전문 및 인권이사회 심의기록과 북한의
B규약 최초보고서 (82년)를 파편 송부 부탁드림.　　　　끝 .
　　　　　및 인권이사회 심의기록을

보안통제	(서명)

앙고재	91년1월8일	기안자성명		과 장	국 장	차 관	장 관	(서명)
		UN과 송영환						

외신과통제
(서명)

0034

長官 報告事項

報告畢

1991. 1. 14.

國際機構條約局
國際聯合課 (1)

題目 : 我國 人權報告書 作成

90.7.10. 人權規約 加入에 따라 我國은 人權報告書를 91.7.9.한
提出해야 하는 바, 同 報告書 作成과 關聯하여 아래 報告드립니다.

1. 人權規約(B규약) 報告書 提出 時限

° 最初 報告書는 人權規約 加入後 1年이내에 提出, 2次 報告書 以後는
每 5年마다 提出함. 但, 人權理事會는 追加 報告書를 提出토록 要求할
수 있음.

2. 報告書 作成 要領

가) 報告書 構成

1) Part Ⅰ(一般的 事項) : 市民的, 政治的 權利가 保護되도록 保障
하는 一般的 法律體系에 대한 說明 記述

2) Part Ⅱ(人權規約 各 條項關聯 事項) : 人權規約 各 條項의 權利와
관련 施行되고 있는 司法的, 行政的 또는 其他 措置를 記述

법규과장 :

공람	담 당	과 장	국 장	차 관 보	차 관	장 관

0035

3) Annex ： 人權保障에 관한 關聯 國內 法令等의 條項이 添附되어야 함.

4) 분 량 ： 通常 30페이지 내외로 作成

3. 報告書 作成關聯 考慮事項

가. 法令을 根據로 한 報告書

ㅇ 人權規約에 따른 報告書는 他 人權關聯 說明資料와는 달리 政治的.
文化的 說明을 排除하고 순수히 法令에 根據한 人權保護裝置를 記述
하여야 함.

나. 包括的 人權保障制度 提示

ㅇ 人權規約(B규약)은 市民的.政治的 權利에 관하여 包括的으로 規定
하고 있으므로 法務部, 勞動部, 內務部等 關聯部處의 參與가 필수적임.

다. 關係法令 英文本 整備

ㅇ 國內法令을 根據로 하여 我國의 人權狀況을 說明하여야 하므로 同
報告書에 附錄으로 添附될 各種 法令의 正確한 英譯은 매우 重要함.
따라서 報告書 作成과 더불어 關係法令의 英文本의 整備도 필수적인
作業임.

라. 報告書 時限問題

ㅇ 我國의 人權保障 意志를 闡明한다는 側面에서 可及的 時限을 지키도록
함.(단, 國家保安法等 主要 法令이 發展的으로 整備될 計劃이 있을시
예외로 함)

＊ 報告書 提出時限 (인권규약 가입후 1년)내에 報告書를 提出한 國家는
그리 많지 않음.(人權規約 報告書 제출 시점별 분류 : 별첨1)

0036

4. 向後 推進對策

o   報告書가 순수히 法律的 考慮下에 作成되어야 함을 감안, 法務部에
    關聯部處 該當資料를 취합, 報告書(국문)를 作成토록 의뢰함.
    - 但, 報告書에 添附될 關係法令의 英語本은 關聯部處의 檢討를 거쳐
      法務部가 綜合함.

o   上記 國文資料를 바탕으로 하여 英文飜譯後 關係部處와 最終 檢討後
    提出

o   報告書 作成 日程案 (기한내 제출시)
    - 報告書 作成에 관한 協議 : 1월중 (관련부처)
    - 報告書 作成   : 1-4월중순 (법무부, 관련부처)
    - 報告書 英文飜譯   : 4월-6월중순 (외무부)
    - 最終 檢討 및 提出   : 6월-7월초

添 附 : 各國의 人權報告書 提出時期

                                            - 끝 -

(첨 부)

各國의 人權報告書 提出時期

시 한	국 가 수	주 요 국 명
시한내 제출	13개국	호주, 덴마크, 에쿠아돌, 리비아, 맥시코, 놀웨이, 페루, 스웨덴, 튀니지, 영국등
시한 6개월 초과	13개국	일본, 필리핀, 칠레, 베네주엘라, 핀랜드, 프랑스, 독일, 헝가리, 스페인, 세네갈등
6개월이상 초과	67개국	북한, 인도, 뉴질랜드, 알젠틴, 카나다, 벨기에, 덴마크, 서독, 이태리, 화란, 폴투갈, 폴랜드, 소련, 이집트, 가봉, 자이르 등
계	93개국	

* 북한은 81.12.14. 인권규약 가입후 2년만인 83.10.23. 최초 보고서를
   제출하였고, 84.4.2. 보고서 추가분을 제출함.

0038

長官報告事項

題目 : 我國 人權報告書 作成

> 90.7.10. 人權規約 加入에 따라 我國은 人權報告書를 91.7.9.한
> 提出해야 하는 바, 同 報告書 作成과 關聯하여 아래 報告드립니다.

1. 人權規約(B규약) 報告書 提出 時限

º 最初 報告書는 人權規約 加入後 1年이내에 提出, 2次 報告書 以後는
　毎 5年마다 提出함. 但, 人權理事會는 追加 報告書를 提出토록 要求할
　수 있음.

2. 報告書 作成 要領

가) 報告書 構成

1) Part Ⅰ (一般的 事項) : 市民的, 政治的 權利가 保護되도록 保障
　　　　　　　　　하는 一般的 法律體系에 대한 說明 記述

2) Part Ⅱ (人權規約 各 條項關聯 事項) : 人權規約 各 條項의 權利와
　　　　　　　　　관련 施行되고 있는 司法的, 行政的 또는 其他 措置를 記述

3) Annex : 人權保障에 관한 關聯 國內 法令等의 條項이 添附되어야 함.

4) 분 량 : 通常 30페이지 내외로 作成

0039

3. 報告書 作成關聯 考慮事項

가. 法令을 根據로 한 報告書

ㅇ 人權規約에 따른 報告書는 他 人權關聯 說明資料와는 달리 政治的. 文化的 說明을 排除하고 순수히 法令에 根據한 人權保護裝置를 記述 하여야 함.

나. 包括的 人權保障制度 提示

ㅇ 人權規約(B규약)은 市民的.政治的 權利에 관하여 包括的으로 規定 하고 있으므로 法務部, 勞動部, 內務部等 關聯部處의 參與가 필수적임.

다. 關係法令 英文本 整備

ㅇ 國內法令을 根據로 하여 我國의 人權狀況을 說明하여야 하므로 同 報告書에 附錄으로 添附될 各種 法令의 正確한 英譯은 매우 重要함. 따라서 報告書 作成과 더불어 關係法令의 英文本의 整備도 필수적인 作業임.

라. 報告書 時限問題

ㅇ 我國의 人權保障 意志를 闡明한다는 側面에서 可及的 時限을 지키도록 함.(단, 國家保安法等 主要 法令이 發展的으로 整備될 計劃이 있을시 예외로 함)

* 報告書 提出時限(인권규약 가입후 1년)내에 報告書를 提出한 國家는 그리 많지 않음.(人權規約 報告書 제출 시점별 분류 : 별첨1)

4. 向後 推進對策

ㅇ 報告書가 순수히 法律的 考慮下에 作成되어야 함을 감안, 法務部에 關聯部處 該當資料를 취합, 報告書(국문)를 作成토록 의뢰함.

- 但, 報告書에 添附될 關係法令의 英語本은 關聯部處의 檢討를 거쳐 法務部가 綜合함.

0040

ㅇ 上記 國文資料를 바탕으로 하여 英文飜譯後 關係部處와 最終 檢討後
　提出

ㅇ 報告書 作成 日程案 (기한내 제출시)
－ 報告書 作成에 관한 協議 : 1월중 (관련부처)
－ 報告書 作成　　　　　　 : 1-4월중순 (법무부, 관련부처)
－ 報告書 英文飜譯　　　　 : 4월-6월중순 (외무부)
－ 最終 檢討 및 提出　　　 : 6월-7월초

添 附 : 各國의 人權報告書 提出時期

　　　　　　　　　　　　　　　　　　 - 끝 -

(첨 부)

各國의 人權報告書 提出時期

시 한	국 가 수	주 요 국 명
시한내 제출	13개국	호주, 덴마크, 에쿠아돌, 리비아, 멕시코, 놀웨이, 페루, 스웨덴, 튀니지, 영국등
시한 6개월 초과	13개국	일본, 필리핀, 칠레, 베네주엘라, 핀랜드, 프랑스, 독일, 헝가리, 스페인, 세네갈등
6개월이상 초과	67개국	북한, 인도, 뉴질랜드, 알젠틴, 카나다, 벨기에, 덴마크, 서독, 이태리, 화란, 폴투갈, 폴랜드, 소련, 이집트, 가봉, 자이르 등
계	93개국	

＊ 북한은 81.12.14. 인권규약 가입후 2년만인 83.10.23. 최초 보고서를
   제출하였고, 84.4.2. 보고서 추가분을 제출함.

0042

기 안 용 지

분류기호 문서번호	국연 2031 -	(전화:)	시 행 상 특별취급	
보존기간	영구·준영구· 10. 5. 3. 1	장		관
수 신 처 보존기간				
시 행 일 자	1991. 1. 29.			

보조기관	국 장	전 결	협조기관		문서통제
	과 장	*(서명)*			1991. 1. 30
기안책임자	송영완				발 송 인

경 유		발신명의	
수 신	법무부장관		1991. 1. 30
참 조	법무실장		
제 목	인권보고서 관련자료 송부		

　　　　83.10.24. 및 84.4.2. 2회에 걸쳐 북한이 제출한 바

있는 최초인권보고서 및 인권이사회 심의기록과 87.12.24.

일본이 제출한 제 2차 인권보고서 및 동 심의기록을 별첨

송부하오니 업무에 참고하시기 바랍니다.

　　　첨 부 : 1. 북한의 최초인권보고서

　　　　　　　2. 북한의 최초인권보고서 심의기록

　　　　　　　3. 일본의 2차인권보고서

　　　　　　　4. 일본의 2차인권보고서 심의기록.　끝.

0043

법　　　무　　　부

인권 2031-1487　　　503-7045　　　1991. 1. 31

수신　수신처참조

제목　국제인권규약보고서 작성관련 유관부처 실무자회의 개최

　　　우리 정부는 국민의 인권옹호와 신장을 위한 노력의 일환으로
지난해 7.10 국제인권규약에 가입하였는 바, 동 규약 가입에 따라
우리나라는 '91.7.9까지 인권상황 보고서를 UN 인권이사회에 제출토록
되어 있어 동 보고서 작성을 위한 유관부처 실무자 회의를 아래와 같이
계획하오니 적극 협조하여 주시기 바랍니다.

－ 아　　래 －

○ 일 시 : '91.2.6(수), 14:00

○ 장 소 : 법무부 소회의실 (과천청사 제1동 216호실)

○ 참석범위

　. 회의주재 : 법무부 법무실장

　. 참 석 : 각부처 인권담당관 또는 관련과장

　. 보의의제 : 인권규약보고서 작성에 따른 업무협조

　. 협조사항

　　- 의무부 : 국제인권규약보고서 작성지침 및 가나 보고서
　　　　작성에 관한 의무부측 요청사항

　　- 타부처 : 별도 준비사항 없요.

　　　　법　　　무　　　부　　　장

수신처 : 의무부(참조:국제연합과장), 공보처(참조:), 치안본부
　　　(참조:수사과장), 국방부(참조:총무과장), 교육부(참조:법무담당관),
　　　문화부(참조:법무담당관), 노동부(참조:노정과장).

0044

인권보고서 작성관련 특별 요망사항

91. 2. 6.

과장님 회의참가시
지적하신 요망사항

o 아국의 인권보호 의지가 명백히 드러나는 상세한 보고서 작성

  - 특히, 타국에 입법례가 없는 법령의 경우 <u>동 입법사유, 시행에 따른</u>
    <u>효과등을 명기</u>하여 불필요한 오해방지에 유의

  - 독창적인 인권보호제도, 법령 부각

    (예) 제 24조(미성년자로서 보호받을 권리)의 경우, 관계법령규정 적시와
    더불어 우리나라의 미성년자 보호를 위한 총체적 노력으로서 1957년
    어린이헌장 제정, 1992년 어린이날 선포등을 적시함이 바람직

o 법령등의 영문본 검토 철저

  - 각 개별 인권보호를 규정한 법령내용은 인권보고서의 핵심

  - 특히, 최근 개정된 법령, 영문번역이 불완전한 법령등에 대한 철저한
    검토 요망 (동 법령은 일체의 수정없이 그대로 보고서에 수록 예정)

o 인권이사회에서의 심의를 감안한 보고서 작성

  - 아국 인권보고서는 91년 10월 또는 92년 3월 인권이사회에서 18명의
    국제적인 인권전문가의 심의에 부쳐짐. 동 심의시 인권전문가들은 각종
    질문을 아측에 제기하고 아측은 이에 답변해야 함을 감안, 예상질의를
    고려한 보고서 작성이 필수적임.

o 보고서에 수록될 내용과 더불어 <u>설명자료 또는 참고자료도</u> 함께 작성함이
  바람직

o 전문용어 또는 특별히 표현에 유의해야 할 부분은 영문 표기 병행 요망

0045

人權規約 加入에 따른 人權報告書 作成

1. 我國의 人權報告書 提出時限

ο 經濟的, 社會的 및 文化的 權利에 관한 國際規約 (A규약) :
  92.6.30.한 (발효일로 부터 2년째되는 6.30.시한)
  - 2次 報告書부터는 5年간격으로 提出

ο 市民的, 政治的 權利에 관한 國際規約 (B規約) :
  91.7.9. 발효일로 부터 1년이내)
  - 2次 報告書부터는 5年간격으로 提出
  - 報告書 審議 : 人權理事會 (B規約 當事國 會議에서 選出된 4년
                任期의 18名의 委員으로 構成)에서 審議됨.
                同 理事會는 年 3回 開催

2. 報告書 作成 要領

가. 報告書 構成
   1) Part Ⅰ(一般的 事項) : 市民的, 政治的 權利가 保護되도록 保障
                하는 一般的 法律體系에 대한 說明 記述
     - 憲法에 의한 基本的 人權保障內容
     - 規約 條項과 國內法과의 關係
     - 人權問題 管轄部處
     - 人權侵害를 主張하는 個人이 취할 수 있는 措置
     - 規約上의 제규정 이행보장을 위한 國家의 措置等

0046

2) Part Ⅱ(人權規約 各 條項關聯 事項) : 人權規約 各 條項(27개조항)의
  權利와 관련 施行되고 있는 司法的, 行政的 또는 其他 措置를 記述
  - 各 個別 人權의 保護를 위한 裝置를 國內法令 規定을 들어
    상세히 기술
  - 法令 또는 慣行으로 취해지고 있는 人權制限措置 說明
    (시한적 조치 포함)
  - 人權伸張을 위하여 취한 措置에 관한 事項
3) Annex : 人權保障에 관한 關聯 國內 法令의 條項을 報告書에 添附
4) 분 량 : 通常 30-50페이지 정도로 作成

3. 報告書 作成時 留意事項

가. 法令을 根據로 한 報告書
  º 人權規約에 따른 報告書는 他 人權關聯 說明資料와는 달리 政治的,
    文化的 說明을 排除하고 순수히 法令에 根據한 人權保護裝置를 記述
    하여야 함.

나. 包括的 人權保障制度 提示
  º 人權規約(B규약)은 市民的.政治的 權利에 관하여 包括的으로 規定
    하고 있으므로 法務部, 內務部, 國防部, 勞動部, 敎育部等 關聯部處가
    所管部處 該當事項에 관한 資料蒐集 및 執筆, 報告書에 첨부될 關係
    法令 選擇等을 擔當하고 法務部가 이를 綜合토록 함.

다. 關係法令 英文本 整備
  º 人權報告書는 國內法令을 根據로 하여 我國의 人權保障裝置를 說明
    하여야 하므로 同 報告書에 附錄으로 添附될 各種 法令의 正確한
    英譯은 매우 重要함. 따라서 報告書 作成과 더불어 關係法令의
    英文本의 整備도 필수적인 作業임.

0047

라. 報告書 時限問題

　o 我國의 人權保障 意志를 闡明한다는 側面에서 可及的 時限을 지키도록
　　함. (단. 國家保安法等 主要 法令이 發展的으로 整備될 計劃이 있을시
　　예외로 함)

　* 報告書 提出時限 (인권규약 가입후 1년)내에 報告書를 提出한 國家는
　　그리 많지 않음. (人權規約 報告書 제출 시점별 분류 : 별첨1)

4. 報告書 作成日程 (期限內 提出時)

가. 報告書 作成協議　：　2월초 (관련부처)

나. 報告書 作成　：　2-4월 (법무부. 관련부처)

　o 法務部가 關聯部處 該當資料를 취합. 報告書(국문)를 作成하고
　　報告書에 添附될 關係法令의 英語本도 關聯部處의 檢討를 거쳐
　　法務部가 綜合함.

다. 報告書 英文飜譯　　：　4월-6월중순 (외무부)

라. 最終 檢討 및 提出　：　6월-7월초

添 附 ： 1. 各國의 人權報告書 提出時期

　　　　 2. 人權事務局으로부터 接受한 報告書 作成 指針 (번역문)

0048

各國의　人權報告書　提出時期

시　　　한	국 가 수	주　　요　　국　　명
시 한 내 제출	13개국	호주, 덴마크, 에쿠아돌, 리비아, 멕시코, 놀웨이, 페루, 스웨덴, 튀니지, 영국등
시한 6개월 초과	13개국	일본, 필리핀, 칠레, 베네주엘라, 핀랜드, 프랑스, 독일, 헝가리, 스페인, 세네갈등
6개월이상 초과	67개국	북한, 인도, 뉴질랜드, 알젠틴, 카나다, 별기에, 덴마크, 서독, 이태리, 화란, 폴투갈, 폴랜드, 소련, 이집트, 가봉, 자이르 등
계	93개국	

* 북한은 81.12.14. 인권규약 가입후 2년만인 83.10.23. 최초 보고서를 제출하였고, 84.4.2. 보고서 추가분을 제출함.

0049

인권규약 제40조에 의한 규약당사국 보고서 작성지침

(인권이사회사무국 지침 내용)

1. <u>Part Ⅰ : 일반적 사항</u>

ㅇ 본부분에서는 규약당사국내에서 시민적, 정치적 권리가 보호되도록 보장하는
일반적 법률체계에 대한 설명을 기술함. 특히 하기내용을 포함해야 함.

   a) 규약에서 언급되고 있는 개개의 권리들이 헌법에서 또는 별도의
   "권리장전(Bill of Rights)"에서 보호받도록 규정되어 있는지
   여부와 또한 동 권리의 침해시에 대비하여 헌법 또는 권리장전에
   여하한 규정이 기술되어 있는지 그 내용

   b) 인권규약이 규정들이 재판소, 사법기관, 행정기관에 의해 직접
   원용되고 강행될 수 있는지 또는 규약이 관계 기관에 의하여
   집행되기 위하여는 국내법 또는 행정규정으로서의 국내법령
   으로의 전환 과정을 거쳐야 하는지 여부

   c) 인권문제의 관할부처 (사법, 행정, 기타 기관등)는 어떠한
   기관이 있는가?

   d) 인권침해를 주장하는 개인이 취할 수 있는 조치는?

   e) 인권규약의 제규정의 이행보장을 위해 국가가 취한 조치는?

2. <u>Part Ⅱ : 인권규약 Ⅰ. Ⅱ. Ⅲ의 각 조항에 관련된 사항</u>

ㅇ 본부분에는 인권규약의 각 조항과 관련하여 기술하여야 함.

   a) 각각의 권리와 관련, 시행되고 있는 사법적, 행정적 또는 기타
   조치들

   b) 인권에 대하여 법령 또는 관행으로서 취해지고 있는 제한조치
   (한시적인 조치 포함)

0050

c) 국가의 관할하에 있는 개인의 권리 향유에 영향을 미치는 요인
   또는 문제점등

d) 인권신장을 위하여 취해진 조치에 관한 사항

3. 보고서에는 관련 법령등의 사본이 첨부되어야 함. 관련법령 등을 첨부하지
   않을 경우에는 동 관련 법령을 참조치 않아도 이해될 수 있도록 보고서가
   상세히 작성되어야 함.

4. 인권위원회는 규약당사국의 최근 인권상황의 검토를 위하여 규약 제40조
   (1) (b)의 규정에 따라 추가보고서 제출을 요청할 수 있음.

0051

법 무 부

인권 2031-1932   503-7045   1991. 2. 9

수신 수신처참조

제목 국제인권규약 보고서 작성자료 제출의뢰

　　　국제인권규약 가입에 따라 정부는 '91.7.9까지 UN에 인권보고서를
제출토록 되어 있습니다. 따라서 당부에서는 국제인권규약 보고서 작성계획을
수립하고, 동 계획에 따라 '91.2.6 인권관련부처 회의를 개최하여 보고서
작성에 따른 방안을 논의한 바 있습니다.

　　　동 회의 결과에 따라 동 보고서 내용중 귀부(처)의 소관사항을 작성,
'91.3.31까지 당부(참조:인권과장)로 송부하여 주시기 바랍니다.

첨부 : 1. 국제인권규약 보고서 작성계획 1부

　　　　2. 국제인권규약 보고서 B규약 내용 작성에 따른 소관부처 1부

　　　　3. B규약 제40조에 의한 규약당사국 보고서 작성지침, 요약 1부

　　　　4. 국제인권규약(B규약)에 의한 일본의 최초 인권보고서 1부

　　　* 첨부물은 당일회의에 참석하지 않은 기관에만 배포하며
　　　　기타 상세사항은 법무부 인권과로 문의하시기 바람. 끝.

법 무 부 장 관

수신처 : 외무부(참조:국제연합과장), 내무부(참조:치안본부수사과장),
　　　　국방부(참조:법무관리관), 교육부(참조:교직과장), 문화부(참조:
　　　　종무실장), 보건사회부(참조:법무담당관), 노동부(참조:노정
　　　　과장), 체신부(참조:법무담당관), 공보처(참조:법무담당관),
　　　　정무제2장관(참조:제1조정관), 국가안전기획부(참조:대공수사국장).

주 제 네 바 대 표 부

재네(정) 2031-234   1991. 3. 8

수신 : 장관

참조 : 국제기구조약국장

제목 : 인권규약 관련 자료 전달 요청

    인권규약 보고서 작성과 관련, 별첨 참고 자료를 법무부 인권과로 전달하어
주시기 바랍니다.

첨부 : 상기 참고자료 1부.   끝.

주   제   네   바   대

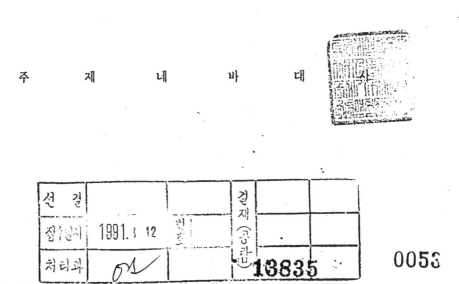

법　　무　　부

인권 2031- **3485**　　503-7045　　1991. 3. 13.

수신 : 수신처 참조

제목 : 국제인권규약 보고서 작성과 관련 참고자료 송부

　　1. 인권 2031-1932('91.2.9), 인권 2031-2764('91.2.28), 인권 2031-3209('91.3.8)와 관련입니다.

　　2. 인권규약 보고서의 효과적이고 체계적인 작성과 심의시 예상질의 답변준비를 위하여 별첨과 같이 "이탈리아 최초 인권보고서"를 송부하오니 보고서 작성 및 관련자료 검토시 참고하시기 바랍니다.

첨부 : 이탈리아 최초 인권보고서 1부. 끝.

법　　무　　부　　장

수신처 : 외무부(참조:국제연합과장), 내무부(참조:치안본부 수사과장), 국방부(참조:법무관리관), 교육부(참조:교직과장), 문화부(참조:종무실장), 보건사회부(참조:법무담당관), 노동부(참조:노정과장), 체신부(참조:법무담당관), 공보처(참조:법무담당관), 정무제2장관(참조:제2조정관), 국가안전기획부(참조:대공수사국장).

6865

0054

법　　　무　　　부

인권 2031-　　　　　　　503-7045　　　　　　1991. 3. 18
　　　　3721
수신　수신처참조

제목　국제인권규약보고서 작성자료 제출협조

　　　1. 인권 2031-1932('91.2.9), 인권 2031-2764('91.
2.28), 인권 2031-3209('91.3.8), 인권 2031-3447('91.
3.13), 인권 2031-3485('91.3.13)과 관련입니다.

　　　2. 인권규약보고서의 체계적인 작성을 위해 귀부(처) 관련조항에
대하여 심의시 예상되는 질문사항(예시)을 일부 도출하여 송부하오니
보고서 작성 및 관련자료 검토시 참고하시기 바랍니다.

　　　첨부 :　질문사항(예시) 1부.　　끝.

　　　　　　　　　법　　　무　　　부　　　장　　　관

수신처 : 외무부(참조:국제연합과장), 내무부(참조:치안본부 수사과장),
　　　　교육부(참조:법무담당관), 문화부(참조:종무실장), 보건사회부
　　　　(참조:법무담당관), 노동부(참조:노정과장), 공보처(참조:
　　　　법무담당관).

　　　　　　　　　　　　　　　　7324

　　　　　　　　　　　　　　　　　　　　　　　　0055

외 무 부

[제 1 조]

o 남아프리카, 나미비아, 팔레스타인 인민들의 자결권을 위한
  투쟁과 관련하여
  - 한국정부는 어떤 입장, 위치에 있는지

o 정부는 남아프리카의 "어파트헤이드" 정책에 대하여 어떤
  구체적 조치를 취했는지
  - 간접적 투자를 규제하기 위한 어떤 고려가 취해졌는지
  - 직접적 투자에 대한 제재규정이 있는지, 만약 있다면
    어떤 조치가 취해졌는지 (구체적 사례가 있는지)
  - 남아프리카에 대한 경제적, 금융적 제재를 가할 것을
    고려한 사실이 있는지

[제 20 조]

o 민족적, 인종적 또는 종교적 증오의 사주를 비난하는 국제조약
  들에 대한 아국의 태도는 어떠한가

[제 26 조]

o "어파트헤이드 범죄의 진압과 처벌에 관한 국제협약"을 비준
  했는지 또는 비준할 의도가 있는지

0056

법　　　무　　　부

인권 2031-3893　　　503-7045　　　　1991. 3. 21

수신　수신처참조

제목　국제인권규약보고서 작성자료 제출협조

　　　1.　인권 2031-1932('91.2.9),　인권 2031-2764('91.
2.28),　인권 2031-3209('91.3.8),　인권 2031-3447('91.3.
13),　인권 2031-3485('91.3.13),　인권 2031-3721('91.3.18)
과 관련입니다.

　　　2.　인권규약보고서의 체계적인 작성을 위해 귀부(처) 관련조항에
대하여 심의시 예상되는 질문사항(예시)을 일부 도출하여 송부하오니
보고서 작성 및 관련자료 검토시 참고하시기 바랍니다.

첨부 :　질문사항(예시) 1부.　　　끝.

　　　　법　　무　　부　　장　　관

수신처 :　외무부(참조:국제연합과장),　내무부(참조:치안본부 수사과장),
　　　　국방부(참조:법무담당관),　교육부(참조:법무담당관),　문화부
　　　　(참조:종무실장),　보건사회부(참조:법무담당관),　노동부
　　　　(참조:노정과장).

7714

02

0057

o 정치적 망명자의 지위 및 처우

o 정치적 망명신청의 접수, 처리절차 및 붑허하는 경우에 대한
  당사자의 이의신청처리절차 등

o 법률이 없다면 제정할 의사가 있는지

o 우리나라 현재의 인권관련 조약의 가입실태 및 전망

[제 12 조]

o 외국인의 지위에 관한 실질적 상황은
  - 관행적으로 어떤 난점, 문제점들이 실제로 일어났는지
    (법률하에서의 지위에만 언급함은 부족)

o 외국인의 추방근거 및 시기는

o 난민보호는 어떻게 하고 있는가

0058

수신 : UN 인권규약보고서 작성 관계관님 제위

최근 저희과에서 협조요청드린 인권보고서 작성건에 관하여
관계관님들께서 다소 불분명할 점이 있는 것으로 생각되어
첨언드리고자 합니다.

1. 먼저 규약 해당조문 (영문 및 국문이 다 있음)을 숙독한 다음
   그 조문이 우리나라의 경우 어떻게 실천, 집행되고 있는지를
   검토하셔서 그 내용을 개조식 또는 서술식으로 간략하게 정리해
   주시기 바랍니다.
   대체적으로는 헌법, 법률, 명령 등 성문법과 제도 및 관행 등을
   거론하는 것이 일반적일 것입니다.
   헌법과 법률의 경우 조문을 기재함으로써 족할 것이고,
   제도나 관행을 거론한다면 연혁, 실적 등을 간략히 설명하면
   될 것입니다.
   다만, 설명도중 법률전문용어가 있을 경우 괄호안에 영문을
   표기하여 주시면 영문번역시 도움이 되겠습니다.
   또한 해당 관계관님들께서는 도움이 될만한 관련 자료를 갖고
   계실 것입니다. 국회 답변자료, 법률개정 연구자료, 유권
   해석자료, 실.국에서 자체적으로 생산한 자료 등....
   이러한 자료는 그대로 복사하여 첨부해 주시면 됩니다.

0059

2. 일반적으로는 별문제가 없을 것입니다만, 규약이 요구하는
   내용을 우리나라가 제대로 실천하지 못하는 경우가 골치일
   것입니다.
   이 경우는 우선 직접적으로는 실천하지 못하지만 간접적으로
   나마 노력한다고 생각되는 법령, 제도, 관행이 있다면 이를
   설명하고 그런것조차 없다면 왜 실천하지 못하는지를 설득력
   있게 설명하여 주시기 바랍니다.
   법체계의 상이, 민족고유관습 등이 주로 거론 될 것입니다.

3. 규약이 규정하는 권리를 제한하는 법령, 제도가 있을 경우
   이를 간략히 소개하고 아울러 제한의 정당성을 설득력 있게
   설명하면 될 것입니다.

4. 협조전에는 규약의 조문을 표시하고 그 밑에 특정항목을
   기재하였는데, 이것은 예상질문사항입니다.
   예상질문사항은 앞으로도 계속 추가될 것입니다.
   이 예상질문사항에 대하여는 답변을 생각하셔서 작성해
   주시는데, 이 부분은 보고서에 반영되는 것이 아니라
   (일부분은 반영되겠지만) 후일의 청문회를 대비하는 것이니
   정성드려 답변을 쓰실 것이 아니라 자료가 있으면 그 자료를
   복사하여 첨부하는 식으로 해 주시면 되겠습니다.

0060

이러한 작업을 위하여 일본 및 이태리의 보고서를 참고하시도록

보내드렸으며, 벨기에 보고서도 곧 보내드릴 예정입니다.

인권과에서는 각 관계관님들께서 보내주실 내용과 자료를

토대로 보고서 작성 및 영문번역 작업을 할 것입니다.

작업을 진행하다보니 시간에 쫓기고 인권과 작업량이 너무

방대하여 제대로 보필을 못해 드리는 감이 있어 미안하게 생각

합니다.

양해하여 주시고 기한내 제출을 위해 적극 도와주시기 바랍니다.

1991. 3. 21.

인권과장 류 공 호 배

0061

법 무 부 인 권 과

1991. 3 . 27.

아래 문건을 수신자에게 전달하여 주시기 바랍니다.

제 목 : ~~국제인권규약인명서~~ 작성을 위한 행정위러

수 신 : 외무부 국제연합과

(수신처 FAX NO: 720-0686)

발 신 : 법무부 인권과

표지포함 총 2 매

0062

법   무   부

인권 2031- **4128**   503-7045   1991. 3. 27

수신 외무부장관

참조 국제기구조약국장

제목 국제인권규약보고서 작성을 위한 협조의뢰

　　1. 당부에서는 국제인권규약 가입에 따른 보고서를 관련부처와
협조하여 작성중에 있습니다.

　　2. 동 보고서 작성에 참고가 되하여 아국이 지금까지 인권과 관련
하여 유엔 또는 국제기구에 가입함에 따라 우리 정부가 제출한 <u>자료 (보고서,
답변서, 헌장 등)</u>를 송부 요청하오니 적극 협조하여 주시기 바랍니다.

　　3. 또한 S. Africa, Namibia 에 관한 우리 정부 입장과
취해온 정책, 실적 등에 관한 자료도 있으면 송부하여 주시기 바랍니다.

법   무   부   장

협조문용지

분류기호 문서번호	국연 2031- 111 ( )		결 재	담 당	과 장	국 장
시행일자	1991. 3. 29.					(서명)
수 신	중동아프리카국장	발 신	국제기구조약국장			
제 목	대 남아프리카공화국 정책					

1. 아국은 90.7.10자로 인권규약에 가입함에 따라

시민적, 정치적 권리에 관한 규약(B규약)관련 인권보고서를

91.7.9한 제출하여야 합니다.

2. 동 인권보고서는 법무부에서 각 부처 관련사항을

취합·작성예정인 바, 당부 해당자료 작성에 참고코자 하오니

하기 사항을 91.4.3(수)한 당국에 통보하여 주시기 바랍니다.

- 아   래 -

가. 아국의 대남아프리카 기본정책

나. 대남아프리카 인적·물적 교류실적

다. 아국과 나미비아와의 관계 (개략적으로 기술)

라. 기타 참고사항.   끝.

0064

법　무　부

인권 2031- 4285　　503-7045　　　　1991. 3. 30
수신　수신처참조
제목　국제인권규약보고서 작성관련 참고자료 송부

　　　1. 인권 2031-1932('91.2.9), 인권 2031-2764('91.2.28),
인권 2031-3209('91.3.8), 인권 2031-3447('91.3.13),
인권 2031-3485('91.3.13), 인권 2031-3721('91.3.18),
인권 2031-3893('91.3.21), 인권 2031-4127('91.3.27)과
관련입니다.

　　　2. 인권규약보고서의 체계적인 작성을 위해 별첨과 같이 "벨기에
최초 인권보고서"를 송부하오니 보고서 작성 및 관련자료 검토시 참고하시기
바랍니다.

　　　3. 그리고 인권규약 내용중 귀 소관부분 이외에도 그동안 4회에 걸쳐
보내드린 소관별 질문사항(예시)에 대한 답변 및 관련자료를 상세하게
보내주시기 바랍니다 (보고서 작성시 매우 필요함)

　　　4. 참고로 벨기에 보고서는 UN에서 내용이 충실하다고 평가된
보고서로 우리의 인권규약보고서도 벨기에 보고서를 중점적으로 참고하여
작성함이 바람직할 것임을 첨언합니다.

첨부 :　벨기에 최초 인권보고서 1부.　　끝.

법　무　부　장　관

수신처 :　외무부(참조:국제연합과장), 내무부(참조:치안본부 수사과장),
　　　　　국방부(참조:국제법과장), 교육부(참조:법무담당관),
　　　　　문화부(참조:종무실장), 보건사회부(참조:법무담당관),
　　　　　노동부(참조:노정과장), 체신부(참조:법무담당관),
　　　　　공보처(참조:법무담당관), 정무제2장관실(참조:제2조정관).

0065

법　　무　　부

인권 2031- 4367   503-7045   1991. 4. 2
수신 수신처참조
제목 국제인권규약보고서 작성협조

　　　1. 인권 2031-1932('91.2.9), 인권 2031-2764('91.2.28),
인권 2031-3209('91.3.8), 인권 2031-3447('91.3.13),
인권 2031-3485('91.3.13), 인권 2031-3721('91.3.18),
인권 2031-3893('91.3.21), 인권 2031-4127('91.3.27),
인권 2031-4285('91.3.30)과 관련입니다.

　　　2. 국제인권규약(B규약)을 각 조문별로 세분하여 집필하여야 할
내용의 소제목을 별첨과 같이 잠정 정리하고, 소관부서 사항을 통보하오니
귀 소관사항에 대한 인권규약보고서(초안)를 별기에 최초인권보고서(기히
송부) 및 일본제2차 인권규약보고서 내용을 참고하여 '91.4.8까지 작성,
송부하여 주시기 바랍니다.

　　　3. 아울러 상기 소제목 이외에도 우리나라 보고서에 들어가야 할
사항으로 판단되는 귀 소관 전문사항에 대하여도 상세히 기술하여 주시기
바랍니다.

첨부 ： 1. 원고 소제목 1부
　　　　2. 일본제2차 인권규약보고서 1부.

　　　　법　　무　　부　　장　　관

수신처 ： 외무부(참조：국제연합과장), 내무부(참조：치안본부 수사과장),
　　　　국방부(참조：국제법과장), 교육부(참조：법무담당관),
　　　　문화부(참조：종무실장), 보건사회부(참조：법무담당관),
　　　　노동부(참조：노정과장), 체신부(참조：법무담당관),
　　　　공보처(참조：법무담당관), 정무제2장관실(참조：제2조정관).

0066

제 1 조

[1항]

o 관계법령

. 헌법전문중 "밖으로는 항구적인 세계평화와 인류공영에
  이바지함으로써"
. 헌법 제5조 제1항

o 아국 정부의 민족자결주의 원칙에 대한 기본정책

. 그 내용 및 국제사회에 있어서의 구체적 정책실시 실적

o 중동문제 특히 팔레스타인 문제와 관련한 아국 정부의
  기본정책, 구체적 수행내용 등

o 남아프리카의 어파트헤이드 정책에 대한 기본정책 및
  그 수행내용

o 이태리 보고서 7 , 9 , 18

0067

기 안 용 지

분류기호 문서번호	국연 2031-	(전화 :　　　　　)	시 행 상 특별취급	
보존기간	영구·준영구. 10. 5. 3. 1.	장	관	
수 신 처 보존기간				
시 행 일 자	1991. 4. 15			

보조기관	국　장	전　결 ~	협조기관	중동아프리카과장:	문 서 통 제 접 수 1991. 4. 17	
	과　장					
기안책임자	송 영 완				발 송 인	

경　유		발신명의		
수　신	법무부장관			
참　조				

제　목	국제인권규약 보고서 작성

　　　　대 : 인권 2031-4367 (91.4.2.)

　　　대호 국제인권규약보고서 작성과 관련, 당부 소관자료를

벌첨 송부합니다.

　　　첨 부 : 국제인권규약 제1조 관련자료 1부.　　　끝.

0068

법 　 무 　 부

인권 2031- **5128**　　　　　　503-7045　　　　　　1991. 4. 17.

수신　수신처 참조

제목　국제인권규약 보고서 (가안)에 대한 검토 요청

　　　1. 본 보고서는 작년 7.10 가입한 국제인권규약의 지침에 따라
우리나라의 인권보장제도 및 그 운용실태에 관하여 국제연합에 제출하는 최초의
보고서로, 국제적인 시각에서 외국인이 우리의 전반적인 인권상황을 이해할 수
있도록 노력하였으며, 영문번역을 전제로 하여 작성하였습니다.

　　　2. 본 보고서는 외무부, 내무부, 국방부, 교육부, 문화부, 보건사회부,
노동부, 공보처, 정무제2장관실 등 관계부처로부터 협조받은 자료 등을 토대로
하였으나 미진한 점이 많을 것으로 사료되어, 일응 가안으로 하였으며,
계속하여 관계부처의 검증과 의견을 수렴, 미비점을 보완할 계획입니다.

　　　3. 따라서 귀 소관부분의 보고서 내용에 대한 검토의견을 별첨양식에
의거 1991. <u>4. 23</u>까지 송부하여 주시기 바랍니다.

첨 부 :　1. 인권보고서 (가안) 1부.

　　　　　2. "양식" 1부. 끝.

법 　 무 　 부 　 장 　 관

수신처 :　외무부 (참조:국제연합과장), 내무부 (참조:치안본부 수사과장),
　　　　　국방부 (참조:국제법과장), 교육부 (참조:법무담당관), 문화부 (참조:
　　　　　법무담당관), 보건사회부 (참조:법무담당관), 노동부 (참조:국제협력
　　　　　과장), 공보처 (참조:법무담당관), 정무제2장관실 (참조:제2조정관).

0069

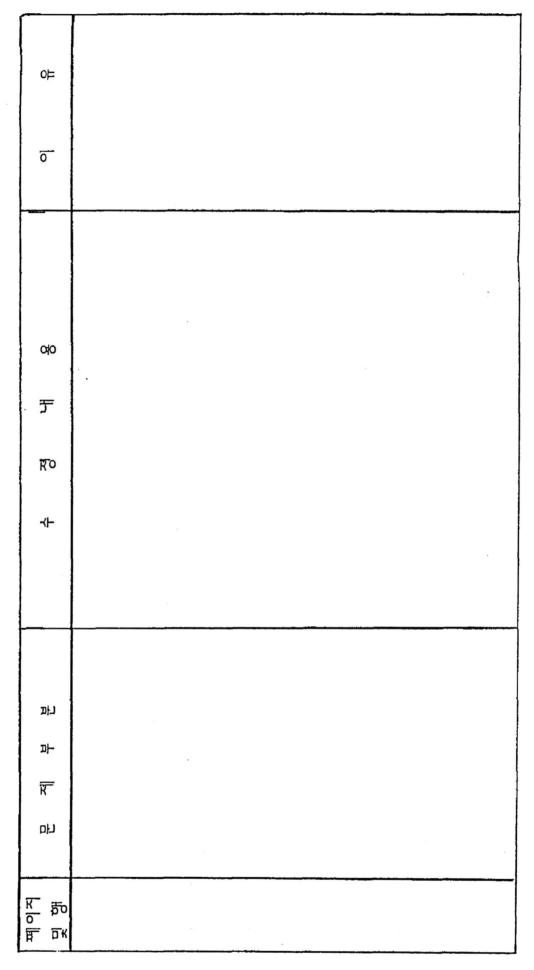

연월일	내용수정	관련자처벌	게재지면

0200

기 안 용 지

분류기호 문서번호	국연 2031-	(전화 :)	시 행 상 특별취급	

(전화 :   )

		장	관

보존기간	영구·준영구. 10. 5. 3. 1.		
수 신 처 보존기간			
시행일자	1991. 4. 19.		ん

보조기관	국 장	전 결	협조기관		문 서 통 제	
	과 장	ШД			(1991. 4. 20)
기안책임자		송 영 완			발 송 인

경 유 수 신 참 조	주제네바대사	발 신 명 의	(스탬프 1991. 4. 20)

제 목	국제인권규약 보고서(가안) 송부

1. 법무부는 각부처로부터 자료를 접수하여 표제보고서

(가안)를 작성한 바, 동 책자를 송부하오니 미비점 또는 보고서

작성시 유의해야 할 사항에 대한 귀견을 ~5.15까지~ 회보하여 주시기 바랍니다.

2. 동 가안을 법무부에서는 각부처의 추가 의견을 취합하여

첨삭후 최종안을 작성할 예정임을 알려드립니다.

첨 부 : 표제 보고서 가안(책자) 1부. 끝.

0071

분류기호 문서번호	국연 2031- 15k ( )	협조문용지	결 재	담당	과장	국장
시행일자	1991. 4. 19.					
수 신	중동.아프리카국장	발 신	국제기구조약국장 (서명)			
제 목	국제인권규약(B규약) 보고서 검토 의뢰					

연 : 국연 2031-111 (91.3.29)

대 : 아프이 20221-69 (91.4.2)

1. 법무부는 아국의 국제인권규약 보고서에 아국의 대남아공

정책 및 대팔레스타인 정책을 포함, 보고서 가안을 별첨과 같이 작성

송부하여 온 바, 동 책자중 제1조 해당부분(PP. 19-22)을 검토하신후

귀국 의견을 별첨 양식에 의거 4.22.한 당국으로 송부하여 주시기

바랍니다.

2. 상기 검토시 피압박민족(쿠르드족등)에 대한 아국정부의

지원실적등 아국의 민족자결정책 및 난민 구호정책 집행내용이 포합될

수 있도록 협조하여 주시기 바랍니다.

첨 부 : 국제인권규약(B규약) 최초 보고서. 1부. 끝.

0072

1505-8 일 (1)
85. 9. 9 승인 "내가아낀 종이 한장 늘어나는 나라살림"
190㎜×268㎜(인쇄용지 2급 60g / ㎡)
가 40-41 1990. 7. 9.

78   한국 인권문제 시민적·정치적 권리 국제규약 인권보고서 1

아국 인권보고서(가안) 검토

1991. 4. 23.
외 무 부

1. 정   정 (73 page)

대한민국은 1950.10.14. 집단살해죄의 방지 및 처벌에 관한 협약(Convention
on the Prevention and Punishment of the Crime of Genocide)의 가입서를
기탁하여 동 협약은 1951.1.12. 우리나라에 대하여 발효하였다.

2. 유엔 고문피해자 구호기금(United Nations Voluntary Fund for Victims
   of Torture)에 대한 아국정부의 기여금 납부 실적

   ○ 1988년 : $5,000
   ○ 1989년 : $5,000
   ○ 1990년 : $5,000
   합   계 : $15,000

3. 이락난민 구호기금에 대한 기여금 납부

   ○ 아국정부는 유엔안전보장이사회 결의 688(1991)호에 호응하여 인도적
     견지에서 1991.4.17. 유엔사무총장에게 쿠르드족 및 기타 이락 난민의
     구호기여금 30만불을 제공하였다.

양	91년	단 당	과 장	국 장
고	4월			
재	23일			

0073

법 무 부

인권 2031- **5567** 503-7045   1991. 4. 26

수신   수신처참조

제목   국제인권규약보고서 (제2고)에 대한 검토요청

　　　1. 본 제2고는 기히 발간한 보고서 가안에 대하여 외무부, 내무부,
국방부, 교육부, 문화부, 보건사회부, 노동부, 공보처, 정무제2장관실 등 행정
각 부와 검찰, 국가안전기획부, 경찰 등 수사담당부서에서 보내주신 의견
을 최대한 반영하면서 가안의 내용을 국제적, 외교적 감각에 맞도록 보완
한 것입니다. 다만, 전체 체제와의 관련상 일부 부처의 의견을 반영
하지 못한 부분도 있음을 양지하시기 바랍니다.

　　　2. 본 제2고는 관계부처에 다시 한번 검증을 부탁드려 최종적인
검토를 거친 다음 보고서 체제 및 문구 등의 손질을 끝으로 확정지을 예정
입니다.

　　　3. 따라서 귀 소관부분의 보고서 내용에 대한 최종 검토의견을
별첨 양식에 의거 1991.5.1까지 송부하여 주시고 아울러 영문번역을
전제로 한 것이니만큼 소관 전문용어에 대하여는 영문표기를 병행하여
주시기 바랍니다.

첨부 :　1. 인권규약보고서 (제2고) 1부.
　　　　2. "양식" 1부.　끝.

법 　 무 　 부 　 장 　 관

수신처 :　외무부 (참조 : 국제연합과장), 내무부 (참조 : 치안본부 수사과장),
　　　　국방부 (참조 : 국제법과장),　교육부 (참조 : 법무담당관),
　　　　문화부 (참조 : 법무담당관),　보건사회부 (참조 : 법무담당관),
　　　　노동부 (참조 : 국제협력과장), 공보처 (참조 : 법무담당관),
　　　　정무제2장관실 (참조 : 제2조정관).

0074

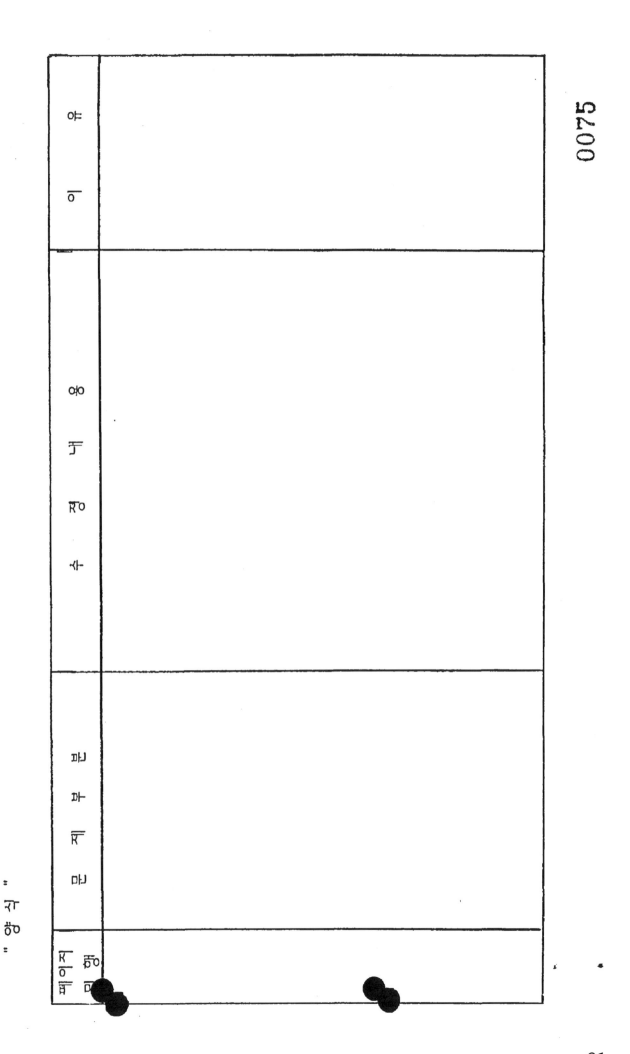

항목:			
제어지	항목	판 단 관 리	내 용 수 정 수	이 안

분류기호 문서번호	아프이 20221-97	협조문용지 (720-4170)	결 재	심 의 관		
				담 당	과 장	국 장
시행일자	1991. 4. 29.					
수 신	국제기구조약국장	발 신	중동아프리카국장	(서명)		
제 목	국제인권규약(B규약) 보고서 검토					

대호 국제인권규약 보고서 검토의견과 피압박 민족에 대한

아국 정부의 지원실적 및 난민구호 정책 집행 내용을 하기와 같이

통보합니다.

  1. 나미비아와의 수교일자 90.3.31을 90.3.21로 정정

  2. 쿠르드족 등 이라크 난민 지원 실적

      가. 정부차원

          ㅇ 유엔의 난민구호 활동에 30만불 제공

          (91.4.29 유엔 사무총장에게 전달)

      나. 민간차원

          ㅇ 대한 적십자사에서 국제적십자 위원회(ICRC)와

          국제적십자 연맹(LRCS)의 걸프전 희생자 및 난민구호

          활동에 총27만불 제공(91.4월)

  3. 이란 유입 난민지원 실적

// 계   속

0076

○ 걸프사태 관련 이란 유입 난민구호를 위해 이란정부에

앰블란스 8대(15만불 상당) 지원(91.4월). 끝.

인권규약 가입에 따른 보고서 작성

91. 5. 9.
국제연합과

1. 인권보고서 작성 및 제출(잠정일정)
   - ㅇ 91.2.15-4.30.   인권보고서 (국문) 작성(각부처 작성, 법무부 종합)
   - ㅇ <u>91.5.1-6.25.</u>   인권보고서 영문작업 (외무부)
   - ㅇ 6.25-6.30.   영문본에 대한 각부처 의견 종합
   - ㅇ 7월초   주제네바대표부 경유, 인권사무국에 보고서 제출
   - ✱ 보고서 심의시기는 종래의 예에 비추어 92년 하반기에 이루어질
     가능성이 큼

2. 보고서 제출시기
   - ㅇ B규약 가입에 따른 제출시한은 금년도 7.9. (단, A규약은 92.6.30.이 시한)
   - ㅇ 제출시한에 맞추어 보고서를 제출한 국가는 그렇게 많지 않음.
     - 우리로서는 금후 개혁입법의 처리결과에 따라 보고서내용이 일부
       수정될 소지가 있을 것으로 보임.

3. 보고서 번역
   가. 번역 주체
   - ㅇ 각부처 관련사항은 해당부처에서 영역(초안)을 하고 외무부와
     공보처 협조하에 타국의 보고서 작성 예를 참조, 일부 수정하여
     완성함이 가장 바람직하나,
   - ㅇ 금차 보고서는 최초 보고서이고, 아국의 인권상황을 전세계에
     공식문서로 밝히는 최초의 문서이므로 외무부에서 작성키로 함.
     (단, 2차 보고서 이후는 각부처에서 해당부분 작성)

0078

나. 법령 및 전문용어 번역

    ㅇ 각종 법령, 규칙, 예규등의 영문작업은 외무부에서 할 수 없는
      사안이므로 필히 해당부처에서 완료해야 하며, 본문내용중의 전문
      용어등은 각부처에서 영역하여야 함.

      - 금번 보고서 번역에 있어서 특히 이점이 준수되어야 할 것임.

4. 보고서 체제

    ㅇ 보고서 내용은 가급적 간단, 명료하게 작성함이 바람직함.

    ㅇ 추후 동 보고서 심의시 편의상 본문에서 언급되는 주요 법령조문은
      본문내에 포함시킴이 편리함. (동 조문등을 Annex로 첨부할 경우,
      인권보고서 심의시 수시로 Annex를 참조해야 하는 번거로움이 예상됨)

5. 개혁입법 문제

    ㅇ 보안법, 경찰법, 안기부법등이 아국 보고서 심의이전(92년 하반기
      예상) 개정될 가능성에 대비문제

      - 보안법등은 본문상에 많이 취급되고 있지는 않으나 아국법령중
       대외적으로 가장 많이 알려져 있는 법중의 하나이므로 보고서
       심의시 집중 논의될 가능성이 있음.

아주 인권외교사업법령

國際人權規約報告書 作成結果 報告

1991. 5.

法 務 部

0080

1. 作成經過

○ 1991. 2. 5   관계기관 실무책임관 회의

○ 1991. 2. 7   법무부 실무작업반 편성

○ 1991. 4.15   제1고 작성

○ 1991. 4.25   제2고 작성

○ 1991. 5. 3   최종본 작성

* 국제인권규약보고서 작성일지 ------ 별책

2. 主要骨子

○ 규약규정에 따라 일반적 사항 및 27개 조문의 개별적 설명을
  총 323개 항목으로 기술, 90 종목의 법규 및 관련 대법원판결,
  헌법재판소판결, 행정지침 등 인용 (총 139쪽)

○ 우리나라 법체계 및 관련 제도.관행을 중점적으로 설명하고
  신체의 자유(제9조), 양심의 자유(제18조), 표현의 자유(제19조),
  결사의 자유(제22조) 등에서 우리나라의 인신구속제도,
  국가보안법 및 노동조합 관련부분 등을 설명

* 국제인권규약보고서 요지 ----- 별책

0081

3. 向後 補完計劃

o 국회의 개혁입법 개정논의를 기다려 관련부분 보완

o 영문작업 과정에서 필요할 경우 문구 등 표현방법 손질

4. 英文化 作業 (意見)

가. 방 향

o 외교적 측면과 법률적 측면을 모두 충족시키는 영문화
  작업 필요

o 정확한 영문번역으로 보고서 심의시 문제제기 최소화

나. 의 견

o 외무부내의 영어능통 외교관 또는 외교안보연구원에
  의뢰하는 방법 등으로 가안 작성 (주관 - 국제기구조약국)

o 법무부에서 심층적으로 의견 개진

o 외국인(공보처 해외공보관) 또는 국제법률전문가의
  감수를 거쳐 최종확정

0082

長官報告事項

報告畢

1991. 5. 14

國際機構條約局
國際聯合課（25）

題目 : 國際 人權規約 加入에 따른 報告書 作成

我國은 90.7.10. 3個의 國際人權規約에 加入함에 따라 同 規約 規定에 따른 人權報告書를 提出해야 하는 바, 同 報告書 作成 關聯事項을 아래 報告드립니다.

1. 報告書 提出時期

○ 市民的 및 政治的 權利에 관한 國際規約（B規約） 提出時限 : 91.7.9.

○ 經濟的, 社會的 및 文化的 權利에 관한 國際規約（A規約） 提出時限

: 92.6.30.

* A 規約 報告書는 今年 下半期에 關聯部處間 作成問題 協議 豫定

2. B規約 人權報告書 作成 및 提出日程

○ 91.2.15-5.10. : 人權報告書（국문）作成

(각부처 작성, 법무부 종합)

○ 5.10-6.25. : 人權報告書 英文作業（외무부）

○ 6.25-6.30. : 英文本에 대한 各部處의 意見綜合

○ 7月初 : 駐제네바代表部 경유, 人權事務局에 提出

* 報告書 審議는 92年 下半期에 이루어질 것으로 豫想됨.

공	담 당	과 장	국 장	차 관 보	차 관	장 관
람						

0083

3. B規約 人權報告書 構成

o 我國 人權保障 制度에 관한 一般的 事項 및 B規約 本文 27個 條項의
   個別的 說明을 總 323個 項目으로 기술, 90 種目의 法規 및 關聯 判例,
   行政指針等 引用 (총 139쪽)
o 改革立法 內容 反映

4. 當部措置事項 (英文本 作成日程)

o 5.10-6.5. : 英文作業
o 6.5-6.25. : 英文本 감수 (國際法 專門家)
   - 同 期間中 수시로 法務部에 영역본 (초안)을 送付하여 法務部側
     意見 수렴 예정

5. 人權報告書 補完計劃

o 改革立法이 確定됨에 따라 現在 法務部에서 關聯法 改正部分을 補完中
   인 바, 英文作業中 同 補完部分 반영 예정
o 英文本과는 別途로 人權報告書에 引用된 國內法令 各 條項을 拔萃하여
   별책 (부록) 인쇄, 추후 人權理事會에서의 我國報告書 審議에 對備

                                                        - 끝 -

長 官 報 告 事 項

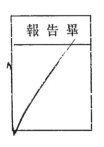

報 告 畢

1991. 5. 14
國際機構條約局
國際聯合課（25）

題目 ： 國際 人權規約 加入에 따른 報告書 作成

我國은 90.7.10. 3個의 國際人權規約에 加入함에 따라 同 規約 規定에
따른 人權報告書를 提出해야 하는 바, 同 報告書 作成關聯 進行事項을 아래
報告드립니다.

1. 報告書 提出時期

○ 市民的 및 政治的 權利에 관한 國際規約(B규약) 提出時限 ： 91.7.9.

○ 經濟的, 社會的 및 文化的 權利에 관한 國際規約(A규약) 提出時限

： 92.6.30.

＊ A 規約 報告書는 今年 下半期에 關聯部處間 作成問題 協議 豫定

2. B 規約 人權報告書 作成 및 提出日程

○ 91.2.15-5.10. ： 人權報告書（국문）作成

(각부처 작성, 법무부 종합)

○ 5.10-6.25. ： 人權報告書 英文作業 (외무부)

○ 6.25-6.30. ： 英文本에 대한 各部處의 意見綜合

○ 7月初 ： 駐제네바代表部 경유, 人權事務局에 提出 計劃

＊ 報告書 審議는 92年 下半期에 이루어질 것으로 豫想됨.

0085

3. B規約 人權報告書 構成

o 我國 人權保障 制度에 관한 一般的 事項 및 B規約 本文 27個 條項의
  個別的 說明을 總 323個 項目으로 기술, 90 種目의 法規 및 關聯 判例,
  行政指針等 引用 (총 139쪽)

o 改革 立法內容 反映

4. 當部措置事項 (英文本 作成日程)

o 5.10-6.5. ： 英文作業

o 6.5-6.25. ： 英文本 감수 (國際法 專門家)
  - 同 期間中 수시로 法務部에 영역본 (초안)을 送付하여 法務部側
    意見 수렴 예정

                                              - 끝 -

0086

주 제 내 바 대 표 부

제내(정) 2031-24   1991. 5. 17.

수신 : 외무부장관

참조 : 국제기구조약국장

제목 : 국제 인권 규약 보고서 (가안) 검토 의견

          대 : 국언 2031-14489

        대호, 법무부에서 작성한 국제 인권 규약보고서 (가안)에 대한

당관 검토 의견을 별첨 송부합니다.

        첨 부 : 당관 검토 의견 1부. 끝.

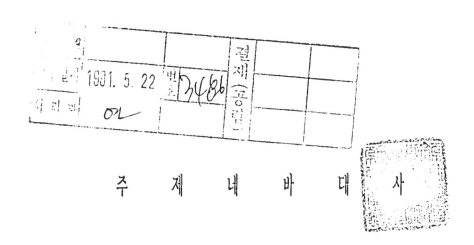

주 제 내 바 대 사

0087

국제 인권 규약 보고서(가안) 검토의견

I. 추가할 사항

1. **일반적 사항**

   B. 규약과 국내법과의 관계

      O 규약관련 위법 행위 발생시 개인이 규약을 근거로 고소
        또는 고발을 제기할 수 있는지 여부

   C. 인권 문제의 관할 기관

      O 대법원과 헌법 재판소의 관계

2. **제 4조**

   O 비상 계엄하의 군사재판의 역할

3. **제 12조**

   O 남북한간의 여행 자유에 관한 입법 및 행정조치 현황

II. 삭제 요망사항

1. **제 2조**

   O Para 15, 16 : (장애인 복지 시책 시행에 관한 장애 요인)
     - 동 관습에 대한 정부의 구체적 시책 내용이 결여되어 있음.

0088

2. 제 3조

　　O Para 17-19 (여성 발전 기본 계획 및 남녀차별 개선 지침)

　　　　- 보고서 심의시 불필요한 질문을 야기할 가능성이 있음.

　　O Para 27 : "직급이 높을 수록 ......불과하다 "

　　　　- 불필요한 설명임.

　　O Para 35 : "교과목의 개정과 함께 ....병행하고 있다"

　　　　- 성차별적 가르침의 현황 및 이에대한 개선방안에 대한
　　　　　언급이 없음.

3. 제 6조

　　O Para 17-24, 27-29(모자보건을 위한 조치, AIDS 관리)

　　　　- 동 조와의 관련성이 희박함.

4. 제 8조

　　O Para 3. "한편 사회 보호법 제 7조 제 1항은 ....지급하고 있다"

　　　　- 불필요한 설명임.

5. 제 9조

　　O Para 3 (임의 동행 문제)

　　O Para 4는 다음과 같이 수정함

0089

"피의자 조사등을 위한 임의 동행 절차에 대해서는 아래와 같이 동 요건, 절차 및 시간을 엄격히 제한하여 임의 동행의 남용과 이로인한 인권 침해를 최소화 하고 있음.

　　'관련 조문'

다음으로 ....연구 추진중에 있다."

- 긍정적 서술이 바람직함.

6. __제 14조__

0 Para 4. (b) (변호인 접견권과 수사권)
- 타국의 입법례를 인용하는 것이 적절치 않으며, 가정상황하의 사례에 대한 정부 의견을 제시할 필요는 없음.

0 Para 11. (사회 안전법 폐지)
- 논란이 되었던 과거 사례를 참고로 언급할 필요는 없음.

7. __제 16조__

0 Para 3. (특별한 경우의 제한)
- 구체적 설명이 추가되거나, 또는 삭제되는 것이 바람직함.

8. __제 18조__

0 Para 10. (국가보안법상 불고지죄와 양심의 자유)
- 보고서 심의시 동 문제가 제기될 경우 언급되는 것이 바람직하며, 타국 입법례의 언급은 적절치 않음.

0090

Ⅲ. 기타 참고 사항

1. 제 2조 Para 19 (모든 형태의 인종차별 철폐에 관한 국제협약 (CERD)
   제 14조 적용문제)

   - 아국이 표제 협약보다 광범위한 성격의 인권 규약 및 동 선택
     의정서에 가입한 이상, 협약 제 14조의 적용을 수락하는 것이
     바람직하다는 다수 건해가 90. 8월 제 5,6차 아국 보고서 심의시
     제기된바 있음.
   - 아국에서의 인종차별 사례가 드물며, 또한 선택의정서에 가입하였음을
     고려, 상기 제14조의 수락을 적극적으로 검토하는 것이 바람직함. 끝.

0091

국제인권규약 최초보고서 수정내용
==================================

I. 본 보고서 수정내용은 5.10 개최된 "인권문제 실무협의회" 회의결과를
   반영한 것임

II. 수정내용

조항	페이지	현 행	수 정
제3조	34-35	50. - 51.	50. 1948년 大韓民國 정부수립 이전까지는 大韓民國의 전통사회는 봉건적 儒敎思想에 젖어 男性爲主의 差別이 女性의 삶을 지배하였다. 그러나 1948.7.17 공포된 大韓民國 憲法은 남녀간의 平等을 인정함으로써 國家生活의 많은 분야에서 男性과 더불어 女性이 同等하게 참여할 수 있도록 문호를 개방하였다.
	35	54.	54. 내용 삭제
	38	61.	61. 1988.2.25 政務長官(제2)실이 발족되어 女性이 長官으로 취임하였다. 同 長官室에서는 女性問題를 해결하기 위하여 政策을 입안하고 실행하는 기능을 수행하는 등 여성과 관련된 업무에 중점을 두고 있다.

0092

조항	페이지	현 행	수 정
제3조	38-39	64.	64. 女性政策審議委員會 (The National Committee of Women's Policies)가 1983. 12.8 國務總理室 산하에 설치되었다. 이 委員會는 여성업무에 관한 최상위의 政府委員會로서 특히 여성과 관련된 基本計劃과 綜合政策을 수립하고 관계 행정기관간의 여성분야 施策을 조정하는 기능을 수행한다. 委員會는 25명 이내의 委員으로 구성되어 있는데 國務總理를 委員長으로 하여 관계부처의 長官 및 女性問題 專門家들이 委員으로 참여하고 있다. 女性問題를 다루는 기타 政府委員會로는 淪落女性善導委員會 (The Committee to Provide Guidance to Women in Prostitution)와 婦女指導協議會 (The Council of Women's Guidance)가 있다.
		65.	65. 내용 삭제
		66.	66. 내용 삭제
		67.	67. 내용 삭제

0093

조 항	페이지	현 행	수 정
제3조	45	88.	88. 내용 삭제
		89.	89. 내용 삭제
제7조	65	144.	144. 大韓民國 大法院은 다음과 같은 판결에 보듯이 고문 등에 의하여 강요된 자백에 대한 증거능력을 부인하여 刑事被疑者 또는 被告人의 自白을 얻기 위한 고문, 폭행,협박,구속의 부당한 장기화를 실질적으로 금지하고 있다. 被告人들이 檢察 이전의 수사과정에서 고문 등으로 임의성 없는 자백을 하고, 그 후 檢事의 조사단계에서도 임의성 없는 심리상태가 계속되어 동일한 내용의 진술을 하였다면 비록 檢事앞에 조사받을 당시는 고문 등 자백을 강요당한 바 없었다고 하여도 檢事앞에서의 자백은 결국 임의성 없는 진술이 될 수 밖에 없다 (大法院 判決 1981.10.13 선고, 81 도 2160). (b). 내용 삭제

0094

조항	페이지	현 행	수 정
제9조	70	155.	155. 이러한 지적에 대응하여 大韓民國 정부는 다각적인 개선노력을 추진중에 있다. 먼저 임의동행을 규정하고 있는 警察官職務執行法을 1988.12.31, 1991.3.8. 두차례에 걸쳐 개정한 바 있는데, "警察官의 임의동행요구를 당해인은 거절할 수 있다"(제3조 제2항 후단), "동행을 한 경우 警察官은 당해인의 가족 또는 친지 등에게 동행한 警察官의 신분, 동행장소, 동행목적과 이유를 告知하거나 본인으로 하여금 즉시 연락할 수 있는 기회를 부여하여야 하며, 辯護人의 조력을 받을 권리가 있음을 고지하여야 한다"(제3조 제5항), "동행한 경우 警察官은 당해인을 6시간을 초과하여 警察官署에 머물게 할 수 없다"(제3조 제6항)라고 규정하는 등 종래와는 달리 임의동행의 要件과 節次 및 時間을 엄격히 제한함으로써 임의동행의 남용과 이로 인한 人權侵害를 최소화하려고 노력하였다. 다음으로 人身拘束制度 전반에 걸친 합리적 改善方案을 꾸준히 연구하는 한편, 사전에 충분한 증거를 수집하여 拘束令狀을 발부

0095

조항	페이지	현 행	수 정
			받은 後 被疑者를 체포하던가 刑事訴訟法상 緊急拘束制度를 적극 활용함으로써 適法 節次가 최대한 준수될 수 있도록 각별히 노력하고 있다.
제9조	74	162.	162. 憲法 제12조 제6항은 "누구든지 逮捕 또는 拘束을 당한 때에는 適否의 심사를 法院에 청구할 權利를 가진다"라고 규정 하고 있으며, 또한 刑事訴訟法 제214조의2 (拘束의 適否審査), 제214조의3 (再拘束의 제한)은 모든 범죄에 대하여 拘束適否審査 請求를 할 수 있도록 규정하고 있다.
제10조	82	184.	184. 내용 삭제
		185.	185. 내용 삭제
		186.	186. 내용 삭제

0096

조항	페이지	현 행	수 정
제10조	83-84	190.	分類處遇 190. (a) 分類審査 新入少年은 一般保護少年과 分離 收容하고 10일간에 걸쳐 分類調査를 실시하며 保護少年處遇審査委員會의 분류조사결과 밝혀진 제사실과 감별결과를 종합하여 分類收容, 處遇期間, 教育課程 등을 구체적으로 결정한다 (少年院法施行令 제4조, 제11조, 제14조, 제15조). (b) 分類收容 少年院을 기능별로 4개 教科教育. 3개 職業訓練. 1개 女子. 1개 特別. 2개 綜合少年院으로 분류하여 운영하고 保護少年의 성별, 연령, 입원횟수, 공범유무, 비행의 질, 처우기간, 교육과정 등에 따라 시설을 달리하거나 동일시설내에서 分類收容한다 (少年院法 제8조, 同法施行令 제4조, 제11조, 제15조, 제16조).

0097

조 항	페이지	현 행	수 정
	84-85	191.	收容期間 191. 收容期間은 敎化改善의 결과에 따라 신축성을 두는 교육기간으로서 단기로 소년원에 送致된 소년은 6개월이내, 矯正 容易者는 6개월이상 13개월미만, 교정이 곤란한 자는 13개월이상 18개월미만, 特定 强力事犯 등 교정이 극히 곤란한 자는 18개월이상으로 분류하고 교정성적에 따라 수시로 기간을 조정하고 있으나 最長收容 期間은 2년을 초과하지 않고 있다 (少年法 제32조 제1항 제6호,제7호, 少年院法 제 43조 및 제44조, 保護觀察法 제28조 제1항, 少年院生收容指針 제21조 제2항).
	85-86	192. - 194.	收容施設 192. 少年院의 收容密度는 3평방미터당 1명 으로서 여유가 있고 敎育訓練에 필요한 학습기자재를 구비하여 일반학교에 준하여 일과를 진행하며 여가시간에는 TV시청,신문 읽기, 운동경기 등을 자유롭게 하고 있다.

0098

조항	페이지	현 행	수 정
			193. 保護少年에게는 생활 및 교육에 필요한 일체의 물품을 지급하며 소년원마다 의사와 간호사를 배치하여 진료를 하고 원내에서 치료가 곤란한 때에는 外部病院에서 치료를 한다.
			194. 면회는 不良交友 등 교정교육에 해롭다고 인정되는 사람을 제외하고는 전면 허용하고 있으며 면회인원 및 횟수에 제한이 없다 (少年院法 제18조, 同法施行令 제48조, 제50조).
	86	195.	陳情制度 195. 각 少年院마다 이용이 편리한 장소에 請願函을 설치하고 請願事項에 대해서는 신속하게 그 처리결과를 通知하며 월 1회 이상 여론조사를 실시하여 그 결과를 少年院 運營에 반영하고 있다 (少年院法 제10조, 제11조, 同法施行令 제19조, 제20조).

0099

추 록

- 국가보안법 개정에 따른 관련부분 수정 -

0100

O 규약 제18조

국가보안법상 불고지죄와 양심의 자유 (246.항)

- 전책 삭재

RECEIVED FROM 5037046   1991.05.24 11:33   P. 3

O 규약 제 19조

국가보안법과 표현의 자유 (252.항 - 256.항)

- 다음과 같이 수정

0102

(다음)

표현의 자유의 제한

○ 언론·출판의 자유가 민주주의 사회의 초석으로서 우월적 지위를
보장받고 최대한 존중되어야 한다는 원칙에는 이론이 있을 수
없으나 표현의 자유라 하더라도 절대적, 무제한적인 것은 아니다.

○ 규약 제19조 제3항이 규정하는 바와 같이 현행 헌법도 표현의
자유에 대하여 국가안전보장, 질서유지 또는 공공복리를 위하여
필요한 경우에는 법률로써 제한할 수 있게 하고 있다 (제37조
제2항).
따라서 표현의 자유에 관해서도 본질적 내용을 침해하지 않는
한 일정한도 내에서 필요하고 합리적인 제한은 허용된다고 보고
있다.

○ 헌법 제76조에 의하여 대통령이 긴급명령을 발한 경우에는 언론·
출판의 자유도 상술한 일반적인 원칙에 따르지 아니하고 긴급
명령에 의하여 제한을 받게 되고, 헌법 제77조 제3항에 의하여
비상계엄이 선포되면 법률이 정하는 바에 따라 계엄사령관은
포고령에 의하여 언론·출판의 자유에 대하여 특별한 조치를 취할
수 있다 (계엄법 제9조 제1항).

표현의 자유와 국가보안법과의 관계

o 표현의 자유와 관련되어서는 특히 국가보안법과의 관계가 문제
되고 있다.

지금까지 동법을 둘러싸고 인권침해와 관련한 많은 논란이 있었
으며, 국제인권단체 등에서는 표현의 자유를 억압하는데 악용
된다는 주장을 펴왔다.

그러나 대한민국의 분단상황은 복수한 것으로서 전통적. 유교적.
윤리적 사고방식을 가진 단일혈통민족이 외세에 의해 남북으로
분단되면서 이데올로기적으로 대립하게 되었고, 그 과정에서
6.25전쟁으로 3년간 피비린내나는 동족상잔의 비극을 겪었다.

이러한 비극적 경험으로 인하여 대다수 국민은 아직도 남한적화
정책을 최우선 목표로 하고 있는 북한의 위험성을 피부로 느끼고
있으며, 정부를 중심으로 일치단결하여 대처해 나가야 함을 깊이
인식하고 있다.

이와 같은 대다수 국민의 지지하에 정부는 우리의 자유민주주의
체제를 수호하기 위하여 국가보안법을 제정.적용해 나가고 있는
것이다.

o 국가보안법상 특히 표현의 자유와 관련하여서는 반국가단체 및
그 구성원 등의 활동을 찬양.고무.동조한 자나 이적표현물을
제작.반포하는 등의 행위를 한 자를 처벌하도록 규정하고 있는
동법 제7조 제1항, 제5항이 문제되어 왔다.

1991.05.24 11:35

ㅇ 이에 대하여 헌법재판소는 1990.4.2. 국가보안법 제7조 제1항,
제5항은 각 그 소정행위가 국가의 안전.존립을 위태롭게 하거나
자유민주적 기본질서에 위해를 줄 경우에 적용된다고 할 것이므로
이러한 해석하에 헌법에 위배되지 않는다는 결정을 한 바 있으며
(1990.4.2. 89 헌가 113호 결정), 대한민국 정부는 이러한 헌법
재판소의 결정을 존중하여 본 조항의 해석, 적용에 더욱 신중을
기하여 왔다.

ㅇ 1991.5.10 대한민국 국회는 헌법재판소의 이러한 결정취지를
그대로 반영, 국가보안법 제7조 제1항,제5항을 개정하여 "국가의
존립.안전이나 자유민주적 기본질서를 위태롭게 한다는 정을
알면서" 반국가단체 및 그 구성원 등을 찬양.고무한 경우에만
처벌토록 구성요건을 명확히 하여 인권침해의 소지를 배제하였다.
개정된 국가보안법은 1991.5. . 공포.시행되고 있다.

법   무   부

인권 2031-**7472**   503-7045   1991. 6. 7.

수신   외무부장관

참조   국제기구조약국장

제목   국제인권규약보고서 송부

　　　시민적 및 정치적 권리에 관한 국제규약 제40조에 따른 최초

보고서를 별첨과 같이 작성, 송부하오니 유엔 인권이사회에 제출하여

주시기 바랍니다.

첨 부 : 시민적 및 정치적 권리에 관한 국제규약 제40조에 따른
　　　　최초 보고서

법   무   부

0106

0107

국제인권규약 최초보고서 수정내용

===================================

I. 본 보고서 수정내용은 국제인권규약 최초보고서 작성후 수집된 관계부처
   검토의견과 1991.5.10 국회에서 개정된 국가보안법 등을 반영한 것임

II. 수정내용

조항	페이지	현 행 (paragraph)	수 정
제3조	34-35	50. - 51.	50. 1948년 大韓民國 정부수립 이전까지는 大韓民國의 전통사회는 봉건적 儒敎思想에 젖어 男性爲主의 差別이 女性의 삶을 지배하였다. 그러나 1948.7.17 공포된 大韓民國 憲法은 남녀간의 平等을 인정함으로써 國家生活의 많은 분야에서 男性과 더불어 女性이 同等하게 참여할 수 있도록 문호를 개방하였다.
	35	54.	54. 내용 삭제
	38	61.	61. 1988.2.25 政務長官(제2)실이 발족되어 女性이 長官으로 취임하였다. 同 長官室에서는 女性問題를 해결하기 위하여 政策을 입안하고 실행하는 기능을 수행하는 등 여성과 관련된 업무에 중점을 두고 있다.

0108

조 항	페이지	현 행 (paragraph)	수 정
제3조	38-39	64.	64. 女性政策審議委員會 (The National Committee of Women's Policies)가 1983. 12.8 國務總理室 산하에 설치되었다. 이 委員會는 여성업무에 관한 최상위의 政府委員會로서 특히 여성과 관련된 基本計劃과 綜合政策을 수립하고 관계 행정기관간의 여성분야 施策을 조정하는 기능을 수행한다. 委員會는 25명 이내의 委員으로 구성되어 있는데 國務總理를 委員長으로 하여 관계부처의 長官 및 女性問題 專門家들이 委員으로 참여하고 있다. 女性問題를 다루는 기타 政府委員會로는 淪落女性善導委員會 (The Committee to Provide Guidance to Women in Prostitution)와 婦女指導協議會 (The Council of Women's Guidance)가 있다.
		65.	65. 내용 삭제
		66.	66. 내용 삭제
		67.	67. 내용 삭제
	45	88.	88. 내용 삭제
		89.	89. 내용 삭제

0109

조 항	페이지	현 행 (paragraph)	수 정
제7조	65	144.	144. 大韓民國 大法院은 다음과 같은 판결에서 보듯이 고문 등에 의하여 강요된 자백에 대한 증거능력을 부인하여 刑事被疑者 또는 被告人의 自白을 얻기 위한 고문, 폭행,협박,구속의 부당한 장기화를 실질적으로 금지하고 있다. 被告人들이 檢察 이전의 수사과정에서 고문 등으로 임의성 없는 자백을 하고, 그 후 檢事의 조사단게에서도 임의성 없는 심리상태가 계속되어 동일한 내용의 진술을 하였다면 비록 檢事앞에 조사받을 당시는 고문 등 자백을 강요당한 바 없었다고 하여도 檢事앞에서의 자백은 결국 임의성 없는 진술이 될 수 밖에 없다 (大法院 判決 1981.10.13 선고, 81 도 2160). (b). 내용 삭제
제8조	67	150.	150. 규약 제3항(b)에서 말하는 중노동을 수반한 拘禁刑에 해당하는 刑罰로 刑法 제41조는 일정한 노동이 따르는 懲役刑을 규정하고 있으며, 財産刑에 대한 換刑處分으로서의 勞役場 留置에 대하여는 刑法 제70조에 규정되어 있다.

0110

조 항	페이지	현 행 (paragraph)	수 정
제9조	70	155.	155. 이러한 지적에 대응하여 大韓民國 정부는 다각적인 개선노력을 추진중에 있다. 먼저 임의동행을 규정하고 있는 警察官職務執行法을 1988.12.31, 1991.3.8. 두차례에 걸쳐 개정한 바 있는데, "警察官의 임의동행요구를 당해인은 거절할 수 있다" (제3조 제2항 후단), "동행을 한 경우 警察官은 당해인의 가족 또는 친지 등에게 동행한 警察官의 신분, 동행장소, 동행목적과 이유를 告知하거나 본인으로 하여금 즉시 연락할 수 있는 기회를 부여하여야 하며, 辯護人의 조력을 받을 권리가 있음을 고지하여야 한다" (제3조 제5항), "동행한 경우 警察官은 당해인을 6시간을 초과하여 警察官署에 머물게 할 수 없다" (제3조 제6항)라고 규정하는 등 종래와는 달리 임의동행의 要件과 節次 및 時間을 엄격히 제한함으로써 임의동행의 남용과 이로 인한 人權侵害를 최소화하려고 노력하였다. 다음으로 人身拘束制度 전반에 걸친 합리적 改善方案을 꾸준히 연구하는 한편, 사전에 충분한 증거를 수집하여 拘束令狀을 발부

0111

조 항	페이지	현 행 (paragraph)	수　　　　　정
			받은 후 被疑者를 체포하던가 刑事訴訟法상 緊急拘束制度를 적극 활용함으로써 適法 節次가 최대한 준수될 수 있도록 각별히 노력하고 있다.
제9조	74	162.	162. 憲法 제12조 제6항은 "누구든지 逮捕 또는 拘束을 당한 때에는 適否의 심사를 法院에 청구할 權利를 가진다"라고 규정 하고 있으며, 또한 刑事訴訟法 제214조의2 (拘束의 適否審査), 제214조의3 (再拘束의 제한)은 모든 범죄에 대하여 拘束適否審査 請求를 할 수 있도록 규정하고 있다.
제10조	82	184.	184. 내용 삭제
		185.	185. 내용 삭제
		186.	186. 내용 삭제

조항	페이지	현 행 (paragraph)	수 정
제10조	83-84	190.	**分類處遇** 190. (a) 分類審査 新入少年은 一般保護少年과 分離 收容하고 10일간에 걸쳐 分類調査를 실시하며 保護少年處遇審査委員會의 분류조사결과 밝혀진 제사실과 감별결과를 종합하여 分類收容, 處遇期間, 敎育課程 등을 구체적으로 결정한다 (少年院法施行令 제4조, 제11조, 제14조, 제15조). (b) 分類收容 少年院을 기능별로 4개 敎科敎育. 3개 職業訓練. 1개 女子. 1개 特別. 2개 綜合少年院으로 분류하여 운영하고 保護少年의 성별, 연령, 입원횟수, 공범유무, 비행의 질, 처우기간, 교육과정 등에 따라 시설을 달리하거나 동일시설내에서 分類收容한다 (少年院法 제8조, 同法施行令 제4조, 제11조, 제15조, 제16조).

0113

조 항	페이지	현 행 (paragraph)	수　　　정
	84-85	191.	收容期間 191. 收容期間은 敎化改善의 결과에 따라 신축성을 두는 교육기간으로서 단기로 소년원에 送致된 소년은 6개월이내, 矯正容易者는 6개월이상 13개월미만, 교정이 곤란한 자는 13개월이상 18개월미만, 特定强力事犯 등 교정이 극히 곤란한 자는 18개월이상으로 분류하고 교정성적에 따라 수시로 기간을 조정하고 있으나 最長收容期間은 2년을 초과하지 않고 있다 (少年法 제32조 제1항 제6호,제7호, 少年院法 제43조 및 제44조, 保護觀察法 제28조 제1항, 少年院生收容指針 제21조 제2항).
	85-86	192. - 194.	收容施設 192. 少年院의 收容密度는 3평방미터당 1명으로서 여유가 있고 敎育訓練에 필요한 학습기자재를 구비하여 일반학교에 준하여 일과를 진행하며 여가시간에는 TV시청,신문읽기, 운동경기 등을 자유롭게 하고 있다.

0114

조 항	페이지	현 행 (paragraph)	수 정
			193. 保護少年에게는 생활 및 교육에 필요한 일체의 물품을 지급하며 소년원마다 의사와 간호사를 배치하여 진료를 하고 원내에서 치료가 곤란한 때에는 外部病院에서 치료를 한다.
			194. 면회는 不良交友 등 교정교육에 해롭다고 인정되는 사람을 제외하고는 전면 허용하고 있으며 면회인원 및 횟수에 제한이 없다 (少年院法 제18조, 同法施行令 제48조, 제50조).
	86	195.	陳情制度
			195. 각 少年院마다 이용이 편리한 장소에 請願函을 설치하고 請願事項에 대해서는 신속하게 그 처리결과를 通知하며 월 1회 이상 여론조사를 실시하여 그 결과를 少年院 運營에 반영하고 있다 (少年院法 제10조, 제11조, 同法施行令 제19조, 제20조).
제12조	89	204.	204. 내용 삭제

0115

조항	페이지	현 행 (paragraph)	수 정
제14조	94-95	212.	212. 내용 중 "辯護人接見權과 搜査權" 제하의 내용 삭제
제14조	101	222.	222. 내용 삭제
제18조	110	246.	246. 내용 삭제
제19조	114- 115	252. - 256.	表現의 自由의 制限 ○ 言論·出版의 自由가 민주주의 사회의 礎石 으로서 우월적 지위를 보장하고 최대한 존중되어야 한다는 원칙에는 이론이 있을 수 없으나 表現의 自由라 하더라도 絶對的, 無制限的인 것은 아니다. ○ 규약 제19조 제3항이 규정하는 바와 같이 현행 憲法도 表現의 自由에 대하여 國家 安全保障, 秩序維持 또는 公共福利를 위하여 필요한 경우에는 法律로써 制限할 수 있게 하고 있다 (제37조 제2항). 따라서 表現의 自由에 관해서도 本質的 內容을 侵害하지 않는한 일정한도 내에서 필요하고 합리적인 制限은 허용된다고 보고 있다.

조 항	페이지	현 행 (paragraph)	수　　　정
			○ 憲法 제76조에 의하여 大統領이 緊急命令 을 발한 경우에는 言論·出版의 自由도 상술한 一般的인 原則에 따르지 아니하고 緊急命令에 의하여 制限을 받게 되고, 憲法 제77조 제3항에 의하여 非常戒嚴이 宣布되면 法律이 정하는 바에 따라 戒嚴 司領官은 布告令에 의하여 言論·出版의 自由에 대하여 특별한 措置를 취할 수 있다 (戒嚴法 제9조 제1항). 表現의 自由와 國家保安法과의 關係 ○ 表現의 自由와 관련되어서는 특히 國家 保安法과의 관계가 문제되고 있다. 지금까지 同法을 둘러싸고 人權侵害와 관련한 많은 논란이 있었으며, 國際人權 團體 등에서는 表現의 自由를 억압하는데 惡用된다는 주장을 펴왔다. 그러나 大韓民國의 分斷狀況은 특수한 것 으로서 傳統的·儒敎的·倫理的 사고방식을 가진 單一血統民族이 외세에 의해 남북 으로 분단되면서 이데올로기적으로 대립

0117

조항	페이지	현 행 (paragraph)	수 정
			하게 되었고, 그 과정에서 6.25전쟁으로 3년간 피비린내 나는 동족상잔의 비극을 겪었다. 이러한 비극적 경험으로 인하여 대다수 국민은 아직도 南韓赤化政策을 최우선 목표로 하고 있는 북한의 위험성을 피부로 느끼고 있으며, 정부를 중심으로 一致團結하여 대처해 나가야 함을 깊이 인식하고 있다. 이와 같은 대다수 국민의 지지하에 정부는 우리의 自由民主主義體制를 수호하기 위하여 國家保安法을 制定·適用해 나가고 있는 것이다. ㅇ 國家保安法상 특히 表現의 自由와 관련하여서는 反國家團體 및 그 構成員 등의 활동을 讚揚·鼓舞·同調한 자나 利敵表現物을 製作·頒布하는 등의 행위를 한 자를 처벌하도록 규정하고 있는 同法 제7조 제1항, 제5항이 문제되어 왔다.

조 항	페이지	현 행 (paragraph)	수 정
			○ 이에 대하여 憲法裁判所는 1990.4.2. 國家 保安法 제7조 제1항, 제5항은 각 그 소정 행위가 國家의 安全·存立을 위태롭게 하거나 自由民主的 基本秩序에 위해를 줄 경우에 適用된다고 할 것이므로 이러한 해석하에 憲法에 위배되지 않는다는 결정 을 한 바 있으며 (1990.4.2. 89 헌가 113 호 결정), 大韓民國 정부는 이러한 憲法 裁判所의 決定을 존중하여 동 조항의 解釋, 適用에 더욱 신중을 기하여 왔다. ○ 1991.5.10 大韓民國 國會는 憲法裁判所의 이러한 결정취지를 그대로 반영, 國家保安 法 제7조 제1항,제5항을 개정하여 "國家의 存立.安全이나 自由民主的 基本秩序를 위태롭게 한다는 정을 알면서"反國家團體 및 그 構成員 등을 讚揚.鼓舞하거나 利敵 表現物을 製作.頒布하는 등의 행위를 한 자만을 처벌토록 構成要件을 명확히 하여 人權侵害의 소지를 배제하였다. 개정된 國家保安法은 1991.5.31. 公布. 施行되었다.

0119

법   무   부

인권 2031- **7545**   503-7045   1991. 6. 10.

수신 외무부

참조 국제연합과장

제목 국제인권규약보고서 송부

　　　　시민적 및 정치적 권리에 관한 국제규약 제40조에 의거 유엔

인권이사회에 제출할 최초보고서를 별첨과 같이 작성, 송부하오니 업무에

참고하시기 바랍니다.

첨 부 ： 시민적 및 정치적 권리에 관한 국제규약 제40조에 따른

　　　　　최초보고서 30 부. 끝.

법   무   부   장   관

0120

분류번호	보존기간

발 신 전 보

번 호 : WGV-0764   910612 1839 FN   종별 : ____

수 신 : 주   제네바   대사. 총영사 ♣♣♣♣♣
             (국연)

발 신 : 장 관

제 목 : 아국 인권보고서

대 : (1) 제네(정) 2031-488 (91.5.23)

(2) 제네(정) 2031-518 (91.6.7)

1. 법무부는 국제인권규약(B규약) 제 40조에 따른 아국 최초 인권
보고서 영문본은 91.7월초에 작성 완료하여 귀관에 송부할 예정임.

2. 아국 인권보고서 제출 및 심의와 관련, 하기 사항을 인권사무국에
확인하여 회보바람.

가. 인권보고서 제출 부수 및 동 보고서를 책자로 인쇄할 필요성
여부 (보고서는 본문 약 170페이지, 첨부(관련법규정) 약
100페이지 정도로 예상)

나. 대호(1)에 따른 핵심자료 (core document)는 시한이 금년말
인바, 금차 보고서 제출시 이를 함께 작성, 제출해야 하는지
여부

다. 대호(2) 제 42차 인권이사회에서의 수단, 모로코, 마다가스칼,
요르단 인권보고서 심의가 공개로 진행되는지 및 아국대표
참관 가능성 여부

라. 기타 참고사항. 끝.

검 토 필(1991. 6. 30.)

(국제기구조약국장 문동석) 보 안 통 제

앙 고 재	91년 6월 12일	기안자 성명	과 장	국 장	차 관	장 관	외신과통제
		송영완		전필			

0121

원 본 ✓

외 무 부

종 별 :

번 호 : GVW-1097

일 시 : 91 0613 1730

수 신 : 장관(국연)

발 신 : 주 제네바 대사

제 목 : 아국인권 보고서

대: WGV-0764

연: 제네(정) 2031-488

대호, 아래 보고함

1. 보고서는 인권사무국에 1 부 제출하며, 사무국에서 번역 및 편집작업을 하므로 책자로 인쇄할 필요는 없음

2. 연호 핵심자료는 인권보고서와는 별도로 금년말까지 제출하면 됨.

3. 인권 이사회에서의 보고서 심의는 공개로 진행되므로 정부 및 NGO 대표들의 참관이 가능함. 다만 동회의에는 통상적으로 소수 NGO 대표가 참관하며, 정부대표의 참관은 드문 실정임.

4. 아국 보고서 심의에 참고하기 위해서는 아국과 인권보장 수준 및 여건, 법체계가 비슷한 국가의 보고서 심의시 참관 또는 회의 요록을 참조, 동내용을 파악하는 것이 바람직할 것으로 사료됨. 끝

(대사 박수길-국장)

예고: 91.12.31. 까지

검 토 필(1991. 6. 30.)

국기국   1차보   2차보

28680

기 안 용 지

분류기호 문서번호	국연 2031 -	(전화:)	시 행 상 특별취급	지 급
보존기간	영구·준영구· 10. 5. 3. 1	장		관
수 신 처 보존기간				
시행일자	1991.6.21.			

보조기관	국 장	전결	협조기관		문서통제
	과 장	(서명)			
기안책임자		송영완			발송인

경 유			발신명의		
수 신	수신처참조				
참 조					
제 목	국제인권규약 보고서(영문초안)				

   1. 법무부 인권 2031-7545(91.6.10) 관련입니다.

   2. 시민적 및 정치적 권리에 관한 국제규약 제40조에

의거, 유엔 인권사무국에 91.7.9한 제출해야 하는 아국의

최초보고서의 영문본 일부(일반적 사항 - 9조까지)를 별첨

송부하오니 귀부 해당사항에 대한 수정안을 별첨 요령에

따라 영문으로 작성, 6.29한 당부 필착토록 협조하여 주시기

바랍니다.

/계속...

0123

3. 상기 보고서의 영문본 잔여분(10조-27조)은 6.25한

귀부로 송부할 예정임을 알려드립니다.

첨부 : 1. 영문본 수정요령 1부.

　　　2. 아국 최초보고서 영문본(일반적사항 - 9조) 1부. 끝.

수신처 : 법무부(참조 : 인권과장), 내무부(참조 : 치안본부

　　　　수사과장), 국방부(참조 : 법무관리관), 교육부

　　　　(참조 : 교직과장), 문화부(참조 : 종무실장),

　　　　보건사회부(참조 : 법무담당관), 노동부(참조 : 노정

　　　　과장), 체신부(참조 : 법무담당관), 공보처(참조 :

　　　　법무담당관), 정무 제2장관(참조 : 제2조정관),

　　　　~~국가안전기획부(참조 : 대공수사국장)~~

0124

아국 최초 인권보고서(영문본) 수정요령

1. 주요 수정대상

   o 고유명사(부서명, 기구명, 법령명등)

   o 전문용어

   o 법령번역상의 오류

   - 법령중 영문본이 없는 경우 국문 법령의 조문을 가급적 직역
     하였는 바, 동 번역시 법조문의 취지가 오역된 경우 수정요
     (단, 영문본이 있는 법령중에서 동 영역이 미흡한 경우 또는
     내용이 불명확한 경우, 보고서에는 가급적 법령의 취지가 전달
     되도록 이를 수정하여 인용함)

   o 내용 중복 또는 삭제

   - 내용상 불필요하게 중복된 부분 또는 필히 포함되어야 할 내용이
     영역시 삭제된 부분

   o 내용상의 의미 부정확

   - 보고서 내용상 국내적으로는 통상 쓰이는 용어로 설명되어 아국인
     에게는 별도 부연설명이 필요하지 않으나, 이를 아국의 관습,
     통념 또는 법체계에 밝지않은 외국인의 시각으로 볼때 부연설명
     되어야 정확한 의미가 전달될 수 있는 부분

   o 번역상의 오류

   - 번역이 잘못된 부분

   o 기타사항

   - 기타 보고서 번역상 문제점

2. 수정 양식

    O 수정요망 내용을 필히 영문으로 하기양식에 작성, 제출하여 주시기
       바람.

page	paragraph	수정을 요하는 부분	수 정 안

0126

기 안 용 지

분류기호 문서번호	국연 2031-	(전화:)	시 행 상 특 별 취 급	
보존기간	영구 68790 10. 5. 3. 1		장 관	
수 신 처 보존기간				
시행일자	1991.6.24.			

보 조 기 관	국 장	전결	협 조 기 관		문서통제
	과 장				
	기안책임자	송영완			발 송 인
경 유			발 신 명 의		
수 신	주제네바 대표부				1991. 6.
참 조					외무부
제 목	아국 인권보고서				

   1. 시민적 및 정치적 권리에 관한 국제규약 제40조에

따른 아국 인권보고서 국문최종본 및 영문번역본 일부(일반적

사항 - 본문 9조까지)를 별첨 송부합니다.

   2. 아국 인권보고서 영문번역과 관련, 내용수정 또는

보완.삭제가 필요할 경우 동 귀견을 6.30한 본부로 전문

보고하여 주시기 바랍니다.

   3. 영문번역문 완결본은 91.7.1. 귀관행 파편 송부할

예정임을 참고하시기 바랍니다.   /계속/

0127

첨부 : 1. 아국 인권보고서(국문최종본) 3부.

2. 영문번역문 일부 1부. 끝.

발 신 전 보

	분류번호	보존기간

번 호 : WGV-0827 910625 1911 ED 종별 : _____

수 신 : 주 제네바 대사. ♣♧♧♧ (김종훈 서기관님)

발 신 : 장 관 (유엔과 송영완 배)

제 목 : 업 연

연 : 국연 2031-22790

1. 아국 인권보고서는 현재 마무리 작업중인 바, 7.1. 파편 최종본을
   보내드릴 계획임.

2. 동 보고서는 당초 법무부측과 50page 내외로 작성키로 하였으나
   부득이 총 160page 정도의 방대한 분량이 되어 번역작업에 시간이
   많이 지체되고 있음. 동 보고서는 미국에서 수학한 유능한
   변호사가 감수를 하고 있으나, 그곳에서 미(영)국인이 한번더
   review하는 것이 바람직 할것으로 사료됨.

3. 보고서를 검토할 충분한 시간을 못드려 죄송함. 끝.

보안통제	𝓤𝓎

앙고재	91년 6월 25일	기안자 성명		과 장	국 장	차 관	장 관	외신과통제
	선과	송영완					𝓤𝓎	

0129

기안용지

분류기호 문서번호	국연 2031 - 3012-6	(전화:)	시 행 상 특별취급	지 급
보존기간	영구·준영구· 10. 5. 3. 1	장	관	
수 신 처 보존기간				
시행일자	1991.6.26.			

보조 기관	국 장	전결	협 조 기 관		문서통제
	과 장	*(서명)*			*(날인)*
기안책임자		송영완			발송인

경 유			발 신 명 의	
수 신	수신처참조			*(날인)*
참 조				
제 목	국제인권규약 보고서(영문초안)			

　　1.　국연 2031-28680(91.6.21) 관련입니다.

　　2.　시민적 및 정치적 권리에 관한 국제규약 제40조에 따른

아국의 최초인권보고서 영문본 잔여분(10조-27조)을 별첨 송부

하오니 귀부 해당사항에 관한 수정안을 연호 요령에 따라 영문

으로 작성, 당부로 송부하여 주시기 바랍니다.

　　3.　상기 아국의 최초인권보고서 영문수정본은 각부처의

의견 취합후 91.7월초에 귀부로 송부할 예정임을 알려드립니다.

　　　　　　　　　　　　　　　　　　　　　　　　　　　　/계속/

0130

첨부 : 영문본 잔여분(10조-27조). 끝.

수신처 : 법무부(참조 : 인권과장), 내무부(참조 : 치안본부

수사과장), 국방부(참조 : 법무관리관), 교육부

(참조 : 교직과장), 문화부(참조 : 종무실장),

보건사회부(참조 : 법무담당관), 노동부(참조 :

노정과장), 체신부(참조 : 법무담당관), 공보처

(참조 : 법무담당관), 정무 제2장관(참조 : 제2조정관)

0131

내 무 부

수사 20310-   (313-0712)   1991. 6. 29.

수신 외무부장관   (3년)

참조 국제조약국장

제목 국제인권규약 보고서 검토통보

　　　국연 20310 - 28680 (91. 6. 22) 의거 당부소관 검토한바, 특이 수정
할 사항없기 통보합니다.　끝.

내 무 부 장

02 / 20210   0132

정 리 보 존 문 서 목 록					
기록물종류	일반공문서철	등록번호	2020110102	등록일자	2020-11-20
분류번호	734.23	국가코드		보존기간	영구
명 칭	시민적.정치적 권리에 관한 국제규약(B규약) 한국 최초 인권보고서 제출 및 심의, 1991-92. 전5권				
생 산 과	국제연합2과	생산년도	1991~1992	담당그룹	
권 차 명	V.2 1991.7-12월				
내용목차	* 1991.7.31. 시민적.정치적 권리에 관한 인권보고서 유엔인권사무국에 제출				

0001

기 안 용 지

분류기호 문서번호	국연 2031 - **24308**	(전화:)	시 행 상 특별취급	
보존기간	영구·준영구· 10. 5. 3. 1	장		관
수 신 처 보존기간				
시행일자	1991. 7. 1.			

보 조 기 관	국 장	전결	협 조 기 관			문서통제 견열 1991. 7. 01
	과 장	uy				
기안책임자		송영완				발 송 인

경 유			발 신 명 의		발송 1991. 7. 01 외부무
수 신	주제네바 대사				
참 조					
제 목	아국인권보고서				

연 : 국연 2031-22790(91.6.24)

1. 연호, 아국 인권보고서 잔여분(본문 10조-27조)을 별첨

   송부하니, 검토후 수정요망사항을 ~~통~~회보바랍니다.

2. 본부는 상기 아국 인권보고서 영문본 내용에 관한 각 부처

   의견을 취합중이며, 영문번역상의 오류시정을 위한 ~~주국관어~~ 외부

   감수를 시행중인 바, 금후 귀관에서의 수정요망사항도

   접수하여 인권보고서 최종영문본을 작성예정이니 참고

   바랍니다.   /계속/

0002

첨부 : 영문번역문 잔여분(본문 10조-27조). 끝.

0003

✓냥

공　　보　　처

법무 2031-1376　　　　720-0986　　　　1991. 7. 1.

수신　외무부장관

참조　국제연합과장

제목　국제인권규약보고서(영문초안) 수정안 통보

1. 외무부 국연 2031-30126('91.6.26)의 관련입니다.

2. 아국의 최초인권보고서 영문초안에 대한 우리처의 수정안을 별첨과 같이
통보합니다.

첨부 : 수정안 1부.　끝"

공　보　처　장　관

(기획관리실장 전결)

0004

공 보 처 수 정 안

page	paragraph	수정을 요하는 부분 (외무부안)	수 정 안 (공보처안)	근 거
113	15-16 재줄	the Committed on Broadcast (방송위원회)	the Broadcast Committee (방송위원회)	.영문법령의 방송법 (법제처발행)제3장 에 Broadcast Committee로 표기 되어 있음
"	18 재줄	The Committee on Broadcast (방송위원회)	The Broadcast Committee (방송위원회)	. "
"	21 재줄	The Association of the Broadcast Culture Promo- tion (ABCP) (방송문화진흥회)	Foundation For the Broad cast Culture (FFBC) (방송문화진흥회)	.고유명사로서 동 진흥회에서 Foundation For the Broadcast Culture로 쓰고 있음
"	23 재줄	ABCP (방송문화진흥회의 약자)	FFBC (방송문화진흥회의 약자)	
"	23-24 재줄	Association of the Broad- cast Culture Promotion Act (방송문화진흥회법)	Foundation for Broadcast Culture Promotion Act (방송문화진흥회법)	.방송문화진흥회는 사단법인이 아니라 재단법인이므로 Association보다는 Foundation으로의 표기가 바람직함 (법제처 영미담당 법제연구관의 견임)
114	1 재줄	ABCP	FFBC	
"	3 재줄	ABCP	FFBC	
"	10 재줄	Covnéant	Covenant	.Spelling 오자
116	13 재줄	adminstration	administration	. "

0005

정무이 2031 - 238   720-2264   1991. 7. 1

수신 수신처참조

제목 국제인권규약 보고서 영문초안 수정사항 송부

　　　1. 국연 2031-28680 ('91. 6. 22) 및 국연 2031-30126 ('91.
6. 26)과 관련입니다.

　　　2. 국제인권규약 보고서 영문초안 수정사항을 별첨과 같이
송부하오니 참고하시기 바랍니다.

별첨 : 국제인권규약 보고서 영문초안 수정사항 1부.　　끝.

　　　　정　　　　무　　　　장

수신처 : 외무부장관, 법무부장관.

　　　　　　　　　　01 20643

0006

Page	Paragraph	수정을 요하는 부분	수 정 안
31	52 - 6행	... Since 1991.	... Since March 1991. (추가사항) · 1989. 2월 모자복지법 제정 · 1991. 1월 영유아보육법 제정
33	57 - 상단	THE STATUS OF WOMEN UNDER LABOR LAW	STATUS OF WOMEN UNDER LABOR LAWS
33	58 - 상단	UNDER CRIMINAL LAW	UNDER THE CRIMINAL LAW
33	58 - 1행	women under criminal	wonen under the criminal
33	59 - 상단	THE WOMEN PROBLEM	WOMEN'S AFFAIRS
33	59 - 1행	The office of 2nd Minister of State for Political Affairs	The office of Minister of Political Affairs(2)
33	60 - 1행	The Women Social Welfare Division	The Women's Welfare Division
33	60 - 2행	the Women and Children Division	the Women and Minor Labor Division
34	60 - 2행	"	"
34	60 - 4행	center	office
34	61 - 1행	On the local ~ and provinces in 1988.	A Family Welfare Bureau was established in all 15 local administrations in 1988.
34	61 - 4행		Social 삭제
34	62 - 1행	The National ~ to Women	The National Committee on Women's Polices
34	62 - 5행	related authorities.	related government authorities.
34	62 - 6행	members of experts on ~ Ministers.	member of Ministers concerned and experts on women's issues.

(2-1)

Page	Paragraph	수정을 요하는 부분	수 정 안
34	62 - 10행	women are the Committee	women are 근로여성위원회 , the Committee
35	65 - 3행 이후		* 모자복지 추가
37	70		* 정부 각종 위원회에 여성 위원 참여 확대조치 추가

(2-2)

국 　 방 　 부

법무24001- *671*　　　(790-4613)　　　　1990.*7.1*

수신 외무부장관

제목 국제인권규약 보고서(영문초안)검토 결과 통보

　　1. 관련근거 : 가. 국연2031-28680('91. 6. 22)
　　　　　　　　　나. 국연2031-30126('91. 6. 26)

　　2. 위 관련근거에 의거 국제인권규약 보고서(영문초안)을 검토한
결과 특별한 의견이 없음을 통보합니다.　　끝.

국 　 방 　 부 　 장 　 관

　　　　| 법무관리관　　전결 |

아V·21039　　　　　　　　　　　　**0009**

교   육   부

법무 2031- 181   (720-3415)   1991. 7. 4

수신 외무부장관

제목 국제인권규약보고서(영문초안)에 대한 의견

1. 국연 2031-28680('91.6.22) 및 2031-30126('91.6.26)의 관련입니다.

2. 국제인권규약보고서 영문본 중 우리부 해당부분에 대한 검토의견을 별첨과 같이

보내드립니다.

첨부 : 국제인권규약(영문)초안에 대한 의견 1부. 끝 .

교   육   부   장

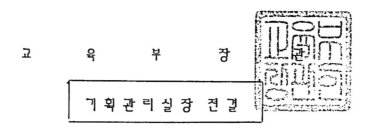

0010

국제인권규약보고서 (영문초안)에 대한 의견

page	paragraph	수 정 을 요 하 는 부 분	수 정 안
22	(3)	Preference in the employment of teachers (89 - ....1990) Article 11(1) of Educational Public Offical Act, - -over the graduates from the private teachers' college over the graduates from the private teachers' college in the employment of teachrs, - - - - -	Preference in the employment of teachers in the Educational Public Official Act (89 -....1990) Article 11(1) of Educational Public Official Act, - - - over the graduates from the private teachers' college in the employment of teachers,- - -
37	71	there were 181,083 female public officials out of 764,563 officials(23.7%) and 111,831 or 61.5% of female officials were involved in education.	there were 181,083 female public officials(23.7%) out of 764,563 officials and 111,831 or 61.5% of the female officials were teachers.
38	72	and the numbers of female teachers continues to rise.	and the number of female teachers continues to rise.
39	77	82. According to Article 31 (1) - - - - - -	77. According to Article 31 (1)- - - -

0011

주 제 네 바 대 표 부

재네(정) 2031-611   1991. 7. 5

수신 : 장관

참조 : 국제기구조약국장

제목 : 아국인권 보고서

대 : 국연 2031-22790 (91. 6.24)

　　　　대호, 아국인권 보고서(전반부)에 대한 당관의 검토 결과를 별첨 송부

하오니 최종 영문본 작성에 참고 하시기 바랍니다.

　　　　첨부 : 동 보고서 (전반부) 1부.　끝.

　　　　　　주　　제　　네　　바　　대

선 결			결재(공람)		
접수일시 1991. 7. 9					
처리과	38012				

0012

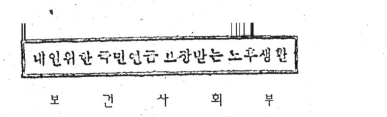

보 건 사 회 부

법무 20310-   503-7525   1991. 7. 5.
                    9438

수신 외무부장관

제목 국제인권보고서 영문본 수정안 제출

　　　1. 국연2031-28680('91.6.22)호 및 2031-30126('91.6.26)호와
관련입니다.

　　　2. 당부관련 국제인권보고서 영문본 수정안을 별첨과 같이 제출합니다.

첨부 : 국제인권보고서 영문본 수정안 1부. 끝.

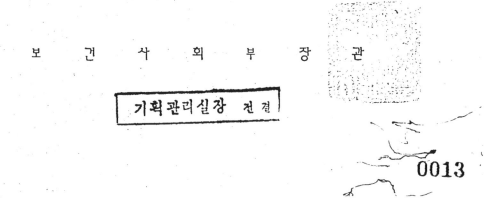

어 2143

　　　보 건 사 회 부 장 관

기획관리실장 전결

0013

국 제 인 권 보 고 서 영 문 본 수 정 안

1 9 9 1 . 7 .

보 건 사 회 부

0014

page	paragraph	수정을 요하는 부분	수 정 안
55	TiTle	MOTHER	Maternal and
55	115 - 3	Mother	Comprehensive Maternal and
55	115 - 4	Mother	Maternal and
55	115 - 4	Offices	Centers
55	115 - 4	Mother	Maternal &
55	115 - 4	infirmaries	Clinics
55	115 - 7	children	infants
55	115 - 7	infants	children
55	115 - 8	worker	workers
55	115 - 8	medical	health
55	117 - 1	Mother-Child	Maternal &
55	117 - 1	Booklet	Health Handbook
55	117 - 2	mother-child health care	MCH
55	117 - 3		and preserves records of MCH services
55	118 - 1	Mother-Child Health Office	MCH Centers
56	119 - 2	mother-child health care	MCH
56	119 - 2	program	programs
56	119 - 3	sanitary	health
56	121 - 1	U5	infant
56	121 - 3	U5	infant
56	121 - 5	U5	infant
57	121 - 6	U5	infants

5-1

0015

page	paragraph	수정을 요하는 부분	수 정 안
58	Title	GET RID OF INFECTIOUS	PREVENT AND CONTROL COMMUNI-CABLE
	125 – 1	get rid of	prevent and control communicable
	125 – 2	infectious	notifiable communicable
	125 – 3	infectious	
	125 – a	autonomous entity infectious curing	government the communicable treating
	125 – b	infectious	communicable
	125 – c	infectious	communicable
	125 – d	infectious	the communicable
	126 – 1	infectious	the communicable
59	Title	treatment	Prevention and Control
	127 2.	treatment	Prevention and control
	127 – 3 .	AIDS patients infection	persons with AIDS/HIV transmission
	127 – 4	under	into
	127 – 6	Delibecation	Review Connittee
	127 – (1)	AIDS infected per son medical	Rerson with HIV the sexually transmitted disease
	127 – (2)	AIDS infected person possivility	Person with HIV risk
	127 – (3)	AIDS infected person AIDS infected person desired	Person with HIV a Person with HIV requests

ξ-2

0016

page	paragraph	수정을 요하는 부분	수 정 안
	127 - (3)	from a facility	in the facilities
	127 - 16	AIDS infected person discovered	Person with HIV identified
	127 - 17	to 138 AIDS infected persons	
	127 - 18	AIDS infected persons	Person with HIV
60	127 - 1	medical	sexually transmitted disease

5-3

0017

영 문 본 검 토 결 과

Page	Paragraph	수정을 요하는 부분	수 정 안
57	124 - 4	Therefore, Some People are Seeking the recognition of brain-death as the legal death.	Therefore, Some People are Seeking the recognition of brain-death as the legal death, this problem is down for a hot discussion.

0018

5-4

Page	Paragraph	수정을 요하는 부분	수 정 안
132	287 첫째줄	13,677,000	14,620,000
	둘째줄	32%	34%
133	287 도 표	90 2000	90 2000
		13,677 12,261	14,620 12,870
		31.9 26.1	34.1 27.5
134	289	"Child Who repuires Protection"	"Child to be Protected"
134	290		
	(a) 둘째줄	Children Counselling centers	Child guidance clini-cs
	"	Special counselors	Professional counsel-ors
	(a) 넷째줄	Children counselling centers	Child guidance clinics
	(a) 여섯째줄	Members of the child-ren committee	Child welfare commit-tee members
	(a) 일곱째줄	Myun and dong (These are units of towns)	Town and villages ✓
135	(c) 첫째줄	Children searching	Child finding centers ✓

0019

5-5

기안용지

분류기호 문서번호	국연 2031 **24962** (전화:)	시 행 상 특별취급	
보존기간	영구·준영구· 10. 5. 3. 1	장	관
수 신 처 보존기간			
시행일자	1991. 7. 8.		m

보조기관	국 장	전 결	협조기관	
	과 장	*uy*		
기안책임자	송영완		

경 유		발신명의	
수 신	주제네바대사		
참 조			

제 목	인권보고서 (영문 수정본)

연 : 국연 2031-24308

1. 연호, 인권보고서 영문초안에 대한 각부처 의견을

취합하여 별첨 수정본을 작성한 바, 문법상의 오류등은 자체적

으로 수정하여 주시기 바라며 용어변경, 표현수정 또는 내용상

첨삭이 필요하다고 인정되는 내용에 대한 귀견을 7.20한 전문

보고하여 주시기 바랍니다.

/ 계속 /   0020

2. 아국 인권보고서 제출은 귀관의 검토의견을 종합하여

영문안을 확정한 후 7.25경 인권이사회에 제출토록 ~~할 보~~ 예정임을

참고하시기 바랍니다. (귀관 검토결과 수정을 필요로 하는 내용이

많지 않을 경우 별첨 영문본을 귀관에서 부분 수정후 유엔에 제출

토록 조치 예정임.)

첨 부 : 영문수정안 1부. 끝.

0021

31607

기안용지

분류기호 문서번호	국연 2031 -	(전화:)	시 행 상 특별취급	
보존기간	영구·준영구· 10. 5. 3. 1	장 관		
수 신 처 보존기간				
시행일자	1991. 7. 8.			

보조 기관	국 장	전 결	협조기관		문서통제 1991. 7. 0
	과 장	*uy.*			
기안책임자	송영완			발송인

경 유		발신명의	발 송 1991. 7. 03 외무부
수 신	법무부장관		
참 조	법무실장		
제 목	아국 인권보고서 (영문)		

연 : 국연 2031-30126

　1.　연호 아국인권보고서 영문초안에 대한 각부처 의견을

취합하여 별첨 수정안을 작성한 바, 동 수정안에 대한 귀견을

7.18.한 당부로 회보하여 주시기 바랍니다.

　2.　별첨 영문 수정안은 7.8. 주제네바 대표부로 송부하였는

바, 동 대표부에서의 재검토 내용 및 귀부 검토의견을 종합하여

7.20경 영문안을 확정하고 동 영문최종안을 늦어도 7.25.경 유엔

인권사무국에 제출토록 주제네바대표부에 지시 예정이니, 영문

0022

수정안에 대한 귀부 의견 회보시 보고서 제출시한 및 영문안

확정을 위한 관계부처 회의개최 필요여부에 관한 귀견도 아울러

회보하여 주시기 바랍니다.

첨 부 : 상기 영문수정안 1부.　　끝.

0023

" 노사관계 안정 "

노   동   부

국제 32220-   (504-7338)   1991. 7. 9.

수신 외무부장관

참조 국제기구조약국장

제목 국제인권규약 보고서 영문본 검토의건

1. 외무부 국인 2031-28080 ('91. 6) 관련입니다.

2. 시민적 및 정치적 권리에 관한 국제규약 제 40조에 따른 최초 보고서
영문본에 대한 당부 검토의견은 첨부와 같이 회신합니다.

첨부 수정양식 1부. 끝.

노   동   부   장

"산업평화 정착"

21985   0024

2. 수정 양식

　○　수정요망 내용을 편히 잉문으로 하기양식에 작성, 재출하여 주시기 바랍.

Page	paragraph	수정을 요하는 부분	수 정 안
31	52	the Equal Opportunities Employment Act	the Gender-equal Opportunities Employment Act
33	60	the Women and Children Division	the Women and Minors Division
34	60	a consulting and guidance center	Women Affairs Guidance Officer
128	line 1	THE LABOR DISPUTE MEDIATION ACT	THE LABOR DISPUTE ADJUSTMENT ACT
	line 8	the Labor Dispute Mediation Act	the Labor Dispute Adjustment Act
	line 16	"	"
129	line 3	"	"
			※ 調整 (Adjustment) 은 斡旋, 調停 (Mediation), 仲裁를 포함한 개념임.

0025

법　무　부

인권 23040-10443　　　503-7045　　　1991. 7. 16

수신　외무부장관

참조　국제기구조약국장

제목　아국 인권보고서(영문)에 대한 수정내용 송부

1.　국연 2031-31607 ('91.7.8)과 관련입니다.

2.　귀부에서 요청한 아국 인권보고서 영문본(수정안) 검토요청에
대한 수정내용을 별첨 송부합니다.

첨부 :　수정내용 1부.　끝.

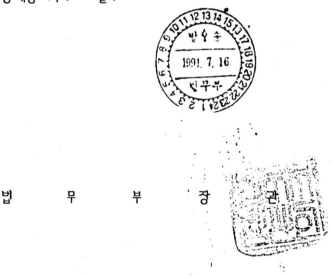

법　무　부　장

0026

page	paragraph	수정을 요하는 부분	수 정 안
1	4	Politidal	political
	5	United Nations1	United Nations
11	4	covenant.	covenant,"
14	16	Question	~~Problem~~
	17	question	problem
	19	question	problem
29	20	file an indictment	~~indict~~ √
30	1	file an indictment	indict √
	5	file an indictment	indict √
	6	file an indictment	indict √
	14	file an indictment, may appeal the decision to	indict, may file an appeal to
	19	may reappeal the decision to	may file a reappeal to
35	19	the costs	~~the expenses~~ √
	20	the cost	the expense √
	23	cost	expense √
	24	cost	expense √

0027

page	paragraph	수정을 요하는 부분	수 정 안
43	6	the custody	fostering and education
	7	child custody	fostering and education
	8	the child custody	fostering and education
50	23	legal procedure	due process of law
52	1-2	crimes for which increased punishment is sentenced, such as	crimes for which punishment ~~are~~ *is* augmented for certain results such as
53	5	to crimes	to the abolition of ~~the~~ crimes
54	21	receive	enjoy
55	18	children	babies
61	4	toture other	toture and other
	12	relating to adjudication	concerning judgement
69	24	attorney	defense counsel
70	13	attorney	defense counsel
72	8	file an indictment	―indict―. ∨
79	21	inmates convicts.	inmates.
83	21	petitioning inmate	petitioner
95	23	cost	―expense―・ ∨

0028

page	paragraph	수정을 요하는 부분	수 정 안
109	2	right	liberty
	15	The detainees in the detention places	Inmates in the correctional facilities
110	13	censorship of	censorship of speech and
112	14	Committe	Committee
118	4-5	사이추가 내용: 신고재는 일반인의 도로, 공원등의 이용과의 충돌을 조정하고, 동일한 장소에서의 여러 집회의 중복으로 인한 혼란을 피하고, 공물관리상 필요한 불가피한 제약으로 인식되고 있다.	영역필요

0029

분류번호	보존기간

발 신 전 보

번   호 : WGV-0944   910724 1527 DQ   종별 :

수   신 : 주 제네바 대사. ❋송영차❋
                (국연)

발   신 : 장 관

제   목 : 인권보고서

연 : 국연 2031-24962

대 : GVW-1373

1. 연호, 인권보고서 내용을 별첨과 같이 수정바람.

2. 본부는 7.24. 상부에 아국 인권보고서 제출관련사항을 보고한 연후, 사무국에의 보고서 제출일자를 귀관에 별도 통보코자 함.

3. 법무부는 유엔사무국에서 아국인권보고서를 유엔회의 문서로 배포되기전까지 동 보고서 전체내용이 국내외 인권단체에 유출됨은 바람직하지 않다는 의견임. 이와관련 본부는 귀관에서 인권보고서를 사무국에 제출하기 직전에 아국의 인권보고서 제출에 관한 간략한 보도자료 (본부 또는 법무부 명의)를 언론에 배포할 예정임을 참고바람.

첨 부 : 인권보고서 수정부분(5매 FAX 송부). 끝.

(WGNA-183)

일반문서로재분류 (1991. 12. 31.)

(국제기구조약국장   문동석)

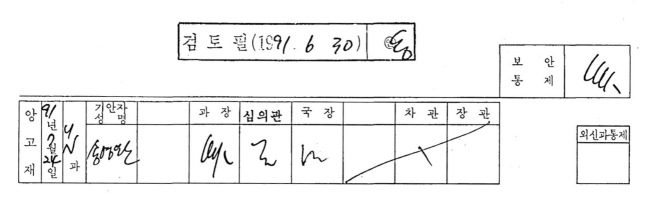

검 토 필 (1991. 6. 30)

		기안자 성명	과 장	심의관	국 장		차 관	장 관	
앙고재	91년 7월 24일	송영식 과							

보 안 통 제	

외신과통제

수 정 내 용

WGVF-0183 910724 1528 DQ

Page	Para	수 정 전	수 정 후
1	4째줄	Politidal	Political
	5째줄	Nationsl	Nations
11	15	Covenant.	Covenant."
43	87(e)		
	6째줄	the custody	fostering and education
	7 "	child custody	"
	8 "	"	"
50	마지막줄	legal procedure	due process of law
52	첫줄	crimes for which increased punishment is sentenced, such as	crimes for which punishment is augmented for certain results, such as
53	110 4째줄	with regard to crimes of abortion,	with regard to the abolition of crimes of abortion,
54	114 6째줄	receive	enjoy
55	5째줄 (소제목)	MOTHER-CHILD HEALTH CARE	MATERNAL AND CHILD HEALTH CARE (MCH)
	115 (괄호속)	(12 Mother-Child Health Centers, 81 Mother-Child Health Offices and 946 Mother-Child Health infirmaries)	(12 Comprehensive Maternal and Child Health Centers, 81 Maternal and Child Health Centers and Child Health Clinics)

0031

Page	Para	수　정　전	수　정　후
55	115.끝줄	medical	health
55	117 첫줄	Mother-Child Booklet	Maternal & Child Health Handbook
	117 2째줄	the mother-child health care programs	the MCH programs, records of MCH services
55	116 4째줄	new-born children	new-born babies
55	118 첫줄	97 Mother-Child Health Offices,	81 MCH Centers,
56	119 2째줄	various mother-child health care programs	various MCH programs
	119 3째줄	sanitary	health
58	(소제목)	MEASURES AND PRACTICES TO GET RID OF INFECTIOUS DISEASES	MEASURES AND PRACTICES TO PREVENT AND CONTROL COMMUNICABLE DISEASES
58	125 첫줄	to eliminate infectious diseases	to prevent and control communicable diseases
	125 (a)3째줄	curing	treating
	125& 126 (8개)	infectious diseases	communicable diseases
59	(소제목)	AIDS Treatment	AIDS Prevention and Control
	127 2째줄	AIDS treatment	AIDS prevention and control
	"	AIDS patients	persons with AIDS/HIV

0032

Page	Para	수 정 전	수 정 후
	127 3째줄	infection.	transmission.
	127(a)	AIDS-infected person medical examination ;	Person with HIV sexually transmitted disease examination ;
	177(b)	AIDS - infected person with a possibility of	Person with HIV with a risk of
	127(c)	AIDS - infected person an AIDS-infected person who desires protection from a protection facility.	Person with HIV a person with HIV who requires protection in the protection facilities.
	127Since 이하(3개)	AIDS - infected person	person with HIV
	127 끝에서 3째줄	medical check-up.	sexually transmitted disease check-up.
61	4째줄	torture other	torture and other
	132 6째줄	relating to adjudication,	concerning judgement,
69	끝줄	an attorney."	a defense counsel."
70	149 3째줄	an attorney.	a defense counsel.
79	172 4째줄	inmates convicts.	inmates.
109	232 2째줄	right	liberty

0033

Page	Para	수 정 전	수 정 후
	233 첫줄	The detainees in the detention places	Inmates in the correctional facilities
110	235 6째줄	censorship of the press	censorship of speech and the press
112	(a)3째줄	Committe.	Committee.
118	255 4째줄 (추가)		In addition, the notification of an assembly or demonstration is considered as inevitable requirement in order to minimize the inconvenience of the general public and protect public facilities and avoid disruption caused by multiple assemblies occuring in one place.
130	287 첫줄 2째줄	13,677,000 32%	14,620,000 34%
131	287도표	90 2000 13,677 12,261 31.9 26.1	90 2000 14,620 12,870 34.1 27.5
132	289	"child who repuires protection"	"child to be protected"

0034

Page	Para	수 정 전	수 정 후
132	290 (a)2째줄	child counselling centers	child guidance clinics
	"	special counselors	professional counselors
	(a)4째줄	child counselling centers	child guidance clinics
	(a)7째줄	members of the Children's Committees	Child welfare Committee members
	(a)8째줄	Eup, Myun and Dong. (these are units of towns)	towns and villages.
133	(c)첫줄	child search centers	child finding centers

0035

외 무 부

종 별 :
번 호 : GVW-1373
수 신 : 장관(국연)
발 신 : 주 제네바 대사
제 목 : 인권보고서

일 시 : 91 0722 1710

대:국연 2031-24962

대호 보고서 115 항 및 118 항(모자보건) 내용중 모자보건센타의 숫자가 상이한바,
재확인후 통보 바람. 끝

(대사 박수길-국장)

국기국

기 안 용 지

분류기호 문서번호	국연 2031- 750	(전화:　　　)	시 행 상 특별취급	
보존기간	영구·준영구· 10. 5. 3. 1	장		관
수 신 처 보존기간				
시행일자	1991. 7. 25.			

보조 기관	국 장	전 결	협 조 기 관	
	심의관			
	과 장	*(서명)*		
기안책임자	송영완			

경 유 수 신 참 조	대통령비서실장 외교안보보좌관, 정책조사보좌관	발신명의

제 목	시민적.정치적 권리에 관한 인권보고서 제출

　　1.　90.7. 아국이 시민적, 정치적 권리에 관한

국제규약(B규약)에 가입함에 따라 동 규약 제 40조에 의거,

아국의 최초 인권보고서를 유엔인권사무국에 제출하여야

합니다.

　　2.　이와관련, 당부는 법무부가 91.6월 귀실주재 관련

부처 회의를 통하여 확정한 아국의 최초 인권보고서를 번역

하고, 관련부처의 검토의견을 종합하여 별첨 영문번역문

최종본을 작성하였습니다.

0037

　/ 계속 /

3. 동 아국 인권보고서 영문본은 주제네바 대사를

통하여 7.31경 유엔 인권사무국에 제출토록 지시코자 하는 바,

보고서 영문본 내용 및 보고서 제출일정등에 관한 의견이

있을 경우 7.30한 당부로 알려주시기 바랍니다.

첨부 : 시민적.정치적 권리에 관한 아국 인권보고서(영문)

　　　　1부. 끝.

0038

기안용지

분류기호 문서번호	국연 2031-		(전화:)	시 행 상 특별취급		
보존기간	영구·준영구· 10. 5. 3. 1		차 관		장 관	
수 신 처 보존기간		대결				
시행일자	1991. 7. 25.					

보조기관	국 장	(서명)	협조기관	제1차관보 (서명)	문서통제
	심의관				
	과 장	(서명)			
기안책임자		송영완			발 송 인

경 유			발신명의		
수 신	내부결재				
참 조					

제 목	시민적.정치적 권리에 관한 인권보고서 제출

   1. 90.7월 아국이 시민적.정치적 권리에 관한 국제

규약(B규약)에 가입함에 따라 동규약 제40조에 의거, 아국의

최초 인권보고서를 유엔 인권사무국에 제출하여야 합니다.

   2. 이와관련, 당부는 법무부가 관련부처의 의견을

취합하여 91.6월 작성한 인권보고서를 번역한 후, 관련부처의

검토의견을 종합하여 별첨 영문 번역문 최종본을 작성한 바,

동 아국 인권보고서 영문본을 7.31경 유엔 인권사무국에

/계속/ 0039

제출토록 주제네바 대사에게 지시하고자 하오니 재가하여

주시기 바랍니다.

첨부 : 표제보고서(영문) 1부. 끝.

0040

Initial Report of the
Republic of Korea under Article 40
of the International Covenant on Civil and
Political Rights

July 1991

Republic of Korea

0041

The Government of the Republic of Korea
submits the following report, which relates to the
progress made in the guarantees of the fundamental
human rights provided for in the International
Covenant on Civil and Political Rights, and in
the enjoyment of these rights, to the Secretary-
General of the United Nations in accordance
with Article 40 of the said Covenant.

I. GENERAL COMMENTS

A.   CONSTITUTIONAL PROTECTION OF CIVIL AND POLITICAL RIGHTS

1.   The first Constitution of the Republic of Korea was proclaimed on 17 July 1948 and there were several amendments to the Constitution until February 1988 when the present Constitution of the Sixth Republic (hereinafter referred to as "the Constitution") was proclaimed. .

As the supreme law of the State, the Constitution, which was adopted upon the desire and consensus of the Korean people, has enormously contributed to the political, economic and social development of the Republic of Korea, and to the protection of human rights of the Korean people.

2.   The Constitution guarantees all the rights provided for in the International Covenant on Civil and Political Rights (hereinafter referred to as "the Covenant"). Article 10 of the Constitution provides, "All citizens shall be assured of human worth and dignity and have the right to pursue happiness. It shall be the duty of the State to confirm and guarantee the fundamental and inviolable human rights of individuals."

In addition, Article 37(1) of the Constitution guarantees the fundamental human rights in an explicit and comprehensive manner stating that "Freedoms and rights of citizens shall not be neglected on the grounds that they are not enumerated in the Constitution."

In compliance with these provisions of the Constitution, the laws and regulations contain more detailed provisions in order to guarantee the rights which are recognized by the Covenant.

3. Generally, the fundamental human rights protected by
    the Constitution are equally guaranteed to all
    foreigners in the Republic of Korea.

    All rights under the Covenant, with the exception of
    the rights which require Korean nationality as a
    condition for enjoyment, such as the right to vote
    or to hold public office, are equally guaranteed to
    all foreigners residing or temporarily staying in
    the Republic of Korea.

4. The Constitution provides that the fundamental human
    rights may be restricted by law only when necessary
    "for national security, the maintenance of law and
    order, or for public welfare." (Art. 37(2) para. 1)

    Concepts such as "national security, the maintenance
    of law and order or public welfare" imply limited
    cases where restrictions on the rights are
    inevitable in order to resolve conflicts among
    individuals in the enjoyment of those rights and to
    guarantee the human rights of each individual to the
    fullest extent.

    With regard to restrictions on the fundamental human
    rights, the Constitution prescribes strict
    limitations on the exercise of the Government's
    power, in order to prevent an abuse of power, by
    providing that "any such restrictions may not
    infringe upon the essential aspects of the
    fundamental human rights." (Art. 37(2) para. 2)

B. RELATIONSHIP BETWEEN THE COVENANT AND THE DOMESTIC LAWS OF THE REPUBLIC OF KOREA

5. Since Article 6(1) of the Constitution provides that "Treaties duly concluded and promulgated under the Constitution and the generally recognized rules of international law shall have the same effect as the domestic laws of the Republic of Korea," the Covenant, which was ratified and promulgated by the Government with the consent of the National Assembly, has the same effect as domestic laws without the enactment of separate domestic legislation.

6. The Korean Government has concluded that the Constitution does not conflict with the Covenant. However, the Government has made reservations on Articles 14(5), 22 and 23(4) of the Covenant which were considered to be incompatible with traditional Korean customs, and the statutory framework and practice based upon the crucial policy objectives of the Republic of Korea. (The reservation on Article 23(4) was withdrawn on 15 March 1991 when the relevant domestic law was amended to conform with the Covenant.)

C. AUTHORITIES HAVING JURISDICTION OVER HUMAN RIGHTS

7. The Constitution guarantees all citizens the right of access to the courts. (Arts. 27 & 101) The judicial power is vested in the Supreme Court, the highest court of the State, and in other lower courts. (Art. 101(2))

   In order to secure independent and just trials, the Constitution provides that "the judges shall rule independently under their own conscience and in accordance with the Constitution and law." (Art. 103)

8. In addition, the Constitution has a provision relating to the organization and competence of the Constitution Court (Arts. 111-113) which has jurisdiction over the following matters:

   (a) Upon a request by the courts, the adjudication of the constitutionality of a law;

   (b) Impeachment;

   (c) Dissolution of a political party;

   (d) Dispute between State agencies, between State agencies and local governments and between local governments;

   (e) Petitions prescribed by law relating to the Constitution.

   In adjudicating the above matters, the Constitution Court has been performing an important and effective role in checking the abusive acts of the Government, securing the independence of the Judiciary and protecting fundamental rights.

9. The Government of the Republic of Korea has a "Human Rights Division" in the Ministry of Justice. The Division has full competence over human rights matters.

   The Human Rights Division is responsible for, inter alia, "the protection of human rights, legal aid, enhancement of the respect for law and order, and affairs relating to private human rights organizations." The Ministry of Justice is planning to reinforce the Division in order to handle more effectively human rights matters which are presently handled by several Government authorities.

10. In the Republic of Korea, the prosecutor has a duty to protect human rights.

As a part of the measures to protect and enhance the fundamental human rights of the citizens, the prosecutor establishes a human rights consultation center in every district attorney's office and its branch offices. The prosecutor also designates a prosecutor in charge of human rights matters to gather information on the instances of human rights violations, and to handle the criminal cases, petitions or secret investigations relating to human rights violations.

11. The Government of the Republic of Korea has several legal aid programs which provide free legal advice, aid for legal costs and an attorney to those who are unable to obtain legal remedies because they are ignorant of the law or cannot afford the legal costs.

The Korea Legal Aid Corporation, established on 1 September 1987 and subsidized by the Government, had dealt with 782,684 cases of legal consultation and 64,328 cases of legal aid by the end of 1990.

12. In the Republic of Korea, there are numerous private organizations for the protection of human rights. The Korean Federal Bar Association is the most prominent of these organizations.

D.   REMEDIES AVAILABLE TO AN INDIVIDUAL WHO CLAIMS AN INFRINGEMENT OF HIS/HER RIGHTS

13. The Constitution and other relevant laws provide numerous remedies to an individual who claims an infringement of his/her fundamental human rights.

Remedies available in case of an infringement of the rights by Government agencies are as follows:

(a) Petition
Generally, an individual who claims an infringement of his/her fundamental rights may obtain remedies by petitioning for the annulment or nullification of the administrative actions, or for the dismissal of the relevant officials under Article 26 of the Constitution. Matters for which petitions are available are prescribed in Article 4 of the Petition Act, and the petitioning method and procedure are prescribed in Articles 6 to 8 of the said Act.

(b) Appeals
An individual, whose rights or interests have been violated by an illegal or unjust administrative action, or by the exercise or non-exercise of Government power by administrative agencies, may use the administrative appeals procedure in order to achieve the proper operation of the administration. (Administrative Appeals Act, Art. 1)

(c) Litigation
Article 107(2) of the Constitution provides that the courts shall adjudicate the constitutionality or legality of administrative actions. The details of the litigation

procedure are prescribed in the Administrative
Litigation Act.

(d) Review of Administrative Decrees and
Regulations

In order to ensure that administrative decrees
and regulations do not violate the fundamental
rights of the citizens, Article 107(2) of the
Constitution provides courts with the power to
review administrative decrees and regulations.
The review of decrees and regulations may be
conducted by the courts when their
constitutionality or legality is at issue in a
trial. The Supreme Court has the power to make
a final review.

(e) Remedies of the Constitution Court

In case of an infringement of fundamental
rights by an unconstitutional administrative
action, an individual may obtain remedies
through a petition to the Constitution Court.
(Refer to no. 8)

(f) Remedies available in case of an infringement
of fundamental human rights and compensation
for damages

An individual, whose fundamental human rights
have been infringed by the unlawful action of a
public official in the course of his/her
official duties, may claim compensation for
damages from the State under the procedures
prescribed by the National Compensation Act.
(Constitution, Art. 29(1))

In case an arrested criminal suspect is not
indicted due to lack of evidence, or an accused
person placed under detention is acquitted by
the court, such persons may claim compensation
from the State (under the procedures prescribed

한국 인권문제 시민적·정치적 권리 국제규약 인권보고서 1

by the Criminal Compensation Act.
(Constitution, Art. 28)

14. Remedies available in case of an infringement of
fundamental human rights by an individual are as
follows:

(a) Complaint or Accusation
In case of an infringement of fundamental
rights by an individual, the person claiming
the infringement is entitled to seek the
withdrawal of the illegal act from the criminal
investigation authorities, i.e., the
prosecutor's office and the police.
For example, through a complaint or accusation
with respect to an unlawful detention or an
infringement of property rights, an individual
can initiate an investigation or prosecution of
the above unlawful acts.
In addition to a complaint or accusation, the
laws of the Republic of Korea provide for other
procedures for requesting an adjudication (Code
of Criminal Procedure, Arts. 260-262), the
details of which will be explained later.
(Refer to No. 133)

(b) Civil Lawsuit for Compensation
An individual, who claims an infringement of
his/her fundamental rights by another person,
can also file a lawsuit to seek compensation
for damages.

(c) Remedies Available to the Victims of a Crime
The Constitution provides for State aid to the
victims of a crime, by stipulating that
"Citizens, who have suffered bodily injury or
death due to criminal acts of others, may
receive aid from the State under the conditions
as prescribed by law." (Art. 30) The State
Aid for Victims of Crime Act, promulgated on 1

July 1988, sets forth detailed methods and procedures for the payment of State aid.

15. Further explanations of the above-mentioned measures to protect human rights, and numerous remedies for the infringements of the rights, will be provided in the "Information Relating to Each Article of the Covenant."

E.   OTHER MEASURES TO ENSURE THE IMPLEMENTATION OF THE PROVISIONS OF THE COVENANT

16. By acceding to the Covenant, the Republic of Korea has expressed its will to participate actively in the concerted international efforts for the protection of human rights. Korea's accession will also contribute to the promotion of respect for human rights in Korea.

17. The Republic of Korea has acceded to the Optional Protocol with a view to enabling its citizens to submit a complaint to the Human Rights Committee. This clearly demonstrates the commitment of the Government of the Republic of Korea to promote respect for and observance of human rights.

18. The Government of the Republic of Korea has made every effort to make the contents of the Covenant fully understood by the Korean people.

Before Korea's accession to the Covenant, the Ministry of Justice held a symposium on the Covenant where people from academic and legal circles participated in a fruitful discussion of the conflicts between the Covenant and domestic laws.

The symposium enhanced public awareness of the Covenant and accelerated the process of accession.

With the accession to the Covenant, the Ministry of Justice has translated into Korean the Covenant, several initial reports submitted by the States Parties to the Covenant in accordance with Article 40 thereof, and selected decisions of the Human Rights Committee.

With the publication and distribution of these translated materials, education on human rights was provided to all levels of public officials - the prosecutors, police, and other law enforcement officers - in order to protect human rights in accordance with the spirit of the Covenant.

19. Every year, the Government of the Republic of Korea designates the week which includes "Human Rights Day" (10th of Dec.), as "Human Rights Week," and holds numerous events such as a commemorative ceremony and symposiums to promote the respect for human rights.

The Government will do its utmost to inform every Korean of the provisions and spirit of the Covenant so that human rights are respected by all individuals. In this respect, there is a positive trend for lawyers as well as agencies such as the Supreme Court and the Constitution Court, to solve legal problems by applying the Covenant in litigation.

INFORMATION RELATING TO EACH ARTICLE OF THE COVENANT

20. The Preamble and Article 5(1) of the Constitution state that the Republic of Korea shall contribute to a lasting world peace and the common prosperity of mankind and shall renounce all aggressive wars.

21. Under the principle of international peace as embodied in its Constitution, the Republic of Korea accepts the principles and the provisions of the United Nations Charter and recognizes that all nations have the right of self-determination and to pursue freely their political, economic, social and cultural development.

    The Republic of Korea has based its foreign policy on the principles enshrined in the Constitution and the United Nations Charter and has made every effort for the complete realization of these principles.

22. With respect to situations where the right of self-determination has not yet been respected or where racial discrimination still persists, the position of the Republic of Korea may be summarized as follows:

23. The Middle East and the Question of Palestine

    The Republic of Korea believes that the question of Palestine should be settled in a peaceful manner by respecting the legitimate rights of the Palestinians and supports a prompt resolution of the question of Palestine in accordance with the Security Council Resolutions 242 (1967) and 388 (1973).

    Since 1950, the Republic of Korea has made, and continues to make, voluntary contributions to the

United Nations Relief and Works Agency for Palestine Refugees in the Near East (UNRWA). The Republic of Korea also contributed to the Arab Student Aid International (ASAI) from 1981-1988.

In addition, since 1978, the Korean Government has participated in activities held under the auspices of the United Nations such as the commemoration of the International Day of Solidarity with the Palestinian People.

In response to UN Security Council Resolution 688 (1991), the Republic of Korea also made a voluntary contribution of US$ 300,000 to the United Nations Relief Activities for Kurdish and other Iraqi Refugees on 17 April 1991.

24. Apartheid in South Africa

The Republic of Korea, in the firm belief that apartheid constitutes a crime against the conscience and dignity of mankind, reaffirms its support for the efforts of the South African people and the international society to establish, through peaceful means, a united, non-racial and democratic society in South Africa in which all people, irrespective of race, colour, sex or creed, will enjoy the same fundamental human rights.

In this regard, the Government of the Republic of Korea welcomes recent developments in South Africa which will foster a climate fully conducive to a peaceful settlement of the problems through negotiation.

The Korean Government believes that these developments are positive steps toward the

0056

elimination of all forms of racial discrimination and the establishment of a united, democratic and non-racial society in South Africa.

The Korean Government, as an expression of its support for and solidarity with the peoples of South Africa, has provided, since 1978, financial assistance to the United Nations Trust Funds and Programmes for Southern Africa and is fulfilling its pledge of 1 million US dollars, pledged in 1987, to the Action for Resisting Invasion, Colonialism and Apartheid Fund.

25. The Republic of Korea fully supports the noble and untiring efforts of the Special Committee Against Apartheid and other relevant organs of the United Nations to achieve the lofty goal of eliminating all forms of racial discrimination and apartheid.

The Republic of Korea established full diplomatic relations with Namibia at ambassadorial level on 21 March 1990 and opened its embassy in Windhoek on 18 June 1990.

ARTICLE 2

26. Respect for the dignity of an individual and non-discrimination are fully reflected in the Constitution. The Preamble of the Constitution states, "... to afford equal opportunities to every person in all fields" and Article 11(1) states, "All citizens shall be equal before the law and there shall be no discrimination in political, economic, social or cultural life on account of sex, religion or social status."

27. Non-discrimination is guaranteed in all aspects of the citizens' lives. (Constitution, Art. 11(1))

28. Political Sphere

All citizens shall enjoy, without any discrimination, the equal right to vote and to hold public office. (Constitution, Arts. 41(1), 67(1), 116(1))

29. Economic Sphere

Unequal treatment in employment, wages and taxation is prohibited.

The right of women to work is guaranteed and they shall not be subjected to unjust discrimination in employment, wages or working conditions. (Constitution, Art. 32(4))

30. Article 5 of the Labor Standard Act provides, "An employer shall not discriminate against the employees on account of sex and shall not discriminate with respect to the terms of employment on the basis of nationality, religion or social status."

Article 1-2 of the Employment Security and Promotion Act provides that "No person shall be discriminated against with respect to employment assistance, occupational guidance and relations for reasons of sex, religion, social status or marital status."

Under Article 17-3 of the said Act, the Minister of Labor is responsible for the enforcement of the non-discrimination principle. The Minister shall endeavour to increase the availability of

occupational and employment opportunities for women,
shall assist in developing occupations suitable for
middle-aged, elderly or disabled persons and shall
assist them in finding employment in the above
occupations.

Articles 4(3) & (4) of the Basic Vocational Training
Act states, "... vocational training for women, the
middle-aged, the elderly and the disabled shall be
considered as important", and Article 11 of the
Labor Union Act provides, "A member of a union shall
not be discriminated against under any circumstances
on account of race, religion, sex, political party
or social status."

31. Cultural Sphere

All citizens shall have an equal right to receive an
education corresponding to their abilities.
(Constitution, Art. 31(1)) However, reasonable
discrimination on the basis of their abilities is
not prohibited.

32. Social Sphere

Any discrimination with respect to residence, travel
or access to public facilities is prohibited. Any
discrimination between legitimate and illegitimate
children, or between men and women in marriage or
family life is also prohibited. (Constitution, Art.
36(1))

33. Equal Treatment and Welfare Policy for Disabled
Persons

The Government of the Republic of Korea has enacted
the "Welfare Law for Persons with Disabilities", in

order to guarantee equal treatment of disabled persons.

The said law prohibits any discrimination against persons with disabilities in employment, education, the grant of a license, residence, access to public facilities, transportation and in all other social activities.

34. In order to ensure that disabled persons enjoy equal opportunities in political, economic, social and cultural activities, the Korean Government has developed and carried out numerous welfare programs, including the grant of a monthly living allowance to persons with severe disabilities who are considered incapable of earning a certain level of income, tax exemptions on automobiles or rehabilitation appliances, and income tax deduction for persons with disabilities.

35. Article 38 of the Welfare Law for Persons with Disabilities provides that national or local governments may establish welfare institutions for disabled persons who suffer difficulties in coping with everyday life. As of the end of 1990, 156 welfare institutions had been established and have been supporting such persons in need.

36. Furthermore, the twelve welfare centers for rehabilitation and vocational training of the disabled have been modernized to provide more opportunities for participation in leisure and social activities.

37. The Minister of Health and Social Affairs, mayors and governors may instruct the relevant public officials to inspect the operational condition,

records and other documents of the welfare
institutions, or may require the founders and
managers of the welfare institutions to submit
reports concerning the managements of the
institutions to the relevant authorities. (The
Welfare Law for Persons with Disabilities, Arts. 41-
42)

PROBLEMS WITH THE IMPLEMENTATION OF THE POLICY ON PERSONS WITH DISABILITIES

38. Due to Confucian tradition and customs, there are
some Koreans who consider it a dishonour to have a
disabled family member and thus tend to conceal the
fact. This tendency creates an obstacle in
establishing and implementing the policy on the
disabled.

39. This obstacle can be overcome by the expansion of
welfare programs and by the enhancement of public
awareness of this Korean tendency.

    The Government of the Republic of Korea is
    determined to guarantee fully the enjoyment of
    fundamental human rights by the disabled.

EQUAL PROTECTION OF THE LAWS

40. The principle of equal protection of the laws is
observed in all legislative, judicial and
administrative activities of the State.

    Under Articles 107(1) and 111(1) of the
    Constitution, the Constitution Court adjudicates
    whether a law violates the Constitution and, also
    whether a law violates the principle of equal
    protection of the laws.

41. Laws and administrative actions which were held unconstitutional by the Constitution Court due to the violation of the equal protection principle are as follows:

(a) Laws which were held unconstitutional

(1) The Bond Provision of the "Special Measures Act Relating to Overdue Loans of Financial Institutions" (89-HUNGA-37, 96 of 24 May 1989)
Article 5-2 of the Special Measures Act was held unconstitutional because it unlawfully restricts, in favor of the financial institutions, the right to appeal the decision to allow a public auction in the case of a financial institution applying for an auction.

(2) Deposit Money Provision of the "National Assembly Members Election Act" (88-HUNGA-6 of 8 September 1989)
Articles 33 and 34 of the National Assembly Members Election Act were declared to be unconstitutional since they discriminate against non-party candidates in favor of party candidates in violation of the principle of equal protection of the laws.

(3) Restrictions on the place of practice in the "Lawyers Act" (89-HUNGA-102 of 28 November 1989)
Article 10(2) and (3) of the Lawyers Act, which contain certain restrictions with respect to the place of practice of lawyers who have practised law for less than 15 years, violates the "equal protection principle" and "the right to choose jobs" provided for in the Constitution.

(4) Special Corporate Liquidation Provision of the "Special Measures Act Relating to Overdue Loans of Financial Institutions" (89-HUNGA-98, 101, 105 of 25 June 1990) Article 7-3 of the Special Measures Act violates the equal protection principle and was thus held to be unconstitutional because, notwithstanding the provisions of the Corporate Liquidation Act, it allows financial institutions to sell the property of a bankrupt company by auction for collection of the debt.

(5) Preference of the National Tax in the "Basic National Tax Act" (89-HUNGA-95 of 3 September 1990) Article 35(1) item 3 of the Basic National Tax Act was held unconstitutional because it provides that national tax shall have priority over any security rights established less than one year after the tax payment due date.

(b) Constitutional Petitions

(1) Non-prosecution (89-HUNMA-10 of 14 July 1989) In case a prosecutor decides not to prosecute a criminal case due to his/her poor investigation, the decision must be revoked because it constitutes a violation of the victim's right of equal protection.

(2) Military prosecutor's decision to suspend the indictment (89-HUNMA-56 of 27 October 1989) Rightful resistance to a superior officer's unjust harsh actions does not constitute the offense of resisting a lawful order. Therefore, the military

prosecutor's decision to suspend, in
violation of the right of equal
protection, the indictment of the
petitioner was held unconstitutional.

(3) Preference in the employment of teachers
in the Educational Public Official Act
(89-HUNMA-89 of 8 October 1990)
Article 11(1) of the Educational Public
Official Act, which gives preference to
graduates from national teachers' colleges
over graduates from private teachers'
colleges in the employment of teachers,
violates the equal protection principle
and is thus unconstitutional.

(4) Provision relating to the legal clerk
examination of the "Enforcement Regulation
of the Legal Clerk Act" (89-HUNMA-178 of
15 October 1990)
Article 3(1) of the Enforcement Regulation
of the Legal Clerk Act violates the equal
protection principle because it prescribes
that the legal clerk examination shall be
held only when the administrative director
of the court determines that additional
legal clerks are needed.

(5) Prohibition of local councilmen from
having an additional job in The Local
Councilmen Election Act and the Local
Autonomy Act (90-HUNMA-28 of 11 March
1991)
Article 28(1) item 7 of the Local
Councilmen Election Act and Article 33(1)
item 6 of the Local Autonomy Act, which
prohibit the directors and officers of the
Agricultural Cooperative, Fisheries
Cooperative and Livestock Cooperative from
concurrently holding the office of local

councilmen, violate the right to hold
public office and the equal protection
principle and were thus held
unconstitutional.

(6) Deposit Money System in the Local
Councilmen Election Act (91-HUNMA-21 of 11
March 1991)
The deposit money system contained in
Article 36 of the Local Councilmen
Election Act infringes upon the right to
hold public office and the right of
equality.

42. Fundamental human rights, with the exception of the
rights which require Korean nationality as a
precondition of enjoyment, such as the right to vote
or to hold public office, are equally guaranteed to
foreigners in the Republic of Korea regardless of
their nationality.

The Republic of Korea ratified the International
Convention on the Elimination of All Forms of Racial
Discrimination on 5 December 1978 and has submitted
reports six times in accordance with Article 9 of
the Convention.

REMEDIES AVAILABLE IN CASE OF AN INFRINGEMENT OF RIGHTS

43. The laws of the Republic of Korea provide effective
remedies to an individual whose rights and freedom
have been infringed.

Infringement of the Rights by Government Agencies

44. Administrative Remedies

    (a)   Petition

        In the case of an infringement of fundamental
rights by Government agencies, under Article 26
of the Constitution an individual may obtain
remedies by petitioning for the nullification
or annulment of the relevant administrative
actions, or for the removal or punishment of
the relevant officials.

        Article 4 of the Petition Act enumerates the
matters for which petitions are available, and
the petitioning procedures are provided for in
Articles 6 through 8 of the said Act. No
person shall be discriminated against or shall
suffer any disadvantages on the grounds that
the person has filed a petition. (Petition
Act, Art. 11)

    (b)   Administrative Adjudication

        An individual, whose rights or interests have
been violated by an illegal or unreasonable
administrative action or an exercise or a non-
exercise of the Government power by the
administrative agencies, may obtain remedies by
applying for an administrative adjudication.
(Administrative Adjudication Act, Art. 1).
Article 107(3) of the Constitution provides,
"An administrative appeal may be conducted as a
procedure prior to a judicial trial. The
procedure of administrative appeals shall be
determined by law and shall be in conformity
with the principles of judicial procedures."

(c) Criminal Compensation

In cases where a criminal suspect or an accused person, who has been placed under detention is not indicted or acquitted by a court, the person is entitled to claim compensation from the State under the conditions prescribed by law. (Constitution, Art. 28). The Criminal Compensation Act prescribes detailed rules on the compensation for victims of unlawful detention.

45. Court Remedies

(a) Administrative Litigation

The Supreme Court shall have the power to make a final review of the constitutionality or legality of administrative decrees, regulations or actions. (Constitution, Art. 107(2))
The Administrative Litigation Act provides remedies to an individual whose rights or interests have been violated by an illegal administrative action or an exercise or non-exercise of Government power by administrative agencies.

(b) Review of Administrative Decrees and Regulations

Article 107(2) of the Constitution protects fundamental rights by providing the Supreme Court with the power to review the constitutionality or legality of administrative decrees and regulations.

(c) Compensation

In cases where a person has sustained damages due to an unlawful act committed by a public official in the course of his/her official

0067

duties, such a person may claim compensation from the State under the National Compensation Act, which was enacted in accordance with Article 29(1) of the Constitution.

46. Remedies Provided by the Constitution Court

(a) Review of the Constitutionality of a Law
The Constitution Court shall adjudicate the constitutionality of a law upon the request of a court. (Constitution, Art. 111(1) item 1.)

If the constitutionality of a law is at issue in a trial, the court in charge of the trial (including the military court) shall request the Constitution Court to adjudicate the constitutionality of the law. In cases where a party to a trial requests an adjudication of the constitutionality of a law, the court shall request, upon its decision, an adjudication by the Constitution Court. (Constitution Court Act, Art. 41(1))

Any law or provisions thereof held unconstitutional shall be null and void from the date of the decision. However, any unconstitutional law or provisions thereof relating to punishment shall be null and void retroactively. (Constitution Court Act, Art. 47(2))

One may apply for a retrial in cases where a conviction was based upon the law or provision thereof as held unconstitutional.

(b) Petitions Relating to the Constitution

The Constitution Court shall adjudicate the petitions relating to the Constitution. (Constitution, Art. 111(1) item 5)

Any person whose fundamental rights guaranteed by the Constitution have been infringed by the exercise or non-exercise of Government power, may request the Constitution Court to adjudicate a constitutional petition. (Constitution Court Act, Art. 68(1))

A ruling in favor of the constitutional petition shall bind all the agencies of the State and the local governments. (Constitution Court Act, Art. 75(1))

In cases where the Constitution Court rules in favor of the constitutional petition against non-exercise of Government power, the relevant administrative agencies shall take new action in accordance with the decision. (Constitution Court Act, Art. 75(4))

In addition, the Constitution Court may nullify the exercise of Government power by which fundamental rights were infringed. (Constitution Court Act, Art. 75(3))

47. Remedies Provided by Special Human Rights Protection Institutions

In addition to the above-mentioned remedies through legal procedures, an individual may seek remedies through human rights consultation or legal aid provided by special human rights protection institutions.

(a) Korean Legal Aid Corporation

The Korean Legal Aid Corporation was
established under the Legal Aid Act in order to
protect fundamental human rights and to
contribute to the promotion of legal welfare by
providing legal aid to those who are either in
economic difficulty or ignorant of the law.
(Legal Aid Act, Art. 1)

(b) The Korean Federal Bar Association

The Korean Federal Bar Association has been
providing legal aid since June 1985 through the
establishment of the Legal Aid Committee and
the Legal Aid Fund. (Lawyers Act, Art. 67)

Infringement of Rights by an Individual

48. Complaint and Accusation

(a) A person who has been injured in consequence of
an offense, and the legal representative,
spouse or relatives of the said person may file
a complaint in order to seek the prosecution of
the offender. (Code of Criminal Procedure,
Arts. 223, 225(1) & (2), 226)

Any person other than the offender and those
with the right to file a complaint, who
believes that an offense has been committed,
may file an accusation. (Code of Criminal
Procedure, Art. 234(1))

(b) A complaint or an accusation shall be filed
with a prosecutor or a police officer in
writing or orally. (Code of Criminal
Procedure, Art. 237(1))

(c) Investigation period
In order to provide prompt remedies, Article 257 of the Code of Criminal Procedure prescribes that if a prosecutor investigates a crime on a complaint or an accusation, he/she shall determine whether or not to indict the case within three months of the filing of the complaint or accusation.

(d) Notice to complainant, accuser or suspect
In cases where a prosecutor decides not to file an indictment with respect to a case based on a complaint or accusation, or to withdraw the indictment or to send the case to another prosecutor's office, the prosecutor shall inform the complainant or accuser of such a decision in writing within seven days after such a disposition has been made. (Code of Criminal Procedure, Art. 258(1))

In cases where a prosecutor decides not to file an indictment or to send the case to another prosecutor's office, the prosecutor shall promptly inform the suspect of such a decision. (Code of Criminal Procedure, Art. 258(2))

(e) Notice of the reasons for the decision not to file an indictment
In cases where a prosecutor decides not to file an indictment with respect to a case based upon a complaint or accusation, the prosecutor, upon the request of the complainant or accuser, shall inform the complainant or accuser of the reasons therefore in writing within seven days after the decision. (Code of Criminal Procedure, Art. 259)

(f) Appeal and reappeal

Any complainant or accuser, who is dissatisfied with a prosecutor's decision not to file an indictment, may appeal the decision to the chief prosecutor of the competent High Prosecutor's Office. (Prosecutor's Office Act, Art. 10(1))

Any appellant who is dissatisfied with a decision to reject the appeal referred to in Article 10(1) of the Prosecutor's Office Act, may reappeal the decision to the Attorney General.

In cases where the chief prosecutor or the Attorney General determines that the appeal or reappeal is well-founded, the decision shall be rectified. (Prosecutor's Office Act, Art. 10(2))

49. Remedies available to a victim of a crime

Under Article 30 of the Constitution, any citizen who has suffered a bodily injury or death due to criminal acts of others may receive aid from the State under the conditions prescribed by law.

In accordance with the provision of the Constitution, the State Aid Act for Victims of Crime prescribes detailed rules for the payment of State aid.

In cases where a victim of a felony, such as murder or robbery, is unable to obtain compensation because the criminal is missing or is unable to compensate for the damages, the State protects the interests of

the victim by paying State aid to the victim or the
bereaved family.

ARTICLE 3

ENHANCEMENT OF WOMEN'S STATUS

50. Until the establishment of the Government of the
Republic of Korea in 1948, women had to endure
sexual discrimination due to prevalent Confucian
tradition. However, the Constitution which was
proclaimed on July 17, 1948, guarantees the equality
of men and women and thus allows for women to
participate equally in social activities.

51. In accordance with the equal protection principle of
the Constitution, the Government of the Republic of
Korea has implemented various measures in order to
eliminate the discrimination against women and as a
result, the status of women experienced a
revolutionary change in political, economic, social
and cultural areas.

52. As a result of strenuous efforts over 30 years,
women have achieved the revision of the
discriminatory family law (Dec. 1989), the enactment
of the Gender-equal Opportunity Employment Act,
which came into force in April 1988, and the
establishment of the Vocational Training Center for
Women, which has been accepting applicants since
March 1991.

The Government and the competent authorities
continue to search for measures to stimulate women's
participation in the major public vocational
training courses.

53. Since its promulgation in 1948, the Constitution has upheld the equality of men and women as a supreme principle of the State, and this is reflected in various provisions of the Constitution.

54. The preamble to the Constitution states, "... to destroy all social vices and injustice, ... and to afford equal opportunities to every person and to provide for the fullest development of the individual capabilities in all fields, including political, economic, social and cultural life by further strengthening the basic free and democratic order..." and thus emphasizes equal treatment and equal opportunity for all citizens.

55. All citizens shall be assured of human worth and dignity and shall have the right to pursue happiness. (Constitution, Art. 10)

All citizens shall have the right to equal protection of the laws and there shall be no discrimination in political, economic, social or cultural life on account of sex, religion or social status. (Constitution, Art. 11)

Women shall not be subjected to unjust discrimination in terms of employment, wages or working conditions. (Constitution, Art. 32) and the State shall endeavour to promote the welfare and rights of women. (Constitution, Art. 34)

In addition, the Government shall endeavour to promote equality between men and women in marriage and family life. (Constitution, Art. 36)

56. The Government of the Republic of Korea has exerted every effort to enact or modify the relevant laws so as to guarantee the equality of men and women and to enhance women's status, and ratified the Convention on the Elimination of All Forms of Discrimination against Women on 27 December 1984.

STATUS OF WOMEN UNDER LABOR LAWS

57. In accordance with the equal protection principle of the Constitution, Article 5 of the Labor Standards Act provides "an employer shall not discriminate against employees with regard to the conditions of employment on the basis of sex."

   In addition, Article 11 of the Labor Union Act provides, "a member of a labor union shall not be discriminated against under any circumstances on account of sex."

   The Equal Opportunity Employment Act is designed to rectify discriminatory practices in employment between men and women and to enhance the social status of women.

THE STATUS OF WOMEN UNDER THE CRIMINAL LAW

58. The sole provision relating to the equality of men and women under the criminal law is Article 241 (adultery) of the Criminal Code, which renders equal punishment to the offenders regardless of their sex.

AUTHORITIES IN CHARGE OF WOMEN'S AFFAIRS

59. On 25 February 1988, the office of Minister of Political Affairs (2) was created and a woman was

appointed as the Minister. The office devises and
implements policies relating to women.

60. The Women's Welfare Division in the Ministry of
Health and Social Affairs, and the Women's and
Minors' Labor Division in the Ministry of Labor are
also in charge of matters relating to women. The
Women's Welfare Division devises an overall plan for
the social welfare of women and the Women's and
Minors' Labor Division is in charge of improving the
employment conditions of working women. In
addition, the Ministry of Labor has a Women's
Affairs Guidance Officer for the special protection
of working women.

61. Family Welfare Bureaus were established in 15 local
administrations in 1988 and women were appointed as
directors. In order to promote the social welfare
of women, these bureaus maintain a close
relationship with the Women's Welfare Division in
the Ministry of Health and Social Affairs.

62. The National Committee on Women's Policies was
established under the control of the Prime Minister
on 8 December 1983.

As the supreme Government Committee concerned with
policies relating to women, it devises the basic
policy and supervises the activities of other
related Government authorities.

This Committee has up to 25 members who are experts
on women's issues and the relevant Ministers. The
Prime Minister is the chairman of the committee.

Other Government Committees concerned with the
policies relating to women are the Committee on

Working Women, the Committee to Provide Guidance to Women in Prostitution and the Council on Guidance to Women.

INCREASE OF CHILDCARE SUBSIDIES

63. The Government, realizing that child care usually prevents married women from working, has established 360 national and public childcare facilities subsidized by the Government, 39 private childcare facilities, 20 office childcare facilities, 1,500 home placement facilities, which between them take care of approximately 48,000 children.

64. The Government enacted the Childcare Act on 14 January 1991.
The important provisions of the said Act are as follows:

(a) The State and local governments shall be responsible for the protection of children who are less than 6 years old. (Art. 3)

(b) The owner of a workplace greater than the prescribed size shall establish an office childcare facility. If the facility cannot be established for unavoidable reasons, it must be jointly established with another workplace or the owner shall pay a childcare allowance to the employees. (Art. 7(3))

(c) The State or local governments may subsidize the costs of childcare, such as the cost of establishing and operating the childcare facilities. (Art. 22)

(d) There shall be a reduction and/or exemption of taxes from the legal guardian's cost of

−39−

0077

childcare for children less than 6 years of age, and for the cost incurred by an owner of a workplace for the establishment and operation of the childcare facility.

65. The Government is planning to establish 1,440 childcare facilities for 17,000 children from low-income families as prescribed by law by 1992, and childcare facilities that can accommodate 1,025,000 children by 1995.

MOTHER-CHILD HEALTH PROTECTION

66. Under the provisions of the Maternal and Child Health Act the Government has improved the maternity protection services and the childcare system.

    The Government has improved the condition of mother-child health protection by establishing 81 maternal and child health centers and the Mother-Child Health Committee was established in the Ministry of Health and Social Affairs in 1987.

SEXUAL EXPLOITATION

67. Prostitution or other forms of sexual exploitation is prohibited by law in the Republic of Korea. Article 303 of the Criminal Code provides, "a person who, through fraudulent means or the power of authority, has sexual intercourse with a woman under his protection or supervision by reason of business, employment or other relationship, shall be punished...."

    In order to eliminate prostitution, the Government enacted the Anti-Prostitution Act in 1961 and its enforcement decree in 1969. The Act prohibits

0078

prostitution (Art. 4), and the intermediation of prostitution (Art. 6), and provides that the Government shall establish guidance centers for women in prostitution (Art. 7), and vocational training and employment guidance centers to support such women in building a new life. Prostitution is a crime under the Criminal Code.

68.   The Government has established 105 consultation centers in the major cities for women in need of protection.

22 employment guidance centers offer vocational training and guidance to women in prostitution in order to support their return to a normal social life.

SOCIAL PARTICIPATION OF WOMEN

69.   Since the establishment of the Korean Government, women have enjoyed equal political rights with men. The Constitution provides that, "all citizens shall have the right to vote under the conditions prescribed by law." (Art. 24) In addition, Article 25 of the Constitution states, "all citizens shall have the right to hold public offices under the conditions as prescribed by law."

70.   Women's participation in the State's policy decisions has increased, but the level of participation is still unsatisfactory. There have been 61 women in the National Assembly so far; 16 members from "the local constituency" and the other 45 members from "the national constituency." Currently, there are 6 women out of a total of 299 members in the National Assembly.

–41–

71. As of December 1989, there were 181,083 female public officials (23.7%) out of a total of 764,563 officials. 111,831 of female officials (61.5%) were teachers.

   The Public Official Employment Regulation, amended by Presidential Decree No. 12730, has deleted the previous provision, which required a separate testing system for men and women, and thus prohibits sexual discrimination in the employment of public officials. Furthermore, since 1991 "education on the equality of men and women" has been adopted as a required subject in the training program for public officials.

72. The field of education is the dominant center of women's social participation. As of April 1990, there were 159,003 female teachers which is 41.33% of all teachers, and the number of female teachers continues to rise.

73. With the increase of members in the political parties, the number of female members has also increased. With regard to the composition of the executive committee of the main political parties, the ruling Democratic Liberal Party has 1 female consultant and 73 female committee members out of 1,698 standing committee members. The opposition New Democratic Party, has 2 female members out of 70 members of the executive committee, and the People's Party has 2 female members out of 20 members of the standing committee.

74. The Government guarantees equal treatment of men and women in the eligibility for and score evaluation of the Korean Bar Examination, which confers the license to practice law in the Republic of Korea.

However, the Confucian custom of sexual discrimination has hindered women from entering the legal field.

With the social changes arising out of modernization and industrialization, women's participation in the legal field has gradually increased. As of 31 March 1991, there were 35 female judges, 2 female prosecutors and 21 female lawyers.

75. There are 2,694 female workers in the press which constitutes 12% of all workers in the mass media. They work as reporters, directors, scriptwriters and administrators.

76. Article 21 of the Constitution, along with other provisions, guarantees that all citizens shall enjoy freedom of assembly and association. Many Korean women participate in the activities of private associations.

EDUCATION OF WOMEN

77. According to Article 31(1) of the Constitution, all citizens shall have an equal right to receive an education corresponding to their abilities.

Furthermore, all citizens who have children shall be responsible for their elementary education at least and other education as provided by law. (Constitution, Art. 31(2))

78. During the course of industrialization, the percentage of school attendance for women, and the percentage of enrolment at the institutions of higher education for women, have increased tremendously.

Since primary school education was made compulsory in 1948, over 99% of children have attended primary school.

As of 1990, the percentage of female students entering high school was 94.96% and the percentage of male students was 96.34%. The percentage of high school female graduates entering college was 32.36%, and the percentage for male students was 33.89% in 1990. In 1988, female students constituted 35.56% of all enroled college students.

79. Since 1989, the discriminatory descriptions and subjects in the textbooks have been corrected in accordance with the principle of equality between men and women. In addition, efforts have been made to eliminate sexual discrimination in education.

STATUS OF WOMEN IN LABOR MATTERS

80. The laws of the Republic of Korea guarantees the equality of men and women with respect to employment. The Constitution provides that all citizens shall have the right and duty to work. (Art. 32(1) & (2)), and that all citizens shall have the freedom to choose their occupations. (Art. 15)

81. The State shall enact laws to guarantee that the standards of employment protect the dignity of the workers and to guarantee reasonable wages for workers. (Constitution, Art. 32(1)) Article 6-2 of the Equal Opportunity Employment Act, amended on 1 April 1989, provides that equal wages shall be paid for equal work, irrespective of sex.

82. Due to rapid industrialization since the 1960s, the number of working women has greatly increased.

−44−

0082

As of 1990, 7,474,000 women out of 15,897,000 women over 15 years of age were working, making the percentage of working women 47%.

Most of the 8,423,000 women who were not working were housewives or students.

83. There are many opportunities for Korean women to receive vocational training.

The Government enacted the Basic Vocational Training Act to promote vocational training for women.

As of 1989, 63,429 trainees have received vocational training in 167 subjects, such as electronics and industrial arts, in 295 institutions i.e., national and local training centers and in-office training centers.

To improve the training for women, the Government is planning to establish a vocational training center for women by 1991.

STATUS OF WOMEN IN OTHER FIELDS

84. As already stated, the Constitution guarantees the equality of men and women in accordance with the equal protection principle. Thus, men and women enjoy equal rights with respect to family allowances, bank loans, mortgages and financial credit evaluations. Moreover, women have the right to participate in all cultural activities including sports.

85. Article 23(1) of the Constitution guarantees the right of property to all citizens, and under the

relevant laws of the Republic of Korea men and women have equal legal competence concerning property.

STATUS OF WOMEN IN MARRIAGE AND FAMILY LIFE

86. The Constitution states that individual dignity and equality of the sexes shall be the basis of marriage and family life. (Art. 36(1))

REVISION OF THE DISCRIMINATORY FAMILY LAW

87. As a result of the struggle of Korean women over 3 decades, the revision of the discriminatory Family Law was passed by the National Assembly in December of 1989.

The amendments to the Family Law are considered fairly satisfactory because they reflect most of the women's requests. The amendments may be summarized as follows:

(a) Adjustment of the Confucian family head system in order to eliminate the discrimination against women under the grand family regime. (The deletion of Arts. 797-799 of the old Civil Code)

(b) Equality in the scope of relatives through extension of the scope of relatives to blood relatives within eighth degree of relationship of both husband and wife. (Civil Code, Art. 777)

(c) Improvement of the inheritance system to allow the successors to inherit equal shares irrespective of sex, age and marital status. (Civil Code, Art. 1009)

(d) Establishment of the right of both husband or wife to seek a division of the joint property on the basis of his or her contribution to the formation of the property. (Civil Code, Art. 839-2)

(e) Establishment of equal parental rights of husband and wife (Civil Code, Art. 909) and the revision of the previous law, which granted fostering and education of a child to his or her father in case an agreement on fostering and education has not been reached, in order to require that the Family Court decide the fostering and education issue. (Civil Code, Art. 837)

ARTICLE 4

88. In case of an emergency that threatens the existence of the State, the President, in order to cope with the emergency situation, may issue emergency orders, may take financial and economic emergency actions and orders, and may proclaim martial law. (Constitution, Arts. 76-77)

89. These emergency powers of the President derive from the duty and responsibility of the President, under Article 66(2) & (3) of the Constitution, to safeguard the independence, territorial integrity and continuity of the State, to protect the Constitution, to pursue the peaceful unification of the homeland and to overcome the crisis of the State.

90. The current Constitution has deleted the emergency powers of the President under the former

-47-

0085

Constitution, and has vested the President with only the power to issue emergency orders, to take financial and economic emergency actions and orders, and to proclaim martial law. (Constitution, Art. 76)

Article 37(2) of the Constitution provides that the freedom and rights of citizens may be restricted by law only when absolutely necessary for national security, the maintenance of law and order, or public welfare, and that such restriction may not infringe upon the essential aspects of fundamental rights. This provision also applies to any restrictions on fundamental rights under the emergency powers of the President.

Therefore, Articles 76 and 77 of the Constitution are consistent with the derogating measures in case of public emergencies pursuant to Article 4, para. 1 of the Covenant.

91. The detailed descriptions of the President's emergency powers are as follows:

Constitution, Article 76

para. 1   In time of internal turmoil, external menace, natural calamity or a grave financial or economic crisis, the President may take in respect to them the minimum necessary financial and economic actions or issue orders having the effect of law, only when it is required to take urgent measures for the maintenance of national security or public peace and order, and there is no time to await the convocation of the National Assembly.

0086

para. 2   In case of major hostilities affecting
           national security, the President may issue
           orders having the effect of law, only when
           it is required to preserve the integrity
           of the nation, and it is impossible to
           convene the National Assembly.

Constitution, Article 77, para. 1

           When it is required to cope with a
           military necessity or to maintain the
           public safety and order by mobilization of
           the military forces in time of war, armed
           conflict or similar national emergency,
           the President may proclaim martial law
           under the conditions prescribed by law.

92. Restrictions on fundamental rights under the
     emergency orders are allowed only by measures
     designed for the maintenance of national security.
     Restrictions under the financial or economic
     emergency orders are allowed only on the financial
     or economic emergency measures, and the restrictions
     under martial law are allowed only on certain
     fundamental rights or powers prescribed in Article
     77(3) of the Constitution - the necessity for
     warrants, freedom of speech, press, assembly and
     association or the powers of the Executive or
     Judiciary.

     Restrictions on fundamental rights are subject to
     the limitation imposed by Article 37(2) of the
     Constitution. In addition, the emergency measures
     are effective only during the period when the
     survival of the State is at stake.

CONTROL ON THE EXERCISE OF EMERGENCY POWERS

93.   The National Assembly, the Courts, and the
       Constitution Court control the exercise of emergency
       powers.

       (a)   Financial and economic emergency actions and
              orders.

       (1)   The National Assembly

              The President shall promptly notify the
              National Assembly of any emergency orders or
              financial and economic emergency actions or
              orders issued or taken by him and shall obtain
              its approval. (Constitution, Art. 76(3))

       (2)   The Court

              Even if the emergency orders or the financial
              and economic orders have been approved by the
              National Assembly, the Court may still request
              a decision of the Constitution Court when the
              constitutionality of these measures is at issue
              in a trial. (Constitution, Art. 107(1))

              Even if the financial and economic emergency
              actions have been approved by the National
              Assembly, the Court still has the power to
              review the constitutionality or legality of
              these measures. (Constitution, Art. 107(2))

       (3)   The Constitution Court

              In cases where the emergency orders or the
              financial and economic emergency orders have
              legal effect due to the approval of the

National Assembly, the Constitution Court may still adjudicate the constitutionality of these orders upon the request of the courts. (Constitution, Art. 111(1) item 1)

In addition, the Constitution Court may adjudicate the constitutionality of the financial and economic emergency actions, which were approved by the National Assembly, in the case of a Constitutional petition relating thereto. (Constitution, Art. 111(1) item 5)

(b) Martial law

The President shall notify the National Assembly of a proclamation of martial law without delay. (Constitution, Art. 77(4)) In the case that the majority of the members of the National Assembly request the lifting of martial law, the President shall comply. (Constitution, Art. 77(5))

94. The above provisions relating to restrictions on fundamental rights in the case of an emergency do not explicitly refer to the absolute fundamental rights of Article 4 of the Covenant.

In terms of Korean legal context, it is understood that absolute fundamental rights fall under "the essential aspect of the freedom or right" referred to in Article 37(2) of the Constitution, and thus cannot be restricted under any circumstances.

95. In the case of an exercise of these emergency powers, the Secretary-General of the United Nations shall be notified of the steps and grounds for the

exercise. Similar notice shall be rendered when the emergency situation ends.

Since the promulgation of the current Constitution, these emergency powers have never been exercised in the Republic of Korea.

ARTICLE 5

96.· The Government of the Republic of Korea does not interpret the Covenant so as to destroy the rights and freedoms recognized by the Covenant or to restrict the rights more severely than as provided for in the Covenant.

On this point, the Constitution states that "All citizens shall be assured of human worth and dignity ... and it shall be the duty of the State to confirm and guarantee the fundamental and inviolable human rights of individuals" (Art. 10) and that "the freedoms and rights of citizens shall not be neglected on the ground that they were not enumerated in the Constitution." (Art. 37(2))

97. No derogation or limitation of fundamental human rights recognized by the Constitution, but not referred to in the Covenant, is allowed on the grounds that they are not stated in the Covenant.

For instance, Article 13(3) of the Constitution provides that no citizen shall suffer unfavorable treatment on account of an act committed by a relative.

ARTICLE 6

THE RIGHT TO LIFE

Paragraph 1

98. The right to life provided for in Article 6, para. 1 of the Covenant is not subject to any restrictions even during a State emergency since it is the supreme fundamental human right. Although the right to life is not explicitly stated in the Constitution, it is implicitly guaranteed by Article 10 of the Constitution which provides for the respect of human dignity and by Article 12(1) which provides for personal liberty.

99. With respect to the right to life, the Supreme Court has stated that "Life once lost is never restored. It is absolute and cannot be exchanged for anything in the world. The life of a man is more precious and solemn than the entire world. It is the basis of the solemn existence of mankind." Thus the Court has clearly indicated that the right to life is the supreme fundamental right. (Supreme Court Decision, 1969.9.19, 67 Do 988)

100. Every individual, regardless of citizenship, has this inherent right to life. Not only life after birth, but also life of a foetus is protected under the laws of the Republic of Korea. (Criminal Code, Chapter 27, the crimes of abortion, Arts. 269-270)

Paragraph 2

101. In the Republic of Korea, all criminal punishment, including the death penalty, are enforced in accordance with the following provisions and a decision of a competent court:

(a) Constitution, Art. 13(1): "No citizen shall be prosecuted for an act which does not constitute a crime under the law in force at the time it was committed."

(b) Constitution, Art. 27(1): the right to be tried in conformity with the law by judges qualified under law.

(c) Criminal Code, Art. 1(1): "The criminality and punishability of an act shall be determined by the law prevailing at the time of the commission of that act."

(d) Criminal Code, Art. 41: types of punishment i.e., death penalty, penal servitude, imprisonment, deprivation of qualification, suspension of qualification, fine, detention, minor fine, confiscation.

(e) Code of Criminal Procedure, Art. 321(1): pronouncement of punishment.

(f) Code of Criminal procedure, Art. 459: "Except as otherwise provided in this Code, a decision shall be executed after it has become final."

As a result of the above rules and procedures, any arbitrary deprivation of life by the State is strictly prohibited.

102. Articles 250-256 of the Criminal Code provides for the punishment of murderers and thus strictly prohibits any arbitrary deprivation of life by an individual.

DEATH PENALTY

103. The Korean laws provide for the death penalty in the Criminal Code and the other related regulations. Crimes subject to the death penalty are strictly limited to crimes that threaten the very existence

of the State such as an insurrection, heinous crimes such as a murder and other designated felonies.

Even with respect to crimes subject to the death penalty, a fair trial by an independent, competent court, the presumption of innocence of the accused, representation by a lawyer, the right of appeal and the right of retrial are fully guaranteed under the following provisions and due process of law are strictly observed:

(a) The right to be tried by a judge designated by law (Constitution, Art. 27(1);

(b) The right to a prompt trial (Constitution, Art. 27(3));

(c) The presumption of the innocence of the accused (Constitution, Art. 27(4));

(d) The right to receive assistance from a counsel or a counsel assigned by the State (Constitution, Art. 12(4));

(e) The right to appeal (Code of Criminal Procedure, Art. 338 para. 1);

(f) The right to a retrial (Code of Criminal Procedure, Art. 429);

(g) Execution of the death penalty (Code of Criminal Procedure, Art. 465).

104. The Special Deliberation Council on the Revision of the Criminal Law, established 21 June 1985, has studied the issue of abolishing the death penalty. The Council has come to the conclusion that it is premature to eliminate the death penalty in view of the criminal situation in Korea where heinous crimes are being committed, such as the recent incident of a gang of burglars breaking into a peaceful home and raping a woman in the presence of her husband and family. However, the Council also concluded that it

would be better to limit the crimes that are subject to the death penalty in consideration of the spirit of the Constitution to respect human dignity and worth, and the international trend toward the abolition of death penalty.

105. Revisions to the Criminal Code are being made in order to limit the crimes which are subject to the death penalty. A new provision, which requires careful consideration when pronouncing the death penalty, has been added to the Criminal Code. In addition, a proposal to eliminate the death penalty for 5 crimes for which punishment is augmented for certain results, such as causing the death of or injury to a person by setting fire to a dwelling structure, is under consideration.

106. The death penalty was eliminated from 15 provisions of the Special Criminal Act i.e., the Act Concerning Additional Punishment for Specified Crimes and the Act Concerning Additional Punishment for Specified Financial Crimes.

107. The average period of time between the final death penalty sentence and execution from 1981 to 1990 was as follows:
    (a) Total: 82 cases;
    (b) Shorter than 1 year: 9 cases (11.0%);
    (c) 1-2 years: 31 cases (37.8%);
    (d) 2-3 years: 20 cases (24.4%);
    (e) 3-4 years: 13 cases (15.8%);
    (f) Longer than 4 years: 9 cases (11.0%).

108. A retrial of a death sentence judgement was held 3 times in 1986 and twice in 1987 and 1988. There was no retrial in 1989 and 1990. In none of these cases was the death sentence judgements reversed.

109. There is a Constitutional petition case pending in the Constitution Court, which contends that Article 338 of the Criminal Code (death penalty for robbers) and Article 57 of the Penal Administration Act (execution of death sentence) are unconstitutional because they violate human worth, dignity and personal liberty.

ABORTION

110. Under chapter 27 of the Criminal Code, it is a crime to have or commit an abortion. However, the Maternal and Child Health Act allows abortions due to medical, eugenic and moral reasons. (Art. 14)

With regard to the abolition of crimes of abortion, the Special Deliberation Council on the Revision of the Criminal Law has concluded overwhelmingly to sustain those provisions criminalizing abortion.

Paragraph 4

111. Under Article 26 of the Constitution, and Articles 4, 6 and 7 of the Petition Act, a person who has been sentenced to death may petition for an amnesty or commutation.

The President may grant an amnesty or commutation under Article 79 of the Constitution and Articles 2, 3, 5 and 8 of the Amnesty Act. However, a general amnesty can be granted only with the consent of the National Assembly. Of all criminals sentenced to death between 1951 and 1990, one was granted an amnesty and 35 had their sentences commuted.

Paragraph 5

112. The age limitation for the death sentence was raised
     from 16 to 18 on 31 December 1988 through the
     revision of the Juvenile Act in conformity with
     Article 5 of the Covenant.

     Under Article 59 of the Juvenile Act, the death
     sentence of a juvenile who is less than 18 years of
     age when the crime is committed, shall be changed to
     15 years of penal servitude.

     Furthermore, Article 469 of the Code of Criminal
     Procedure provides that the execution of a pregnant
     woman who is condemned to death shall be stayed
     until delivery.

     DIFFERENTIAL TREATMENT OF THE CONVICTED PERSONS
     UNDER THE DEATH SENTENCE

113. Article 13 of the Penal Administration Act provides
     that a person sentenced to death shall be committed
     to a detention place for unconvicted detainees.

     The detention of persons sentenced to death is to
     secure the execution of the death penalty, and thus
     it differs from the detention of unconvicted persons
     and the execution of the imprisonment of the
     convicted persons.

114. Article 170 of the Enforcement Decree of the Penal
     Administration Act prescribes that the provisions
     relating to the unconvicted detainees shall apply
     equally to the convicts who received the death
     sentence.

According to this provision, convicts under the death sentence enjoy equal humanitarian treatment as provided to the unconvicted detainees based on respect for human dignity.

In case of request by a convict under the death sentence, various services to relieve the agony and anguish arising from the death sentence are rendered through enlightenment by religious workers and benevolent volunteers.

MATERNAL AND CHILD HEALTH CARE (MCH)

115. In accordance with Article 7 of the Maternal & Child Health Act, the State and local governments have established maternal & child health institutions, (12 Comprehensive Maternal and Child Health Centers, 81 Maternal and Child Health Centers and Child Health Clinics) Under Article 10 of the said Act, maternal & child health institutions have been providing regular medical examinations and immunizations to pregnant women, new-born babies and infants or, when deemed necessary, arranging health-worker home visits and health treatment for them.

116. For the proper health care of pregnant women, regular medical examinations (at least 7 times) are provided and the maternal & child health institutions take care of them during delivery. In addition, mothers and new-born babies are properly taken care of by the maternal & child health institutions.

117. The Korean Government has been issuing a Maternal & Child Health Handbook to pregnant women, which explains the MCH programs, records of MCH services provided by the State.

118. The Government has established 81 MCH Centers, in secluded areas as of December 1990 and the Offices provide medical care i.e., delivery assistance, first-aid treatment and family planning.

119. To cut down the infant mortality rate, the Korean Government is implementing various MCH programs such as regular medical examination, nutritional guidance and health education for pregnant women. In addition, medical examinations and proper treatment for infants between 6 months and 1/2 years of age are being provided.

120. The Korean Government has been providing health care services to 1,323,000 children under 5 years of age (U5's) namely 33% of all the U5's in the Republic of Korea.

Under Article 8 of the Maternal & Child Health Act, the Government provides free health care service to pregnant women, usually from low-income families, if the pregnant woman or her guardian so wishes.

Vaccination is not covered by the medical insurance to which all Korean people have been entitled since July 1989. Thus, the Government provides, without charge, the cost of vaccination for 70% of all children. In the Republic of Korea, children are vaccinated against TB (94%), D.P.T. (97%), Polio (96%) and M.M.R. (89%).

121. With these efforts by the Government, the U5 mortality rate has decreased as follows:

* U5 mortality rate

Year	1970	1984	1986	1989
U5 mortality rate (every 1,000 U5's)	51.0	15.7	12.5	11.0

ORGAN TRANSPLANTS

122. Article 103 of the Civil Code prohibits any organ transplants that violate good morals and social order.

    With advances in medical technology, some organ transplants have been performed after the formal and complete consent of the donor or his/her family.

    According to a Korean Medical Association report, 2,040 kidney transplants were performed from 1969 to 1989.

TRANSPLANTATION OF AN ORGAN FROM A PATIENT IN A STATE OF BRAIN-DEATH

123. According to the Supreme Court precedent in terms of "the heart and lung cease theory", the transplantation of an organ from a patient in a state of brain-death and whose heart and/or lungs still function constitutes a murder under Article 250 of the Criminal Code.

    Even an organ transplant with the consent of the patient or his/her family constitutes the crime of murder upon request or with consent. (Criminal Code, Art. 252)

시민적.정치적 권리에 관한 국제규약(B규약) 한국 최초 인권보고서 제출 및 심의, 1991-92. 전5권 (V.2 1991.7-12월)   237

124. However, the recognition of brain-death as legal death may contribute to saving another life by means of an organ transplant and to mitigating the mental and economic burdens of the patient and the family by terminating the meaningless treatment. Therefore, some people are seeking the recognition of brain-death as legal death.

MEASURES AND PRACTICES TO PREVENT AND CONTROL COMMUNICABLE DISEASES

125. In order to prevent and control communicable diseases and protect human rights of patients, communicable diseases are classified as first, second and third class communicable diseases. The Communicable Disease Prevention Act provides the following:

   (a) State and local authorities establish medical treatment facilities specialized in communicable diseases and pay the costs of preventing communicable diseases and of treating first class communicable diseases;

   (b) People infected with first class communicable diseases or some of the third class diseases shall be treated in isolation. (Communicable Disease Prevention Act, Art. 29, its Enforcement Decree, Art. 5, Enforcement Regulation, Art. 16);

   (c) Patients with first or third class communicable diseases may be temporarily prohibited from working in restaurants, bars, hotels, etc. (Communicable Diseases Prevention Act, Art. 30, Enforcement Regulation, Art. 17);

   (d) Patients with communicable diseases shall not enter public gatherings or other places where they may transmit the disease. (Communicable Disease Prevention Act, Art. 31)

126. The isolation of patients with communicable diseases
     is intended to facilitate treatment of the patients
     in an efficient and effective manner. In practice,
     the consent of the patient, or his/her family is
     required before the patient is isolated.

     The clause that prevents patients from entering
     public places has never been applied.

AIDS Prevention and Control

127. The Government has maintained the minimum
     regulations relating to AIDS prevention and control
     in order to protect the human rights of persons with
     AIDS/HIV and to prevent further transmission.

     Those who fall under the following categories are
     subject to the protective measures by the Government
     upon a strict evaluation for the public interests by
     the Protection Review Committee. (AIDS Prevention
     Act, Art. 14 and its Enforcement Decree, Art. 15)
     (a) Person with HIV who works or is likely to work
          at a place, the employees of which are required
          to take a sexually transmitted disease
          examination;
     (b) Person with HIV with a risk of spreading the
          infection;
     (c) Person with HIV who has no one to depend on and
          who is deemed to be in need of protection, or
          person with HIV who requires protection in the
          protection facilities.

     Since the first person with HIV was discovered in
     1985, no protective measures have been applied to
     the 138 persons with HIV.

시민적.정치적 권리에 관한 국제규약(B규약) 한국 최초 인권보고서 제출 및 심의, 1991-92. 전5권 (V.2 1991.7-12월) 239

Article 18 of the AIDS Prevention Act prohibits the person with HIV from working in restaurants, bars, hotels, etc. Employees of these establishments areas, under the provisions of the relevant laws, are obliged to have a periodic sexually transmitted disease check-up. The Government has been granting subsidies to those infected people who have difficulty in earning a living.

CONVENTION ON THE PREVENTION AND PUNISHMENT OF THE CRIME OF GENOCIDE

128. On 14 October 1950, the Republic of Korea acceded to the Convention on the Prevention and Punishment of the Crime of Genocide, which entered into force on 12 January 1951.

ARTICLE 7

PROHIBITION OF TORTURE AND OTHER INHUMANE TREATMENTS

129. The provisions in the first sentence of Article 7 of the Convention are also reflected in the domestic laws, such as the Constitution and the Criminal Code.

The above Korean laws use a variety of expressions, such as torture, intimidation and other harsh treatment. Taken as a whole, these terms correspond to the same kind of treatment expressed in the Covenant.

130. Under the Constitution, all citizens shall be assured of human worth and dignity (Art. 10) and no citizen shall be tortured or be compelled to testify against oneself in a criminal case. (Art. 12(2))

In cases where a confession is deemed to have been made against the defendant's will due to torture, violence, intimidation, unjustifiably prolonged arrest, or deceit etc., such a confession shall not be admitted as evidence of guilt, nor shall the defendant be punished by reason of such a confession. (Art. 12(7))

The above provisions prohibit torture and harsh treatment, and ensure that suspects will not be subject to such inhumane treatment by prohibiting the admission of confession derived from torture and other harsh treatment.

131. There are numerous laws in the Republic of Korea prohibiting any kind of torture and inhumane treatment by the police and public officials.

132. Article 123 of the Criminal Code prohibits a public official from abusing his/her official authority in order to cause a person to perform an act which the person has no duty to do, or to obstruct the person from exercising his/her rights.

Article 124 of the said Code provides that a person who performs or assists in activities concerning judgement, prosecution, law enforcement or other functions involving restraint of the human body, shall be punished in the case that the person commits the arrest or detention of an individual by abusing his/her official authority.

Article 125 provides that a person, described in Article 124, shall be punished in the case that he/she commits an act of violence or cruelty against a suspect or any other person in the performance of his/her official duties.

-65-

A person who has sexual intercourse with a female held in his custody according to law shall be punished more severely than in the case of normal maltreatment. (Criminal Code, Art. 303, para. (2))

Article 4-2 of the Act Concerning Additional Punishment for Specified Crimes prescribes increased punishment for a person who causes injuries or death to an individual in consequence of committing the crimes stipulated in Articles 124 or 125 of the Criminal Code.

The prosecutor must inspect the detention places more than once every month in order to investigate whether an illegal detention has been made or not. (Code of Criminal Procedure, Art. 198-2) In accordance with the spirit of the above provision, and in order to eliminate cruelty against a person during the course of an investigation, the prosecution strictly guides and supervises the police and the investigators to ensure that they follow the relevant legal procedures.

Article 309 of the Code of Criminal Procedure provides that any confession extracted by torture, violence, threat, unjustifiably prolonged detention or which is suspected to have been made involuntarily, shall not be admitted as evidence of guilt.

REQUEST FOR RULING

133. In the case that the prosecutor decides not to prosecute a case based on a complaint or an accusation with respect to the crimes prescribed in Articles 123 through 125 of the Criminal Code, the person who filed the complaint or accusation may apply to the competent High Court for a ruling on the prosecutor's decision in accordance with the procedures prescribed in Articles 260 through 265 of the Code of Criminal Procedure which are designed to ensure the actual enforcement of the above provisions of the Criminal Code.

In the case that the High Court decides that the case shall be committed to the competent district court for a trial, public prosecution shall be deemed to have been instituted in the case and a special prosecutor appointed by the competent district court shall be in charge of prosecuting the case.

PROHIBITION OF TORTURE AND CRUELTY COMMITTED IN THE PERFORMANCE OF OFFICIAL DUTIES

134. Law enforcement officers are strictly educated never to inflict torture in the performance of their official duties and a Constitution course is a compulsory subject of the educational program for all Government officials.

As the Prosecutor General instructed, 9,303 law enforcement officers and 5,059 members of the prosecutor's office staff have been educated on the above subject in 222 and 410 courses respectively from 1 January 1990 to 31 December 1990.

135. The detainees are equally entitled to file a
     complaint or an accusation with respect to any
     incidence of torture, violence or cruelty.

     In the case that they are victims of the above-
     mentioned unlawful acts, they may obtain
     compensation in accordance with the relevant
     provisions of the Civil Code and if any unlawful
     acts were committed in the performance of official
     duties, they shall be entitled to claim just
     compensation from the State.

136. 29 public officials have been prosecuted for
     inflicting torture: 9 police officers in 1986, 5
     police officers and 4 prison officers in 1987, 4
     police officers in 1988, 5 police officers in 1989,
     and 2 police officers in 1990.

     In the case that prosecution of public officials is
     accompanied by a claim for damage compensation from
     the State or a claim based on the Civil Code, a
     guilty verdict may be accompanied by a court's
     decision to grant compensation for damages.

137. By denying the admissibility of a confession made
     against a defendant's will due to torture in the
     following instance, the Supreme Court has actually
     prohibited torture, violence, intimidation and
     unduly prolonged arrest which are committed in order
     to obtain a confession from a suspect or the
     accused.

     In case the accused had made a confession against
     his will due to torture during investigation by
     police and the accused made the same confession
     under coerced state of mental oppression during
     investigation by the prosecutor, the fact that no

torture was committed during the investigation by the prosecutor does not preclude the conclusion that confessions were involuntary and thus inadmissible. (Supreme Court decision, 13 October 1981, 81-TO-2160)

138. Article 10 of the Constitution protects the right of an individual to not be subjected to a medical or scientific experiment without his/her consent. This right is provided for in the second sentence of Article 7 of the Covenant.

   A medical or scientific experiment carried out without the individual's consent constitutes the crime of bodily injury and the crime of violence. (Criminal Code, Arts. 257, 260)

139. In the spirit of international efforts to protect human rights, the Government is seriously considering the accession to the Convention against Torture and Other Cruel, Inhuman or Degrading Treatment or Punishment.

140. In addition, from 1988 to 1990, the Government contributed US$ 15,000 to the United Nations Voluntary Fund for Victims of Torture, to participate in the concerted efforts of the international community to fight against torture and other harsh treatment or punishment.

ARTICLE 8

141. The Constitution does not explicitly prohibit slavery. However, according to Article 10 of the Constitution, there is no doubt that slavery is unlawful.

-69-

0107

Article 10 of the Constitution protects human
dignity, fundamental human rights and the right to
pursue the free development of oneself.

In accordance with the above provision, the Criminal
Code provides that a person, who forces, through
violence or intimidation, another to perform an act
which the latter does not have a duty to do, or who
kidnaps another, or buys or sells another for the
purpose of transporting him/her out of the Republic
of Korea, shall be subject to penal servitude (Arts.
324, 288, 289, 292, 293). Furthermore, if the
kidnapper under the above provisions kills or causes
the death or the injury of the kidnapped, the person
shall be subject to increased punishment. (Act
Concerning to Additional Punishment for Specified
Crimes, Art. 5-2)

142. Article 12(1) of the Constitution provides that no
person shall be subject to involuntary labor except
as provided by law and through lawful procedures.

In accordance with this provision, the Labor
Standards Act prohibits forced labor and excessive
work (Arts. 6, 55-57) and the Anti-Prostitution Act
prohibits prostitution and enticement or
intermediation thereof and provides for penal
servitude or penalty for those who violate the
provisions of the said Act. (Arts. 4-6, 14-17)

The Employment Security and Promotion Act provides
that a person, who engages in a placement service or
the recruitment of employees using violence, threat,
illegal confinement etc., shall be subject to penal
servitude or a fine. (Art. 29)

Under the Child Welfare Act, a provincial governor
who finds that a person with parental authority
abuses that authority, commits misconduct or cannot
exercise the authority for a significant reason
whatsoever, may request from a court, the forfeiture
of the parent authorities. And a person, who makes
his or her child beg for food or who begs for food
by using the child, shall be subject to penal
servitude or a fine. (Arts. 15, 18, 34)

In addition, any legal act for the purpose of
committing slavery shall be void under Article 103
of the Civil Code.

143. With respect to imprisonment with hard labor set
forth in paragraph 3(b) of the Covenant, the
Criminal Code provides for penal servitude with a
certain amount of labor (Art. 41) and a substitute
term of lockup at a place of hard labor in the case
that a fine is not paid in full. (Art. 70)

144. With respect to labor that is not compulsory labor
under paragraph 3(c) of the Covenant, or alternative
service for conscientious objectors to military
duty, the Constitution provides that all citizens
shall have the duty of national defense under the
conditions prescribed by law. (Art. 39(1))

The Supreme Court has decided that a Jehovah's
Witness, who refuses the duty of national defense,
is subject to the punishment prescribed in the
Military Service Act, and the so-called
"conscientious decision" is not included in the
freedom of conscience protected by Article 19 of the
Constitution. (Supreme Court decision, 22 July
1969, 69-TO-934)

ARTICLE 9

RIGHT TO LIBERTY AND PROHIBITION OF ARBITRARY ARREST AND DETENTION
Paragraph 1

145. Article 12(1) of the Constitution provides "All citizens shall enjoy personal liberty. No person shall be arrested, detained, searched, seized or interrogated except as provided by law. No person shall be punished or placed under preventive restrictions except as provided by law and through lawful procedures."

In addition, Article 12(3) provides that a warrant issued by a judge upon the request of a prosecutor shall be presented in the case of an arrest, detention, seizure or search.

146. In accordance with these provisions of the Constitution, the Code of Criminal Procedure prescribes strict requirements for arrest and detention.

The Court may detain the accused when there are reasonable grounds to suspect that the person has committed a crime and he/she has no fixed dwelling or there are reasonable grounds to suspect that the person may destroy evidence or that he/she may escape. (Code of Criminal Procedure, Art. 70)

In order to place the accused under detention, a warrant containing the following items must be issued and presented to the accused: the name and address of the accused, description of the crime, essential facts of the charge, the place of detention, the date of issue, the effective period

0110

of the warrant, a statement that after the lapse of
the effective period the warrant may not be executed
and must be returned to the court of issuance, and
the name and seal of the judge issuing the warrant.
(Code of Criminal Procedure, Arts. 73, 75, 85)

Under the Code of Criminal Procedure, a prosecutor
or a police officer may detain a suspect with a
warrant issued by a competent court upon a request
by the prosecutor. (Art. 201) However, in the case
that there are a reasonable ground to suspect that
the suspect committed a crime punishable by death,
imprisonment for life or imprisonment of three or
more years, and there are reasonable grounds to
believe that the suspect may destroy evidence or
escape, and it is not possible to obtain a warrant
due to the urgent situation (Art. 206), or in the
case that the suspect committed a crime in the
presence of a police officer (Arts. 211-214), the
suspect may be detained without a warrant. In case
of detention without a warrant, the prosecutor or
police officer must obtain a warrant within 48 hours
or 72 hours from the time of arrest (Art. 207). In
case the warrant is not obtained within the time
period, the suspect shall be released immediately.
(Arts. 207 & 213-2)

147. Although the Code of Criminal Procedure strictly
requires a warrant for arrest, it contains no
provisions requiring a warrant for the temporary
detention of a suspect. Therefore, it has been
pointed out that there is a discrepancy between the
norms of the Code of Criminal Procedure and the
actual practices of investigatory agencies, in that
the agencies sometimes detain a suspect who is
willing to accompany the officer to the police

station, and request the issuance of a warrant for detention after conducting an investigation.

148. In response to the above criticism, the Government is exerting efforts to improve the situation.

First, the Police Officers' Duty Performance Act has been amended twice, on 31 December 1988 and 8 March 1991. By strictly regulating the procedures for the suspect's voluntary submission into police custody in the following way, the amended Act prevents the abuse of the suspect's voluntary submission into police custody and the human rights violations resulting therefrom:
"A suspect may refuse a police officer's request for a voluntary submission into custody." (Art. 3(2))
"In the case of a suspect's voluntary submission into police custody, the police shall notify the family or close relatives of the suspect of the identity of the officer who took the suspect into custody, the place of custody and the reasons for custody, or shall allow the suspect to contact them and shall notify the suspect that he/she has the right to the assistance of a defense counsel."
(Art. 3(5))

"In case of a voluntary submission into police custody, the police may not detain the suspect for more than six hours." (Art. 3(6))

Second, the Government continues to search for ways to improve the entire arrest and detention system. In addition, the Government is making efforts to ensure that suspects are arrested pursuant to a warrant based upon sufficient evidence, or are arrested without a warrant only in the case of an urgent situation prescribed in the Code of Criminal Procedure.

NOTIFICATION OF THE CHARGE AND THE REASONS FOR ARREST

Paragraph 2

149. No person shall be arrested or detained without being informed of the reasons therefor and of his or her right to the assistance of a defense counsel. The family of a person arrested or detained, and other individuals designated by law, shall be notified without delay of the reasons for and the time and place of the arrest or detention. (Constitution, Art. 12(5))

In accordance with this provision, Article 72 of the Code of Criminal Procedure provides that the accused shall not be placed under detention unless the court has informed the accused of the facts of the alleged crime, the reasons for detention and the fact that the accused may select a defense counsel, and unless the court has given the accused the opportunity to defend himself/herself. In addition, Article 88 of the Code of Criminal Procedure provides that the accused shall be informed of the facts concerning the charge against him/her and the fact that the accused may select a defense counsel.

The right of the accused to defend himself/herself was reinforced by Article 87 of the Code of Criminal Procedure, as amended on 28 November 1987, which provides that in the case that the accused is detained, his/her defense counsel shall be notified immediately, in writing, of the reasons for the detention. (Prior to the amendment, the defense counsel was not informed of the reasons for detention and the notice was made in writing within 3 days from the time of detention.)

The Supreme Prosecutor's Office Regulation No. 172 (3 May 1988) prescribes that the detention notification form shall contain the statement of the facts of the alleged crime, and that a copy of the warrant shall be given to the defense counsel upon the counsel's request.

In the case of an urgent arrest without a warrant, the reason why it was impossible to obtain the warrant shall also be given. (Code of Criminal Procedure, Art. 206(1))

SPEEDY TRIAL AND RESTRICTIONS ON DETENTION OF THE ACCUSED

150. All citizens shall have the right to a speedy trial. The accused shall have the right to a public trial without delay in the absence of any justifiable reasons. (Constitution, Art. 27(3)) If a confession is deemed to have been made against the defendant's will due to an unduly prolonged detention, such a confession shall not be admitted as evidence of guilt, nor shall a defendant be punished by reason of such a confession. (Constitution, Art. 12(7)) Under the above-mentioned provisions, the right of an arrested offender to a speedy trial is ensured.

151. The Code of Criminal Procedure contains the following provisions to limit the period of detention reasonably and to allow the suspect to be released at each step of the criminal procedure.

152. The period of detention by a police officer and a
     prosecutor is limited to ten days each i.e., if a
     police officer arrests a suspect, the suspect shall
     be released if he or she is not transferred to the
     prosecutor within ten days, and the suspect shall
     also be released if the prosecutor does not file an
     indictment within ten days. (Code of Criminal
     Procedure, Arts. 202, 203)

     However, detention by a prosecutor may be extended
     at his/her request only once for no longer than ten
     days. In the request, the grounds for such an
     extension shall be stated. (Code of Criminal
     Procedure, Art. 205)

     However, since violations of the National Security
     Law require prolonged investigation and information
     gathering, the detention period may be extended for
     a total of 50 days upon the request of a police
     officer (once) or a prosecutor (twice). (National
     Security Law, Art. 19)

153. The period of detention and trial by a court shall
     not exceed two months. In the case that
     continuation of the detention is especially
     necessary, the period of detention may be extended
     twice by a ruling of the court and the extended
     period of detention shall not exceed two months.
     (Code of Criminal Procedure, Art. 92(1) & (2))

     If the trial does not come to an end during the
     period of detention, the accused must be released
     and the trial shall proceed without the detention of
     the accused.

154. After the indictment, the accused in detention or
     the defense counsel may request release on bail.

-77-

0115

(Code of Criminal Procedure, Art. 94) When request for release on bail has been made, it must be allowed except for certain cases (Art. 95) and if a court deems it proper, it may permit release on bail ex officio. (Art. 96)

Recent figures on the operation of bail system are as follows

(the number of persons)

Kinds Year	Request	Permitted	Not Permitted	Bail ex officio
1989	29,801	17,664	12,137	110
1990	37,585	22,701	14,884	114

REVIEW OF THE LEGALITY OF DETENTION

Paragraph 4

155. Article 12(6) of the Constitution provides that any person who is arrested or detained shall have the right to request the court to review the legality of the arrest or detention. Furthermore, Article 214(2) (Review of the Legality of Detention) and Article 214(3) (Restrictions on Re-arrest) of the Code of Criminal Procedure provide for the right to request the review of the legality of all crimes.

CRIMINAL COMPENSATION

Paragraph 5

156. Article 28 of the Constitution provides that in case
a criminal suspect or an accused person who has been
placed under detention is not indicted as provided
by law or is acquitted by a court, such a person
shall be entitled to claim just compensation from
the State under the conditions prescribed by law.
The Criminal Compensation Act has been enacted in
accordance with this provision.

The Criminal Compensation Act, amended on 28
November 1987, has expanded the types of people who
may seek compensation from the State by providing
that suspects released for lack of evidence are also
entitled to compensation. (Prior to the amendment,
only the accused persons who had been acquitted
could seek compensation from the State.)

Through the revision of the Enforcement Decree of
the Criminal Compensation Act, compensation of 8,000
won per day was increased to 15,000 won per day.

ARTICLE 10

HUMANE TREATMENT OF DETAINED PERSONS

Paragraph 1

157. In accordance with Article 10 of the Constitution,
which guarantees respect for human rights, any
person placed under detention in a prison or other
detention place is accorded humane treatment based
on respect for human dignity.

시민적.정치적 권리에 관한 국제규약(B규약) 한국 최초 인권보고서 제출 및 심의, 1991-92. 전5권 (V.2 1991.7-12월) 255

TREATMENT OF THE INMATES

158. In accordance with the menu determined by the Inmates Meal Regulation Committee composed of nutrition specialists, inmates are provided with meals of 3,150 Kcal per day. (Penal Administration Act, Art. 21, its Enforcement Decree, Arts. 78-82)

159. For sanitarian reasons, sufficient clothes and bedsheets, which are appropriate for the season, are supplied to and are regularly changed for the inmates. (Penal Administration Act, Art. 20, its Enforcement Decree, Arts. 73, 75, 76)

160. In order to take care of the inmates, 2 to 5 doctors, who reside at detention places, provide medical treatment, regular check-ups and epidemic prevention. An inmate may also receive medical attention at his/her own expense upon request of his/her family member or defense counsel. (Penal Administration Act, Arts. 25, 26, 28, 29 and its Enforcement Decree, Art. 97-105)

SEGREGATION

Paragraph 2

161. All persons in the detention places are segregated according to their status, such as whether the person is convicted, adult or juvenile, male or female.

Even within the same detention place, they are accorded separate treatment and accommodation based on the number of times the person has committed a crime, the type of crime, etc.

162. Unconvicted detainees are committed to detention houses whereas convicted detainees are committed to prisons. Even when a prison and a detention house are built in one place, unconvicted and convicted detainees are accorded separated accommodation. (Penal Administration Act, Art. 2(4) & (5))

As unconvicted detainees are presumed innocent until proven guilty (Constitution, Art. 27(4)), they are entitled to prepare and submit trial documents, to communicate with their defense counsels, to have access to general information including the newspapers. Aside from the minimum duty imposed on them so as to secure order at the detention institution, they receive the same treatment as is rendered to civilians. (Penal Administration Act, Arts. 45, 65)

163. Convicted persons who are 20 or more years of age shall be committed to the prisons, while convicted persons who are under 20 years of age shall be committed to juvenile correction centers. In addition, unconvicted detainees who are under 20 years of age shall be separately accommodated within detention places for unconvicted detainees. (Penal Administration Act, Arts. 2-4, Art. 11, Regulation on the Separate Accommodation of Juvenile Detainees)

Basically, juvenile convicts with similar problems are accommodated in the same detention places. Therefore, the juvenile correction center located in Cheonan city accommodates first offenders and the juvenile correction center in Kimcheon city accommodates repeat offenders.

164. Female convicts are accommodated in female prisons and unconvicted female detainees are in segregated

accommodation in detention places. Female detainees are treated in a manner that is appropriate for their physical characteristics. (Penal Administration Act, Arts. 4, 30)

PENITENTIARY SYSTEM

Paragraph 3

165. The purpose of the Penal Administration Act is to reform and rehabilitate convicted persons through vocational training and the cultivation of a sound spirit and work ethic.

166. In order to return convicted persons to a normal life in society, the following education programs are carried out in the correction facilities:
    (a) Restoration of morals through education;
    (b) Access to social information and intellectual education;
    (c) Promotion of self-improvement through technical education and vocational training.

EDUCATION

167. Courses equivalent to elementary, middle and high school education are offered to convicted persons. Juvenile convicts may obtain education from the correspondence high school and exemplary convicts who graduated from high school may enter the correspondence university. There are also study groups for the convicts in order to enable them to pass the qualifying examination to enter schools of higher education.

In addition, in order to correct the criminal tendencies of the convicts, renowned people are invited for moral education (2 weeks per year) and social education (1 week per year). (Penal Administration Act, Arts. 32, 34, its Enforcement Decree, Arts. 112, 113, Cumulative Correction Treatment Regulation, Art. 63, Regulation on the Education of the Convicts)

In 1990, 9 convicts passed the qualifying examination for middle school, 177 convicts passed the qualifying examination for high school and 361 convicts obtained the certificate for high school graduation by passing the qualifying examination.

CONVICTS' RIGHT TO COMMUNICATE

168. According to Article 18 of the Penal Administration Act, an inmate may see his or her relatives and is permitted to see other persons when deemed necessary.

    However, in the interests of inmates, an inmate may see other persons except in limited cases where the meeting is deemed harmful for the rehabilitation of the inmate.

    An unconvicted person may be restricted from communicating with other persons by an order of the court, due to the possibility that necessary evidence may be destroyed. An inmate who has violated prison regulations and is thus under a disciplinary punishment, is prohibited from communicating with other persons. (Penal Administration Act. Art. 46) Even in this case, the convict may communicate with his or her family members if deemed necessary. However, the right to communicate with the defense counsel is never restricted.

169. Inmates may send and receive letters without any. restrictions, except in limited cases where there is a possibility that the relevant evidence may be destroyed or where the order at the prison may be disturbed. (Penal Administration Act, Art. 18, its Enforcement Decree, Arts. 54, 56, 61, Cumulative Correction Treatment Regulation, Arts. 45, 56)

170. Inmates are allowed to enjoy radio and TV programs which contribute to the restoration of their morals and self-improvement. (Cumulative Correction Treatment Regulation, Art. 55) Furthermore, inmates are permitted to read newspapers and books and other publications that are not inappropriate or that do not encourage crimes. (Penal Administration Act, Art. 33)

RELIGION

171. Inmates are free to worship according to their own religion and religious workers are permitted to enter the prison in order to perform religious activities for inmates.

HOME LEAVE

172. Programs of home leave and adaptation to social life have been implemented in order to assist inmates in returning to a normal life in society. These programs are linked with the program of release on parole for exemplary inmates. (Penal Administration Act, Arts. 44, 49-52, its Enforcement Decree, Art. 139, Cumulative Correction Treatment Regulation, Art. 88 and Home Leave Enforcement Regulation)

CIVILIANS' PARTICIPATION IN INMATES' REHABILITATION

173. Renowned people from the community, such as social workers, lawyers and businessmen assist in rehabilitating inmates through religious lectures and mediation of job opportunities.

The Religious Guidance Committee which is composed of pastors, monks and priests, provides religious guidance to inmates through religious education and counselling etc.

TECHNICAL AND VOCATIONAL TRAINING

174. In order to enable inmates to make a living after their release from prison, they are offered vocational training on 54 subjects such as computer, carpentry, etc. As a result, almost all inmates have acquired technician certificates and many have won awards in technical skills competitions.

In addition, the inmates are provided with vocational training according to their work experience, interests and age and are provided with compensation of up to 3,000 won per day for their work in order to assist them to make a living after they return to society. (Penal Administration Act, Art. 39)

In 1990, 3,329 inmates acquired the technician certificate.

OPEN CORRECTION FACILITIES

175. Exemplary inmates in open correction facilities and general correction facilities are permitted to commute to companies in order to receive technical

training. After their release from prison, these inmates are guaranteed a job in these companies.

CULTIVATION OF A SOUND AND STABLE PERSONALITY

176. Juvenile inmates are permitted to participate in sports, singing and speech contests, to watch movies and TV and listen to the radio so that they may cultivate a sound and stable personality.

PAROLE

177. Since a long period of detention and the environment of places of detention significantly affect the character of juvenile inmates, Article 65 of the Juvenile Act provides for a more lenient standard of parole for juveniles than adults. Accordingly, a juvenile inmate who has served the following period may be released on parole:
    (a) 5 years in case of a life sentence;
    (b) 3 years in case of a 15 year sentence;
    (c) One-third of the minimum term of an indeterminate sentence.

REHABILITATION OF JUVENILE OFFENDERS

178. Juvenile offenders between 14 and 19 years of age, who were transferred to a juvenile reformatory in accordance with Article 32(1) No. 6 and 7 of the Juvenile Act (protected juveniles), are treated in a humane manner that provides an appropriate environment for the further development of stable and disciplined character. (Juvenile Reformatory Act, Art. 5)

UPGRADED TREATMENT

179. The treatment of protected juveniles is upgraded
    step-by-step according to improvements in their
    character and behaviour. (Juvenile Reformatory Act,
    Art. 6, its Enforcement Decree, Arts. 5, 6)

SEPARATE TREATMENT

180. (a) Review
        The place and period of detention and
        educational courses for new juvenile inmates
        are determined by the Protected Juvenile
        Treatment Committee after 10 days of review.
        (Enforcement Decree of the Juvenile Reformatory
        Act, Arts. 4, 11, 14 and 15)

    (b) Separate detention
        Juvenile reformatories are classified and
        operated according to the following categories:
        4 educational reformatories, 3 vocational
        training reformatories, 1 female reformatory, 1
        special reformatory and 2 general
        reformatories. The place of detention for the
        juvenile inmates is determined by such factors
        as their sex, age, number of times of entering
        the reformatory, crime. sentence and the
        educational course they are required to take,
        etc. (Juvenile Reformatory Act, Art. 8 and its
        Enforcement Decree, Arts. 4, 11, 15 and 16)

DETENTION PERIOD

181. The detention period for juvenile is flexible and
    depends on their behavior at the detention place.
    The period of detention is as follows:
    (a) 6 months or less for a juvenile inmate under
        the minimum sentence;

—87—

(b) 13 months or more but less than 18 months for a juvenile inmate whose rehabilitation is deemed difficult;

(c) 18 months or more for a juvenile inmate whose rehabilitation is deemed extremely difficult.

In all cases, the maximum period of detention cannot exceed 2 years. (Juvenile Act, Art. 32, para. 1, No. 6 and 7, Juvenile Reformatory Act, Arts. 43 and 44, Protection and Supervision Act, Art. 28(1), Juvenile Reformatory Manual, Art. 21(2))

DETENTION FACILITIES

182. In the juvenile reformatories, each inmate has 3m2 of space. The educational program for juvenile inmates is generally identical with that of regular schools in society. Inmates are permitted to watch TV, read newspapers and participate in sports activities during their leisure time.

183. Protected juvenile inmates are provided with everything they need for their life and education in the detention places. In every juvenile reformatory, there are doctors and nurses to treat the juvenile inmates and if a proper treatment is not possible within the reformatory, the inmates are taken to an outside hospital.

184. A juvenile inmate is permitted, without any restriction, to meet people other than those who are deemed to be harmful to him/her. (Juvenile Reformatory Act, Art. 18, its Enforcement Decree, Arts. 48, 50)

PETITIONS

185. In every reformatory, there are boxes for petitions
     by the juvenile inmates and the petitioning inmate
     is notified of the relevant decision promptly. At
     least once every month, a poll is conducted on the
     conditions of detention and the results of the poll
     are taken into account in operating the reformatory.
     (Juvenile Reformatory Act, Arts. 10, 11 and its
     Enforcement Decree, Arts. 19, 20)

CONTROL OF CORRECTION FACILITIES

186. In order to protect the human rights of convicts in
     the correction facilities and to ensure that they
     receive appropriate treatment, strict controls are
     imposed on every correction facility.

     (a) A public official designated by the Minister of
          Justice inspects correction facilities such as
          prisons, juvenile reformatories and detention
          places at least once a year. (Penal
          Administration Act, Art. 5(1))
     (b) The Board of Audit and Inspection inspects
          correction facilities in order to supervise and
          improve their operation and management. (Board
          of Audit and Inspection Act, Art. 20)
     (c) Judges and prosecutors may inspect the
          correction facilities in order to ensure just
          execution of criminal penalties and to check
          the conditions of the detention of unconvicted
          persons. (Penal Administrations Act, Art.
          5(2))

REMEDIES

187. In case an inmate has any complaints regarding treatment at the prison, he/she may petition the Minister of Justice in writing or the public official who is making the inspection rounds, either in writing or orally. (Penal Administration Act, Art. 6) He/she may also petition the prison chief by requesting an interview. (Enforcement Decree of the Penal Administration Act, Art. 9)

    In any case, the confidentiality of the petition is guaranteed. (Enforcement Decree of the Penal Administration Act, Art. 4, 6)

    In the case of an infringement of human rights, a complaint, accusation, claim for compensation from the State and administrative petition are available in addition to the above-mentioned measures.

    In case a remedy for an infringement of fundamental rights guaranteed by the Constitution is not available through the legal procedures, a constitutional petition may be made to the Constitution Court. (Constitution Court Act, Art. 68)

STANDARD MINIMUM RULES FOR THE TREATMENT OF PRISONERS

188. As has been explained in detail in the preceding paragraphs, the penal administration laws and regulations of the Republic of Korea reflect most of the "Standard Minimum Rules for the Treatment of Prisoners" adopted by the United Nations.

ARTICLE 11

189. Under the Korean legal system, failure to perform contractual obligations may incur civil liability but does not constitute a crime. Thus, no person may be arrested or detained on the grounds that he/she failed to perform contractual obligations.

190. The Special Deliberation Council on the Revision of the Criminal Law in the Ministry of Justice has once considered criminalizing the failure to perform contractual duties in order to punish debtors who can afford to meet their obligations but evade doing so. However, it was concluded that such criminalization is not in accordance with the spirit of the Covenant.

191. The Code of Civil Procedure, amended on 13 January 1990, provides that a court, at the request of a creditor, may order a debtor to submit an affidavit describing his/her property and punish the debtor who refuses to submit the affidavit or presents a false one. (Art. 524(8))

ARTICLE 12

192. Article 14 of the Constitution provides that "all citizens shall enjoy freedom of residence and the right to move at will". Therefore, all citizens are free to move, to emigrate and to travel in and out of the Republic of Korea.

Although the Constitution does not contain an explicit provision, it fully guarantees the right of a citizen to enter his/her own country provided for in Article 12, para. 4 of the Covenant.

193. The right stated in this Article may be restricted in accordance with the following provisions only when it is necessary for national security, public order or public welfare:
   (a) Restriction on the residence of an accused person when execution of his/her detention was suspended. (Code of Criminal Procedure, Art. 101(1));
   (b) Restriction on leaving Korea for a person who is under criminal investigation (Immigration Law, Art. 4) and restriction on the area of activity for those who were granted permission to land. (Immigration Law, Arts. 12(2), 13(2), 14(2);
   (c) Temporary isolation of a patient with an infectious disease. (Communicable Disease Prevention Act, Art. 37);
   (d) Restriction by special measures of the martial law commander. (Martial Law Act, Art. 9)

ARTICLE 13

194. A foreigner, who violates the provisions of the Immigration Law, may be expelled from the Republic of Korea. (Immigration Law, Art. 45)

195. The persons who may be expelled under the Immigration Law are those who threaten the national security or public order, such as:
   (a) A person who entered the Republic of Korea without an entry visa (Art. 45(1) & (3));
   (b) A person who is not permitted to enter the Republic of Korea (Art. 45(2));
   (c) A person who has landed without permission (Art. 45(4));

0130

(d) A person who has violated the conditions set forth in the landing permission (Art. 45(5));

(e) A person who is in Korea after the expiration of a visa (Art. 45(6));

(f) A person who has been released after having been sentenced to imprisonment or a more severe punishment (Art. 45(10));

196. A foreigner may be expelled in accordance with the procedures provided for in Articles 46-64 of the Immigration Law. Any foreigner under investigation for expulsion is guaranteed the right to submit pleadings against his/her expulsion to the competent authority. When an expulsion order is issued, the foreigner shall be informed by the Immigration Office and is guaranteed the right to appeal to the Minister of Justice.

197. In addition, a foreigner under an expulsion order may institute an administrative litigation with respect to the order. If the defendant has complaints about the judgement of the administrative litigation, he/she may appeal to the Supreme Court.

ARTICLE 14

EQUALITY BEFORE THE COURTS, RIGHT TO A FAIR, OPEN AND INDEPENDENT TRIAL

Paragraph 1

198. Article 11 of the Constitution states that, "All citizens shall be equal before the law." Furthermore, right to a fair, open and independent trial is guaranteed by Article 27(1) & (3) and Chapter 5 (Arts. 101-110) of the Constitution.

Article 27(1) of the Constitution states that "all citizens shall have the right to be tried in conformity with the law by judges qualified under the Constitution and the law." The provisions of the Constitution and the Court Organization Act concerning the qualification of the judges are as follows:

(a) Article 42 of the Court Organization Act, which was promulgated in accordance with Article 101(3) of the Constitution, prescribes the qualification of the judges.

(b) Article 104 of the Constitution provides

    (1) that the Chief Justice of the Supreme Court shall be appointed by the President with the consent of the National Assembly

    (2) that the Supreme Court Justices shall be appointed by the President on the recommendation of the Chief Justice and with the consent of the National Assembly

    (3) that judges other than the Chief Justice and the Supreme Court Justices shall be appointed by the Chief Justice with the consent of the Conference of the Supreme Court Justices.

(c) In order to ensure the independence of the court, the Constitution prescribes the term of office and the retirement age of the judges (Art. 105) and further guarantees the independence of the judges by stating that "no judge shall be removed from office except by impeachment or by a sentence of imprisonment or heavier punishment..." (Art. 106)

(d) The Constitution also provides that "Judges shall rule independently according to their conscience and in conformity with the Constitution and law."

0132

(e) Judges may be precluded from adjudicating a case for reasons prescribed by law.

Article 27(3) of the Constitution provides that "All citizens shall have the right to a prompt trial" and that "The accused shall have the right to a public trial without delay in the absence of justifiable reasons to the contrary."

Article 109 of the Constitution also provides that "Trials and decisions of the courts shall be open to the public. Provided, however, that when there is a danger that such trials may undermine the national security, or disturb public safety and order or may be harmful to public morals, trials may be closed to the public by a court decision."

199. The Court Organization Act and the Code of Criminal Procedure contain detailed provisions to enforce the principle of open trials. Article 57 of the Court Organization Act provides that if a court decides to close a trial to the public because an open trial might endanger national security, public peace and order or good public morals, the court must indicate the reasons therefor and may admit to the trial those it deems appropriate.

The record of the trial shall state whether or not the trial was open to the public and if it was not open to the public, the reasons why it was held in closed session. (Code of Criminal Procedure, Art. 51(2), item 5) When the principle of open trials is violated, this may be the subject of an appeal. (Code of Civil Procedure, Art. 394(1), Code of Criminal Procedure, Art. 361-5 item 9)

However, Article 13 of the Non-Contentious Cases Act states that "Trials of non-contentious cases shall not be open. However, the court may permit anyone whom it deems appropriate to attend the trial" and the Code of Civil Reconciliation Procedure provides that "Reconciliatory procedures shall not be open. However, the judge in charge of the reconciliation may permit anyone whom he/she deems appropriate to attend the hearing."

PRESUMPTION OF INNOCENCE

Paragraph 2

200. While the presumption of innocence was not explicitly provided for in the earlier Constitutions, Article 27(4) of the current Constitution provides that an accused person shall be presumed innocent until proven guilty. Article 275-2 of the Code of Criminal Procedure also provides for the presumption of innocence. Article 118(2) of the Rules of Criminal Procedure also states that documents or any other articles, which may cause the court to have a presupposition on the case, shall not be attached to the indictment. Under the above-mentioned provisions, presumption of innocence is the resolute principle of criminal procedure.

RIGHT OF THE ACCUSED IN A TRIAL

Paragraph 3

201. Regarding the right of the accused in a trial, Korean laws provide for the following safeguards:

(a) Right to be promptly notified the details of crime the accused is suspected to have committed.

When a suspect or an accused is arrested or detained, he/she shall be immediately notified of the reasons for the arrest or detention. (Code of Criminal Procedure, Arts. 72, 88, 209) In the case of a public trial, the court shall send, at least five days prior to the first trial date, a copy of the indictment to the accused or his/her defense counsel. (Code of Criminal Procedure, Art. 266)

In the case that there is a change in the charges during a trial, the court shall promptly notify to the accused or his/her defense counsel of the reasons thereof. In the case that the change is deemed to place the accused at a further disadvantage, the court may, ex officio or upon the request of the accused or his/her defense counsel, grant a recess for a period necessary for the accused to prepare his/her defense. (Code of Criminal Procedure, Art. 298(3) & (4)) Such provisions ensure that the accused and his/her defense counsel are informed of the facts concerning the charges against the accused in advance and prepare their defense against the charges.

(b) Right to have sufficient time and appropriate conveniences for the preparation of defense and the right to communicate with his/her defense counsel.

Article 12(4) of the Constitution provides that any person who is arrested or detained shall

시민적.정치적 권리에 관한 국제규약(B규약) 한국 최초 인권보고서 제출 및 심의, 1991-92. 전5권 (V.2 1991.7-12월) 273

have the prompt assistance from a defense counsel and Article 12(5) further provides that no person shall be arrested or detained without being informed of the reasons therefor, and of his/her right to the assistance from defense counsel.

In this connection, Article 34 of the Code of Criminal Procedure states that the defense counsel may interview the accused or suspect who is in detention, deliver to or receive from the accused or suspect any documents and other materials and have a doctor treat the accused or the suspect.

The Supreme Court has recently decided that the right to communicate with the defense counsel may not be restricted. (Supreme Court decision on 28 March 1991, 91-MO-24) The decision is consistent with the spirit of the Constitution and the Code of Criminal Procedure.

(c) Right to a speedy trial.

Article 27(3) of the Constitution guarantees the right to a speedy trial. As has been stated in Article 9, para. 3 of the Covenant in this report (see para. 152), the Code of Criminal Procedure strictly limits the detention period of the accused and the detention for a trial may not extend for more than six months, even for the trial of the most serious crime.

(d) Right to appear in the trial and right to a defense counsel appointed by the State.

The accused has the right to appear in the
trial and state facts favorable to his/her
case. When the accused does not appear on the
trial date, the trial cannot be commenced.
(Code of Criminal Procedure, Arts. 276, 286)
However, the trial may be convened without the
appearance of the accused in the following
exceptional cases (Code of Criminal Procedure,
Arts. 277, 306, 330, 365, Special Act for
Speedy Proceedings, Art. 23):

(1) Where the offense charged is a
    misdemeanour;
(2) Where it is evident that the charged is to
    be dismissed;
(3) Where an accused refuses to make a
    statement, leaves the court without
    permission or is ordered by the judge to
    leave the court for the maintenance of
    court order;
(4) Where the accused does not appear in the
    court more than twice without a proper
    reason;
(5) Where the accused cannot be located for
    more than six months. However, in the
    case that the offense charged is
    punishable by death or imprisonment or
    confinement of more than three years,
    public trials shall not be conducted
    without the presence of the accused.

In case a defendant in a criminal trial is
unable to secure a defense counsel, the State
shall assign a counsel, free of charge, for the
defendant as prescribed by law. (Constitution,
Art. 12(4)) Article 33 of the Code of Criminal
Procedure provides that the court shall, ex

officio, appoint a counsel in the following
cases:

(1)   Where the accused is a minor;

(2)   Where the accused is seventy years of age
      or more;

(3)   Where the accused is a deaf or a mute;

(4)   Where the accused is suspected of being
      mentally unsound;

(5)   Where the accused is unable to select a
      counsel because of poverty or any other
      reason.

Furthermore, in case the offense charged is
punishable by death or imprisonment of more
than three years, public trials shall not be
conducted without defense counsel. In case a
defendant in a military court has no counsel,
the court shall appoint a counsel ex officio.
(Code of Criminal Procedure, Arts. 282, 283,
Military Court Act, Art. 62(1))

(e)   Right to examine evidence and witnesses.

Under the Code of Criminal Procedure, the
prosecutor, the accused or his/her defense
counsel may apply for the examination of the
evidence and the judges shall ask the accused
for his/her opinion in the results of the
examination and shall inform the accused of
his/her right to apply for the examination of
the evidence (Arts. 293, 294). The prosecutor,
the accused or his/her defense counsel may
raise objections regarding the examination of
the evidence (Art. 296) and may be present
during the examination of witnesses. (Art. 163)

In the case that the judge recognizes that a
witness cannot sufficiently testify in the

presence of the accused, the accused may be
ordered to leave the court (the defense counsel
may remain at the court). However, the court
shall inform the accused or his/her defense
counsel of the witness' testimony if it
contains unexpected and serious statements
which are disadvantageous to the accused.
(Art. 164) Furthermore, Article 310-2 of the
Code of Criminal Procedure strictly limits the
probative value of hearsay evidence and
provides that the accused shall have the right
to cross-examine witnesses.

(f)   Right to an interpreter.

If a person is not versed in the Korean
language, he/she shall be provided with an
interpreter. (Code of Criminal Procedure, Art.
180, Court Organization Act, Art. 62(2)) If a
person required to make a statement is deaf or
mute, any interpreter shall be provided and
letters, signs or marks not in the Korean
language shall be translated. (Code of
Criminal Procedure, Arts. 181, 182)

The State pays for the cost of interpretation
including travel and accommodation costs of the
interpreter.

(g)   Right to be silent and right not to be
compelled to testify.

Article 12(2) of the Constitution states that
no citizen shall be tortured, or shall be
compelled to testify against himself/herself in
criminal cases. Furthermore, Article 12(7)
provides that in the case that a confession is

deemed to have been made against a defendant's will due to torture, violence, intimidation, unduly prolonged arrest or deceit, etc., such a confession shall not be admitted as evidence of guilt, nor shall a defendant be punished by reason of such a confession.

In criminal cases, confessions made against the defendants' will and a disadvantageous confessions without supporting evidence cannot be taken as evidence of guilt. (Code of Criminal Procedure, Arts. 309, 310))

Article 289 of the Code of Criminal Procedure provides that the accused may refuse to answer questions and Article 200(2) of the Code states that the prosecutor or the police officer shall notify the suspect in advance he/she may refuse to answer questions.

SPECIAL TREATMENT FOR JUVENILE OFFENDERS

Paragraph 4

202. The Juvenile Act contains special provisions that promote healthy and sound upbringing of juveniles.

JUVENILES TO BE PROTECTED

203. Protected juveniles are defined as follows (Juvenile Act. Art. 4(1)):
    (a) Juveniles between the age of 14 and 19 who have committed a crime;
    (b) Juveniles between the age of 12 and 13 who have committed acts against the criminal laws and decrees; and

(c) Juveniles between the age of 12 and 19 who may
     be prone to commit acts against the criminal
     laws and decrees.

INVESTIGATION

204. In investigating juvenile cases, medical science,
     psychology, pedagogy, sociology and other
     professional disciplines are used to examine the
     character, personal records, family background, and
     other circumstances of the juvenile. (Juvenile Act,
     Art. 9)

     When the Juvenile Department (the Juvenile
     Department of the Family Court or the Juvenile
     Department of a District Court) or an investigator
     investigates a juvenile with respect to the facts of
     the crime, the Juvenile Department or the
     investigator shall notify that he/she may refuse to
     make any incriminating statement. (Juvenile Act.
     Art. 10)

     In its investigation or trial, the Juvenile
     Department or the investigator takes into account
     diagnosis by psychiatrists, psychologists, social
     workers, educators and other experts as well as
     classification results and opinions by the Juvenile
     Classification Office. (Juvenile Act, Art. 12)

     When a criminal case involving a juvenile is related
     to another ordinary case, the trial of the juvenile
     shall be conducted separately from the other case if
     such separation does not cause any obstruction to
     the trial proceedings of the juvenile case.
     (Juvenile Act, Art. 57) The trial of the juvenile
     case shall be conducted in a kind and gentle manner
     and particular emphasis should be placed on the

0141

evaluation of the juvenile's physical and mental condition, character, career, family background and other circumstances. (Juvenile Act, Art. 58)

The judge and clerk shall be present during the trial and the investigator, guardian and assistant of the juvenile may attend and state their opinions concerning the case. (Juvenile Act, Arts.23, 25)

The trial shall not be made public. However, when deemed appropriate, the judge may permit certain persons to attend the trial. (Juvenile Act, Arts. 23, 24, 25)

PROHIBITION OF REPORTING

205. Regarding the cases involving protected juveniles and criminal cases under investigation or a trial in accordance with the Juvenile Act, facts or photographs which may identify the juveniles by means of their names, ages, occupations, appearances and other things shall not be published in newspapers or other publications nor shall they be broadcast. In case of violation of this provision, the authors, editors, publishers or broadcasters shall be punished by an imprisonment of less than one year or a fine not exceeding 3,000,000 won. (Juvenile Act, Art. 68(1) & (2))

RIGHT TO APPEAL

Paragraph 5

206. The judicial power is vested in the courts, and the courts are composed of the Supreme Court, which is the highest court of the State, and the other lower courts. (Constitution, Art. 101(1) & (2))

0142

In accordance with this provision, the Code of Criminal Procedure contains detailed provisions on the appeal to the High Court and the Supreme Court (Part III), and on the retrial and the extraordinary appeals (Part IV).

Through those provisions the right of the accused to appeal or reappeal is fully guaranteed and when evidence which may prove the innocence of the convict is newly discovered after the end of a trial, the convict may request a retrial.

207. The Korean Government has made a reservation on paragraph 5 of Article 14 of the Covenant, because Article 110(4) of the Constitution and Article 534 of the Military Court Act, which stipulate that military trials under extraordinary law may not be appealed except in case of death sentences, are not in conformity with the Covenant.

AMNESTY AND CRIMINAL COMPENSATION

Paragraph 6

208. With regard to amnesty and criminal compensation, explanations have been already given in the description paragraph of Article 9, para. 5 of the Covenant. (See para. 156) In this connection, no criminal compensation is provided in the case of an amnesty in the Republic of Korea.

DOUBLE JEOPARDY

Paragraph 7

209. Article 13(1) of the Constitution clearly expresses the principle against double jeopardy (ne bis in

idem) by providing that no citizen shall be prosecuted for an act which does not constitute a crime at the time the act was committed, nor shall he/she be placed under double jeopardy.

Thus, a case involving a retrial of the crime for which a final judgement of acquittal has already been rendered, must be dismissed. (Code of Criminal Procedure, Art. 326 item 1)

The principle against double jeopardy also applies to misdemeanour cases where the accused has already been sentenced to confinement or a fine.

210. However, the principle against double jeopardy can not be forced upon another country as considerable differences might exist in legal systems and laws from one country to another. Article 7 of the Criminal Code provides that a sentence imposed abroad may be the basis for mitigating or eliminating the sentence in Korea for the same crime. It is for this reason that the Korean Government has made a reservation on Paragraph 7 of Article 14 of the Covenant.

ARTICLE 15

NULLA POENA SINE LEGE, NULLUM CRIMEN SINE LEGE

211. Article 13(1) of the Constitution stipulates that no citizen shall be prosecuted for an act which does not constitute a crime under the law in force at the time it was committed

212. The prohibition of ex post facto laws is guaranteed by the provisions of the Criminal Code.

0144

Article 1 of the Criminal Code reaffirms the principle and further provides that if a law is changed after the commission of an act and such an act thereby no longer constitutes a crime under the new law, or the punishment for the act under the new law is less severe than under the previous law, the new law shall apply and that if a law is changed after the sentence for a crime has become final and such act thereby no longer constitutes a crime under the new law, the punishment shall not be executed. Therefore, the accused are guaranteed the benefits of the new law.

RETROACTIVE EFFECT OF A DECISION OF UNCONSTITUTIONALITY

213. Article 47(2) of the Constitution Court Act provides that any law decided to be unconstitutional shall lose its effect from the decision date and that the law relating to any penalty shall lose its effect retroactively. Thus, retroactive effect of a decision of unconstitutionality is acknowledged only with respect to laws relating to criminal punishment. In accordance with this provision, a retrial may be requested with respect to a conviction based on the law which was held unconstitutional. (Constitution Court Act, Art. 47(3))

ARTICLE 16

214. Article 10 of the Constitution provides that, "All citizens shall be assured of human worth and dignity and shall have the right to pursue happiness and it shall be the duty of the State to confirm and

guarantee the fundamental and inviolable human
rights of individuals."

Article 37 of the Constitution states, "Freedoms and
rights of citizens shall not be neglected on the
grounds that they are not enumerated in the
Constitution and the freedoms and rights of citizens
may be restricted by law only when necessary for
national security, the maintenance of law and order
or public welfare. Even when such restriction is
imposed, no essential aspect of the freedom or right
shall be violated."

These provisions of the Constitution guarantee that
human rights shall be respected in all the laws and
regulations.

In this connection, Article 3 of the Civil Code
provides that "All persons can enjoy rights and
assume duties during their lives."

215. All persons, irrespective of their nationality, are
entitled to be treated as human beings. Therefore,
human worth shall not be denied to criminals,
patients of mental disease, embryos and deformed
children.

RESTRICTIONS OF THE RIGHTS IN EXCEPTIONAL CASES

216. Article 16 of the Covenant should not be interpreted
to prohibit any restrictions on the right of minors,
mentally disabled persons and foreigners.

217. Article 43 of the Criminal Code prescribes
restrictions on the rights of the persons who are
convicted.

0146

(a) A person who is sentenced to death or life imprisonment shall be deprived of the following:

(1) Qualification to become a public official;

(2) Right to vote and to be elected under public law;

(3) Qualification concerning a business under public law, for which necessary conditions have been prescribed by law;

(4) Qualification to become a director, auditor, manager, inspector or custodian of a juristic person.

(b) Qualifications (1) through (3) shall be suspended for a person who is sentenced to an imprisonment for a limited term until the sentence is fully served or exempted.

218. (a) Capacity of a Minor

The Civil Code prescribes restrictions on the legal capacity of a Minor in Article 5 which states, "A minor shall obtain the consent of his/her legal guardian in order to perform any juristic act, except for an act to merely acquire a right or to be relieved of an obligation. Any act performed in violation of this provision is voidable."

(b) Capacity of a person with limited financial capacity

The Family Court must adjudge a person with a severe mental or physical disease or spendthrift who is liable to bring his/her family to bankruptcy as a person with limited financial capacity. (Civil Code, Art. 9)

The capacity of a person with a limited capacity shall be that of a minor.

(c) Capacity of an incompetent

The Family Court must adjudge a person with a mental disorder an incompetent. The judicial acts of an incompetent may be voidable. (Civil Code, Arts. 12 & 13)

ARTICLE 17

219. Article 16 of the Constitution states "All citizens shall be free from intrusion into their place of residence. In the case of search or seizure in a residence, a warrant issued by a judge upon request of a prosecutor shall be presented." The Criminal Code also prohibits arbitrary entry by State agencies into the residence of citizens. (Arts. 319-322)

Any persons who, without a justifiable reason, conceals himself/herself in an uninhabited and unguarded house, shall be punished by Article 1 item 1 of the Minor Offense Punishment Act.

220. The rights to privacy of the citizens shall not be infringed upon. (Constitution, Art. 17) A doctor, lawyer or any other person who discloses another person's secrets which have come to his/her knowledge in the course of practising his/her profession, shall be punished. (Criminal Code, Art. 317, Code of Criminal Procedure, Art. 149, Code of Civil Procedure, Art. 286)

The right to privacy, which includes the right to non-disclosure, without good reason, of the past events that may injure the honour and reputation of a person, is protected in Korea.

221. The honour and credibility of an individual are protected as follows:

    (a) A person, who defames another by disclosing facts concerning the other person or defames a dead person by publicly alleging false facts, shall be punished. (Criminal Code, Arts. 307-309)

    (b) A person, who injures the credibility of another person, shall be punished. (Criminal Code, Art. 313)

    (c) A person whose credibility or reputation is damaged may seek compensation for mental distress (Civil Code, Art. 751) and may also request the restoration to the original state. (Civil Code, Art. 764)

222. Article 18 of the Constitution provides that the right to privacy of correspondence shall not be infringed upon.

Under the Criminal Code, a person, who violates the right to privacy of another person by opening his/her letter, document or drawing sealed or protected in other ways, shall be punished. (Art. 316)

The Postal Act and the Korea Telecom Corporation Law also guarantee the secrecy of correspondence in accordance with the spirit of the Constitution. No one, who engages or had engaged in the postal services or telecommunication services, shall divulge any information obtained in the discharge of his/her duties. Offenders shall be subject to imprisonment or a fine. (Postal Act, Arts. 3, 51, 51-2, Korea Telecom Corporation Law, Arts. 9, 20)

223. The Government is about to operate a nationwide administrative telecommunication network with a view to improving public administration. In this regard, the Enforcement Decree of the Resident Registration Law is being amended so that only a person, his/her family or representative is allowed to review the person's certificate of Resident Registration or request a copy thereof. At the same time, the Personal Information Protection Act is to be legislated, which will provide an individual with the rights to request information on himself/herself and to seek compensation for the infringement of his/her rights.

224. The Telecommunication Privacy Act will soon be legislated, which will provide that the censorship of correspondence and wiretapping shall be prohibited "except in limited cases where they are inevitable for the purpose of investigating felonies and where the court grants permission to do so." Evidence acquired from illegal censorship or wiretapping shall not be admitted in a trial.

ARTICLE 18

225. The Constitution provides that all citizens shall enjoy freedom of conscience (Art. 19) and freedom of religion. (Art. 20)

0150

The Constitution does not expressly provide for the freedom of thought. However, it is considered that the conscience stated in Article 19 of the Constitution, covers not only non-metaphysical thought (moral, ethical decision and perception of moral duty) but also metaphysical thought (creed and values). Thus, all the rights stated in Article 18 of the Covenant are guaranteed by the Constitution.

226. Freedom of conscience includes the right not to be forced, coerced or interfered with in making conscientious decisions and the right to be silent on what has been decided in one's conscience.

The right to be silent does not include the right not to testify on simple facts as a witness in a criminal trial (Code of Criminal Procedure, Art. 161). However, no citizen shall be compelled to testify himself/herself in a criminal case (Constitution, Art. 12(2)) and, in certain cases, refusal to testify as a witness is allowed. (Code of Criminal Procedure, Arts. 147-150)

227. The Constitution Court has held that a court's order to the press to make a public apology for damaging the honour and reputation of an individual violates the Constitutional rights of conscience and is thus unconstitutional. (89-HUNMA-160 of 1 April 1991)

228. Conscientious objection to the military service has been explained in the description of Article 8, para. 3 of the Covenant. (See para. 144)

229. Freedom of religion comprises the following rights:
(a) Right to manifest one's religious creed;
(b) Right to hold religious ceremonies, to preach and to worship;

—113—

(c) Right to congregate and to assemble for
    religious purposes;

(d) Right to engage in a missionary work;

(e) Right to render religious education.

Freedom of speech in the course of religious
activities is also guaranteed. Hence, religious
groups are not discriminated against in their
publication and distribution of religious
literature. (Constitution, Art. 21)

In Korea, there are a variety of broadcasting
institutions, newspapers and publications run by
religious groups.

230. In accordance with Article 37(2) of the
     Constitution, the right to carry out religious
     activities may be restricted for the maintenance of
     public order. This restriction is consistent with
     para. 3 of Article 18 of the Covenant.

231. Article 20(2) of the Constitution provides that "No
     State religion shall be recognized and church and
     State shall be separated."

     Therefore, religion is separated from the Government
     and the State shall not perform any religious
     education or engage in any religious activities.

     Article 5(2) of the Education Act provides that the
     public schools shall not conduct any religious
     education.

     The State is prohibited from rendering special
     economic and financial assistance in favor of a
     religion and from discriminating against a religion.
     However, the State may subsidize the costs for the

0152

management of cultural properties such as old churches or temples. (Cultural Properties Protection Act, Art. 28)

232. Under Paragraph 4 of Article 18 of the Covenant, the Parties undertake to respect the liberty of parents or legal guardians to ensure the religious and moral education of their children in conformity with their own convictions. No law which restricts the above liberty exists in Korea. Article 913 of the Civil Code states that a person with parental authority has the liberty to protect and educate a child. In accordance with this provision, parents or legal guardians are guaranteed the liberty to provide moral and religious education for their children according to their own conviction.

In Korea, the religion of a parent is not automatically transferred to his/her child. In addition, a child who attends a private school established by a religious group is free to choose his/her own religion. Therefore, everyone is entitled to choose his/her own religion in accordance with his/her own conviction.

233. Inmates in the correctional facilities are also free to choose and change their religion.

Article 31 of the Penal Administration Act provides that in the case that an inmate requests an admonition based on his/her religion, the prison authority shall allow it.

In accordance with this provision, religious workers of various denominations, have requested membership to the Religious Guidance Committee and perform weekly religious ceremonies, jointly or

individually, by denomination, and deliver lectures
to those who are in detention.

ARTICLE 19

234. The right under Paragraph 1 of Article 19 of the
Covenant is guaranteed under Article 19 of the
Constitution which provides for freedom of
conscience.

Freedom of conscience is an absolute fundamental
right which is not subject to any kind of
restriction.

No law which places restrictions on this right
exists in Korea.

235. The rights referred to in Paragraph 2 of Article 19
of the Covenant are guaranteed under Article 21(1)
of the Constitution which provides that all citizens
shall enjoy freedom of speech, press, assembly and
association and Article 22(1) which provides that
all citizens shall enjoy freedom of education and
arts.

Article 21(2) of the Constitution provides that
censorship of speech and the press shall not be
recognized.

236. Freedom of expression is the essence of mental
freedom and the cornerstone of democracy. However,
it is not an absolute fundamental right. Thus, it
is subject to restrictions.
The duties and responsibilities in the exercise of
this right are specified in Article 21(4) of the

0154

Constitution, which provides that the exercise of freedom of expression shall not violate the honour or rights of other persons or undermine public morals or social ethics and that, should the exercise of freedom of expression violate the honour or rights of other persons, claims may be made for the damage resulting therefrom.

Under the Broadcast Act and the Act Relating to the Registration of Periodicals, correction of the report is available as a remedy for infringements committed by the press, publishing firms or broadcasting companies. (Act Relating to the Registration of Periodicals, Arts. 16, 20, Broadcast Act, Arts. 41, 42)

237. The following provisions prohibit the abuse of freedom of expression by the press or the publishing firms:
  (a) Defamation through printed materials (Criminal Code, Art. 309);
  (b) Disclosure of other's occupational secrets (Criminal Code, Art. 317);
  (c) Distribution of obscene pictures, etc. (Criminal Code, Art. 243);
  (d) Incitement of crimes relating to insurrection and foreign aggression (Criminal Code, Arts. 90(2), 101(2), 120(2), National Security Law, Art. 4(1) item 6, 7);
  (e) Intrusion into another's privacy (Civil Code, Art. 751) etc.

238. The purpose of the Broadcast Act is to help the
     formation of public opinion in a democratic manner,
     to improve national culture and to contribute to the
     promotion of public welfare by guaranteeing freedom
     of press and the public functions of broadcasting
     companies. (Broadcast Act, Art. 1) Under the Act,
     freedom of broadcast is guaranteed and no person
     shall regulate or interfere with the making of a
     program or the operation of a broadcasting company
     without complying with the conditions prescribed by
     law. (Art. 3)

In Korea, there are three kinds of broadcasting
companies, public, private and special. Public
broadcasting companies are invested by the State or
special public legal corporations but operate
independently. Private broadcasting companies are
corporations operated by an individual or a company.
Special broadcasting companies are operated and
subsidized by the State, local governments or
religious groups for the limited purposes of
education and transportation information, etc.

The operators of public broadcasting companies must
be socially and politically neutral figures. There
are two public broadcasting companies in Korea: the
KBS and the MBC.

(a) The Executive Board of the Korea Broadcasting
     System (KBS) is composed of 12 members who are
     appointed by the President of the Republic of
     Korea on the recommendation of the Broadcast
     Committee. The president of the KBS is
     appointed by the President of the Republic of
     Korea on the recommendation of the Executive

Board. The Broadcast Committee is composed of 9 members of whom the Executive, the National Assembly and the Judiciary recommend 3 persons each.

(b) The Foundation for the Broadcast Culture (FFBC) is the major stockholder of the Munhwa Broadcasting Company (MBC). The FFBC, established under the Foundation for Broadcast Culture Promotion Act, is a special corporation. The Executive Board of the FFBC is composed of 10 members of whom the National Assembly and the Broadcast Committee recommend 4 or 6 persons respectively. The FFBC elects the president of the MBC. The neutrality of the MBC in political and social matters is fully guaranteed.

RESTRICTIONS ON FREEDOM OF EXPRESSION

239. Since freedom of expression is regarded as the cornerstone of democracy, it is fully guaranteed in the Republic of Korea. However, it is subject to restrictions in limited cases.

240. As provided for in Paragraph 3 of Article 19 of the Covenant, freedom of expression is subject to restrictions in accordance with the general principle of restrictions on fundamental rights referred to in Article 37(2) of the Constitution.

The restrictions on the right by law may be imposed only when necessary for national security, the maintenance of law and order or public welfare and even when such restrictions are imposed, no essential aspect of the right shall be violated.

241. If an emergency order is issued by the President under Article 76 of the Constitution, freedom of speech and press may be restricted.

Under martial law, (Constitution, Art. 77(3)), the martial law commander may take special measures concerning freedom of speech and the press. (Martial Law Act, Art. 9(1))

NATIONAL SECURITY LAW AND FREEDOM OF EXPRESSION

242. The National Security Law is a special law to cope with the special situation facing the Korean peninsula. The Korean people suffered a horrifying war for three years (1950-53) started by the North Korean attack on the South. Therefore, most South Koreans are fearful of the North's aggression and are prepared to cope with the special situation of the divided nation. Under these circumstances, the Korean Government promulgated the National Security Law and has applied it to check anti-State activities that threaten the security and democratic system of the Republic of Korea.

243. Article 7(1) of the National Security Law provides that any person, who aids an anti-State organization by praising or encouraging the activities of the anti-State organization, shall be punished. Article 7(5) of the Law provides that any person, who produces or distributes documents, drawings or any other materials for the benefit of an anti-State organization, shall be punished.

244. The Constitution Court has held that Article 7(1) & (5) of the National Security Law is not inconsistent with the Constitution because these provisions are

—120—

0158

applied when the security or safety of the State is in danger or when the offenses undermine the basic order of democracy. (2 April 1990, 89-HUNGA-113)

In accordance with the spirit of the decision, the Government has done its utmost in interpreting and applying these provisions so that the rights and freedoms of the people are fully protected.

245. On 10 May 1991, the National Assembly passed a series of amendments to the National Security Law in order to reduce the scope of its application. In particular, Article 7(1) & (5) of the Act was amended to eliminate the possibility of infringement of human rights by adding "with the knowledge that it will endanger national security or survival, or the free and democratic order" to the previous provisions. The amended National Security Law was promulgated on 31 May 1991.

THE CONVICT'S RIGHT TO INFORMATION

246. Under the Korean penal administration system, convicts are guaranteed the right to gather information, which comprises subscribing to newspapers, reading books, writing and receiving letters, meeting their relatives, listening to radio and watching TV. Explanations have already been provided in Paragraphs 168-170.

RIGHT TO KNOW

247. With respect to right to know, the Constitution Court has held: "It is in violation of the right to know of the claimant, and thus unconstitutional, that the provincial governor of Ichon-kun refused the claimant's numerous requests to obtain and

review a copy of the Certificate of the Real Estate
Registration." (4 September 1989, 88-HUNMA-22)

ARTICLE 20

248. The preamble of the Constitution states, "...to
contribute to lasting world peace and the common
prosperity of mankind..." and Article 5(1) of the
Constitution also provides, "the Republic of Korea
shall endeavour to maintain international peace and
shall renounce all aggressive wars". On account of
the absolute character of the above-mentioned
provisions, no further legislation is required and
the above-mentioned provisions are consistent with
Article 20, Paragraph 1 of the Covenant. Under
Article 112 of the Criminal Code, a person who
violates an order to stay neutral in a war between
foreign countries shall be punished by imprisonment
or a fine.

249. As has been previously stated in this report, all
citizens shall be equally assured of human worth and
dignity without discrimination. In light of this
principle, instigation of national, racial or
religious hatred towards others is subject to
punishment.

Under the Criminal Code, a person, who, in
conspiracy with a foreign country, instigates or
propagates the crime of commencing hostilities or
fighting against the Republic of Korea, or who
instigates or propagates another person to act as a
spy for an enemy country, shall be punished. (Art.
101(2)) A person who wages a private war against a
foreign country shall also be punished. (Art. 111)

250. The Republic of Korea has acceded to the International Convention on the Elimination of All Forms of Racial Discrimination. The explanations thereof have been provided in Article 2 of the Covenant. (See para. 42)

ARTICLE 21

251. Article 21(1) & (2) of the Constitution provides that "All citizens shall enjoy freedom of assembly and association and licensing of assembly and association shall not be recognized."

252. Both juristic persons and natural persons are assured of freedom of assembly. It is also guaranteed to foreigners in the Republic of Korea.

253. Freedom of assembly shall not be violated by any of the State agencies. The violation of that freedom by a private person is also strictly prohibited.

Article 3(1) of the Act Concerning Assembly and Demonstration provides that no person may disturb a peaceful assembly or demonstration by means of violence, intimidation or any other means and Article 3(3) also provides that the sponsor of an assembly or demonstration may, upon finding that there is a possibility of interference with the peaceful assembly or demonstration, notify the police and request protection.

254. The right of assembly is subject to certain restrictions when it conflicts with legal interests or fundamental rights of others, because the exercise of the right has a great impact on public order.

First of all, an assembly or a demonstration should be peaceful and it should be carried out without violating Constitutional order, the rights of others and the morals of society.

While the former Act Concerning Assembly and Demonstration prohibited assembly or demonstration which might have caused substantial social instability, the amended Act has narrowed the scope of restriction and prohibits an assembly or a demonstration designed to achieve the purpose of a political party dissolved by the decision of the Constitution Court, or an assembly or a demonstration which would apparently cause a direct threat to the public peace due to its violent nature.

RESTRICTION ON FREEDOM OF ASSEMBLY

255. Article 21(2) of the Constitution prohibits any requirement of a license for the exercise of freedom of assembly. However, requiring notification of an assembly or demonstration for administrative purposes does not violate the said provision.

In addition, the notification of an assembly or demonstration is considered as inevitable requirement in order to minimize the inconvenience of the general public and protect public facilities and avoid disruption caused by multiple assemblies occuring in one place.

NOTIFICATION OF OUTDOOR ASSEMBLY OR DEMONSTRATION

256. Any person, who intends to sponsor an outdoor assembly or demonstration, shall submit a written notice to the chief of the district police station

forty-eight hours prior to the outdoor assembly or demonstration, describing therein its purpose, date, time, place and estimated number of participants, etc. (Act Concerning Assembly and Demonstration, Art. 6(1))

In case a planned outdoor assembly or demonstration violates the restrictions on time or places, or the notice thereof does not contain the required supplementary information, the chief of police station who has received the notice may notify the sponsor within forty-eight hours after receipt of the notice that the assembly or demonstration is prohibited. (Act Concerning Assembly and Demonstration, Art. 8(1))

A sponsor of an assembly or a demonstration may, within seventy-two hours after the receipt of the notice of prohibition, file an objection thereto to the mayor of Seoul City, mayor of a major city or governor of the province who has jurisdiction over the police district that issued the prohibition notice. The mayor or governor shall rule on such objection within twenty-four hours after receipt of the objection. A petitioner who contests the ruling may file an administrative lawsuit to the High Court which has jurisdiction over the ruling administrative agency. (Act Concerning Assembly and Demonstration, Art. 9)

PROHIBITED TIME AND PLACES FOR OUTDOOR ASSEMBLY AND DEMONSTRATION

257. No person may hold an outdoor assembly or demonstration before sunrise or after sunset unless the sponsor has designated a caretaker of the assembly or demonstration to maintain order and has

notified the relevant authorities of the assembly or demonstration. (Act Concerning Assembly and Demonstration, Art. 10)

When it is deemed necessary for regulating the traffic, an assembly or a demonstration, which is to be held on main streets of major cities may be prohibited. Prohibition is not allowed if the sponsor of an assembly or a demonstration has designated a caretaker who will march with the participants to maintain order. (Act Concerning Assembly and Demonstration, Art. 12)

There shall be no restrictions on assembling relating to academic research and study, arts, sports events, religious services, rituals, fraternization, entertainment, marriages, funerals, ancestral worship, and national celebrations. (Act Concerning Assembly and Demonstration, Art. 13)

PROHIBITION OF ASSEMBLY OR DEMONSTRATION TO PROTECT PUBLIC HEALTH

258. A mayor or governor may restrict or prohibit an assembly or demonstration when it is necessary for the prevention of first-class communicable diseases. (Communicable Disease Prevention Act, Art. 39(1-2))

259. The above-mentioned restrictions on assembly are required for public safety, public order and the protection of rights and freedoms of the citizens. Thus, these restrictions are not inconsistent with Article 21 of the Covenant.

Paragraph 1

260. The Constitution guarantees freedom of association
     in Article 21 (all citizens shall enjoy freedom of
     association), Article 8 (political parties) Article
     20 (religious groups) Article 22 (academic and art
     associations) and Article 22 (labor unions).

261. Freedom of association is guaranteed to all persons
     i.e., citizens, foreigners and legal corporations.

262. Freedom of association includes freedom to form,
     participate in and to withdraw from an association.

RESTRICTION ON FREEDOM OF ASSOCIATION

263. Article 21(2) of the Constitution prohibits any
     requirement of a license for the exercise of freedom
     of association.

     However, freedom of association may be subject to
     restrictions in accordance with the general
     principle of restrictions on fundamental rights
     provided for in Article 37(2) of the Constitution.

     In the case that the President issues an emergency
     order (Constitution, Art. 76) or martial law is
     declared (Martial Law Act, Art. 9(1)), restrictions
     may be imposed by the emergency order or the special
     measures taken by the martial law commander.

264. Although freedom of association should be guaranteed
     to the full extent without any regard to the purpose
     of associations, illegal associations such as anti-
     State organizations (National Security Law, Arts. 2,

3, 7(3)) and criminal organizations (Criminal Code, Art. 114) are prohibited.

LABOR UNION OF PUBLIC OFFICIALS

265. (a) Article 8 of the Labor Union Act guarantees that employees (who live on wages, salaries and/or other income) may freely organize or join labor unions. However, the employers (the owner or the manager of a business or the person who acts for the owner on matters related to the employees) or persons who always act for the benefit of the employer cannot organize or join labor unions. (Labor Union Act, Art. 3(1))

(b) Article 33(2) of the Constitution provides that only those public officials who are designated by law shall have the right to association, collective bargaining and collective action.

In accordance with this provision, the Labor Union Act and the Public Officials Law place restrictions on the exercise of labor union-related rights by public officials. Public officials and teachers or professors of public and private schools, colleges and universities are prohibited from organizing or joining labor unions. (Public Officials Law, Art. 66, Local Public Officials Law, Art. 58, Private School Act, Art. 55)

However, public officials who perform physical labor, such as postmen, laborers in the railroad service and other laborers in the Ministry of Communication, the Office of

National Railroads and the National Medical
Center may organize or join labor unions.

The main reasons for these restrictions are
that public officials have a special duty to
serve the entire people, that they are
responsible for the management of the State and
that their collective actions affect all
citizens.

Therefore, the Korean Government is of the view
that labor rights of public officials should be
reviewed in the context of the benefit of all
citizens and the development of the State.

(c)   Due to the reasons mentioned in Paragraph
      265(b), the Korean Government has made a
      reservation with respect to Article 22 of the
      Covenant.

(d)   In addition, public officials such as members
      of the armed forces, policemen, prison officers
      and fire fighters are not entitled to enjoy
      labor rights. (Members of the Armed Service
      Rules, Art. 38, Police Officer's Service Rules,
      Art. 12, Public Officials Law, Art. 66, Public
      Officials Service Rules, Art. 28)

(e)   Article 33(3) of the Constitution also provides
      that the right to collective action of workers
      employed by important defense industries may be
      either restricted or denied under the
      conditions prescribed by law.

      These restrictions are imposed in order to
      protect the interests of the nation against
      individual interests and thus these limitations

are not in violation of Paragraph 2 of Article 22 of the Covenant.

PRIVILEGES OF A POLITICAL PARTY

266. Political parties are vested with various privileges. Under the Constitution, a political party shall be dissolved in accordance with the decision of the Constitution Court only when the purposes or activities of the political party are contrary to the fundamental democratic order (Art. 8(4)). Political parties may be provided with operational funds by the State. (Art. 8(3))

In this connection, the Political Funds Act has been legislated in order to contribute to the development of democracy by guaranteeing a sufficient supply of political funds to the parties, and by making the receipt and disbursement of political funds open to public scrutiny. (Arts. 4, 5-10, 11, 17-21)

These privileges of the political parties are guaranteed in order to protect their inherent political function.

267. The Republic of Korea is not a Member of the International Labor Organization. However, the Korean Government has continued to make efforts to join the Organization and has, since 1982, been participating, as an observer State, in the works of the ILO. The Korean Government believes that it will join the ILO in the near future.

DISSOLUTION OF LABOR UNION

268. A labor union shall be dissolved for one of the following reasons only:

(a) Occurrence of an event which dissolves the labor union as set forth in its by-laws;

(b) Extinction due to a merger or a division;

(c) A resolution for dissolution adopted at a general meeting or a council of delegates by the affirmative vote of two thirds or more of the union members or delegates present at the meeting or council where two thirds or more of the entire union members or delegates are present; or

(d) In the case where the labor union has no officer and has not carried out any activity for more than two years.

Major reasons for the dissolution of a labor union in Korea are the closure of the company and the resolution of dissolution.

RESTRICTION ON LABOR DISPUTES

269. The provisions of labor laws in most countries, particularly those relating to collective activities are simple in spite of their complicated contents. Therefore, recourse has often been made to opinions of scholars and decisions of the court in order to determine whether or not the activities of a labor union are justified.

270. In the Republic of Korea, where the history of the labor movement is relatively short and decisions by the court on the activities of labor unions are rare, opinions of scholars have usually been referred to in the settlement of conflict arising out of differences in the interpretation of labor laws.

However, the settlement of disputes is sometimes impossible because both parties insist on adopting the interpretation favorable to them.

271. Thus, the Korean Government (Ministry of Labor) has published and distributed a booklet entitled, "A Guide for Better Understanding of Labor Rights", in January, 1990. The book provides detailed explanations on the object and scope of collective bargaining and the restrictions on labor disputes.

272. The Korean Government is making every effort to enhance public awareness of the rights and responsibilities of labor unions and their members.

EX OFFICIO ARBITRATION UNDER THE LABOR DISPUTE ADJUSTMENT ACT

273. If settlement of labor disputes, which are closely related to the national economy and the daily life of citizens, were entrusted entirely to the parties to the disputes, damage and inconveniences could affect not only the parties themselves, but also all citizens, and such labor disputes could also undermine the development of the national economy and threaten public interests.

274. Under the Labor Dispute Adjustment Act, the arbitration of a labor dispute in the public service sector shall be conducted if the labor committee decides to refer a dispute to arbitration ex officio or upon request of an administrative agency. Any act of dispute shall be prohibited for 15 days from the date of referral.

Since the purpose of the arbitration is to prevent the abuse of labor rights by the parties in the

public service sector, the Labor Dispute Adjustment
Act does not violate the provisions relating to
labor rights in the Constitution.

275. The applicability of ex officio arbitration has been
greatly narrowed due to two amendments to the Act
(31 September 1986 and 28 November 1987) which
excluded Government invested enterprises, research
projects sponsored by the Government, coal mining,
industrial fuel business and securities transaction
business from the public service sector.

276. On March 16 1989, a lawsuit requesting the
adjudication of the constitutionality of the ex
officio arbitration system was brought to the
Supreme Court in connection with the strike by
subway workers.

The Supreme Court decided that the labor dispute
acts of the employees in the public service sector
are subject to inherent restrictions. Since Article
31 of the Labor Dispute Adjustment Act legislates
these inherent restrictions and does not violate the
labor rights provided for in the Constitution, it
was held to be constitutional. (Supreme Court
Decision of 15 May 1990, 90-KA-33)

ARTICLE 23

PROTECTION OF THE FAMILY

Paragraph 1

277. In order to guarantee a democratic marriage and
family system, Article 36(1) of the Constitution
provides that marriage and family life shall be

entered into and maintained on the basis of individual dignity and equality of the sexes and that the State shall do its utmost to achieve these goals.

278. Since Article 36(1) of the Constitution binds all State agencies without any further legislation, remedies may be obtained under this provision in the case that the State interferes with a person's marriage and family life.

279. Furthermore, the Civil Code was amended so as to abolish the patriarchal family system, to enforce the principle of individual dignity and equality of the sexes guaranteed by the Constitution and to guarantee the welfare of the family. (proclaimed on 13 January 1990 and enforced from 1 January 1991)

280. In 1988, the Government planned to establish the "mother-child self-support facilities" to accommodate families headed by a mother who did not achieve economic independence after being discharged from the mother-child health care facilities.

According to this plan and after a public discussion held in June 1988, the Mother-Child Welfare Act was legislated in April 1989 in order to support families headed by married or unmarried mothers. The Act became effective in July 1989.

AGE REQUIREMENT FOR MARRIAGE

Paragraph 2

281. Under the Civil Code, any adult may freely enter into a matrimonial engagement (Art. 800) and a man over eighteen years of age and a woman over sixteen

0172

years of age may enter into matrimony. (Art. 807)
A minor shall obtain the consent of his/her parents
in order to enter into matrimony. (Art. 808)

MARRIAGE SYSTEM

Paragraph 3

282. The Korean marriage system guarantees monogamy based
on the free will of each party and prohibits
concubinage and bigamy.

According to Article 815 of the Civil Code, a
marriage shall be based on the free will of each
party and any marriage without the consent of the
parties shall be null and void. In addition, an
annulment of a marriage may be sought if the
declaration of intention to enter into a marriage
was induced by fraud or duress. (Civil Code, Art.
816)

RIGHTS OF SPOUSES

Paragraph 4

283. At the time of accession to the Covenant, the
Republic of Korea made a reservation with respect to
Paragraph 4 of the Covenant, since the Civil Code
prescribes the rights and responsibilities of
spouses in favor of the husband during marriage and
after its dissolution.

However, as the discriminatory provisions were
revised by the amendments to the Civil Code, which
entered into force on 1 January 1991, the
reservation was withdrawn on 15 March 1991.

284. The amendments to the Civil Code provide for equal rights and duties of spouses during marriage and after its dissolution.

    (a) Rights and duties during marriage.

        The amendments guarantee the equality of spouses during marriage through the following Articles: Duty to Cooperate (Art. 826), Joint Liability for Obligations with respect to Household Matters (Art. 832), Joint Responsibility for Living Expenses (Art. 833) and Joint Exercise of Parental Authority with respect to a Minor Child (Art.909).

    (b) Rights and duties after the dissolution of marriage

        (1) In the case of divorce, the parties shall determine, by an agreement, all matters concerning their children. If the parties are unable to reach an agreement, the Family Court may, upon request by a party, decide all matters relating to the children. (Civil Code, Art. 837)

        (2) Under the amendments to the Civil Code, parents who do not raise their children may visit, call and write to their children. (Civil Code, Art. 837-2)

        (3) In the case of divorce, a party may seek the division of joint property according to the party's contribution to the joint property. (Civil Code, Art. 839-2)

0174

ARTICLE 24

PROHIBITION OF DISCRIMINATION AGAINST CHILDREN

Paragraph 1

285. Article 11(1) of the Constitution prohibits any discrimination against children by providing that no citizen shall be discriminated against in political, economic, social or cultural life on account of sex, religion or social status.

286. The term "child" means a person under eighteen years of age under the Child Welfare Act and the Convention on the Rights of the Child. However, a minor under the Civil Code is a person under 20 years of age.

287. The population under 18 years of age was 14,620,000 in 1990 and constitutes 34% of the entire population of Korea. The number of children is declining due to the Government's policy on population and family planning.

(Unit: thousand children)

1980	1990	2000
15,621 (40.7%)	14,620 (34.1%)	12,870 (27.5%)

* The number in the bracket is the population percentage of children in the entire population.

INSTITUTIONAL FRAMEWORK FOR THE PROTECTION OF
CHILDREN

288. The Korean Government has implemented the following
policies for the protection of children:

(a) The Child Welfare Act was enacted in order to
guarantee the welfare of children so that they
are born safely and are brought up in good
health. (Art. 1)

(b) Article 18 of the Child Welfare Act provides
that no person shall hurt, mistreat or exploit
a child or have a child perform or mediate an
obscene act. Any person who violates this
provision shall be punished. (Art. 34)

(c) May 5 has been designated as "Children's Day" a
legal holiday, in an effort to enhance the
nationwide affection for children. (Art. 4)

(d) The Children's Charter of the Republic of Korea
was legislated in 1957 (and amended in 1988)
and the Charter prescribes the requisites for
the welfare of children.

STATE AGENCIES CONCERNED WITH THE WELFARE OF
CHILDREN

(e) The Child Welfare Bureau of the Ministry of
Health and Social Affairs and the Family
Welfare Bureau of local governments are
responsible for implementing the policies on
the welfare of children.

PROTECTIVE MEASURES FOR CHILDREN WHO REQUIRE
PROTECTION

289. Articles 2 & 3 of the Child Welfare Act provides
that the term "child to be protected" means a child
to be protected under this Act if the child is lost,

abandoned or separated from his/her guardian, the guardian is unsuitable for or incapable of bringing up the child, or in other cases prescribed by law.

290. Protective measures under the above provisions are as follows:

   (a) In order to prevent the separation of children from their parents, 51 child guidance clinics with 380 professional counsellors were established in the cities, provinces and factory areas. Child guidance clinics accommodate children previously living in poor conditions in welfare centers or aid them through programs of an adoption or job guidance. Furthermore, 5,400 Child Welfare Committee members are counselling children at each level of towns and villages.

   (b) Children, who are separated from their parents on account of divorce or industrial accidents, are adopted, placed in foster care or accommodated in welfare centers, and the State and local governments subsidizes the costs of medical treatment, education, and raising the children. (Child Welfare Act, Art. 27) As of 1990, 23,450 children were accommodated at 278 protection centers.

   (c) In order to find missing children, there are child finding centers and 182 telephone lines were set up for notification of missing children.

291. The Government subsidizes the expenses needed for a normal life, including medical treatment and education for those children who head a family due to illness, death or other difficulties of their parents. At the end of 1990, the Government was supporting 13,778 such children.

EDUCATION OF CHILDREN

292. In accordance with Article 31(2) of the
Constitution, Article 8 of the Education Act
provides, "all citizens shall have a right to
receive six years of primary education and three
years of secondary education (para. 1), and citizens
who have children under their protection have a duty
to educate them in accordance with Paragraph 1
(para. 2), and the State shall enforce compulsory
education as provided for in Paragraph 2 and shall
take all necessary measures to secure the facilities
therefor. (para. 3)"

In addition, Article 913 of the Civil Code provides
that parents or legal guardians must protect,
educate and raise their children.

CRIMINAL RESPONSIBILITY

293. Under Article 9 of the Criminal Code, a person under
fourteen years of age shall not be punished for
his/her act. The age of a criminal is a critical
factor in determining punishment (Criminal Code,
Art. 51) and if a minor has not committed a felony,
"protective disposition" under the Juvenile Act is
usually ordered rather than a sentence of penal
punishment.

PROTECTION OF WORKING CHILDREN

294. Article 32(5) of the Constitution provides that
special protection shall be accorded to working
children. In accordance with this provision, the
Labor Standards Act and the Child Welfare Act set
forth special measures to protect working children.

(a)   A person who has not reached 13 years of age shall not be employed. (Labor Standards Act, Art. 50)

(b)   No minor under eighteen years of age shall be authorized to engage in any work which is morally detrimental or harmful to health. (Labor Standards Act, Art. 51)

·(c) Working hours for minors between 13 and 18 years of age shall not exceed seven hours a day and forty-two hours a week. (In the case of an adult, it shall be eight hours a day and forty-four hours a week) (Labor Standards Act, Art. 55)

(d)   No minor under eighteen years of age shall be authorized to work between the hours of 22:00 and 06:00 or on holidays.   (Labor Standards Act, Art. 56)

(e)   An employer shall not employ a minor under eighteen years of age to work inside a pit. (Labor Standards Act, Art. 58)

(f)   A person who regularly employs more than 30 minors under eighteen years of age shall establish an education facility. (Labor Standards Act, Art. 63)

(g)   A person shall not have a child under fourteen years of age perform acrobatics to entertain an audience and shall not employ a child under fourteen years of age in a bar or in other entertainment business. (Child Welfare Act, Art. 18 item 3 & 4)

LEGAL STATUS OF ILLEGITIMATE CHILDREN

295. Illegitimate children were accorded unfavorable treatment due to the traditions of Korean society where monogamy and legal marriage were respected.

However, the Korean Government has tried to eliminate discriminatory treatment toward illegitimate children with respect to their legal status and property rights.

The Civil Code does not distinguish an illegitimate child from a legitimate one except in the succession order of the family headship. (Arts. 985, 989)

ADOPTION OF A MINOR

296. In order to adopt a minor, who has neither a parent nor any other lineal ascendants, it was sufficient that the person who wishes to adopt the minor obtain the consent of the minor's guardian under the old Civil Code.

However, the amended Civil Code requires the approval of the Family Court with regard to the consent of guardian in order to prohibit the exploitation of the adopted minor. (Civil Code, Art. 871)

A guardian shall obtain the permission of the Family Court, if he adopts his ward. (Civil Code, Art. 872)

GUARDIAN OF A MINOR

297. If there is no person with parental authority over a minor or if a person in parental authority is unable to exercise the right of representation with respect to the juristic acts or the right of management of the property of a minor, a guardian shall be appointed for the minor. The qualification is set forth in Article 937 of the Civil Code.

0180

Under the Civil Code, the guardian of a minor shall have the same rights and duties as a person who has parental authority with respect to protection, fostering and education of a minor. (Art. 945)

298. In order to participate fully in the efforts of the United Nations to protect children, the Republic of Korea signed the Convention on the Rights of the Child on 25 September 1990 and the Korean Government will ratify it in the near future.

Paragraph 2

299. Article 49 of the Family Registration Act provides that a birth report containing the name, date and place of birth of a new born child shall be filed within one month from the date of birth.

300. For abandoned infants, the chief of district shall determine the child's name and the permanent domicile with the permission of the Court and shall record them in the Family Register. (Family Registration Act, Art. 57)

NATIONALITY OF A CHILD

Paragraph 3

301. Under Article 2 of the Nationality Act, every child including an illegitimate child, an abandoned child and a child of a person without nationality shall acquire Korean nationality if born in the Republic of Korea.

ARTICLE 25

THE SOVEREIGNTY OF THE REPUBLIC OF KOREA

302. Article 1(2) of the Constitution states that the sovereignty of the Republic of Korea shall reside in the people and all state authority shall emanate from the people.

RIGHT TO VOTE

303. Article 24 of the Constitution provides that all citizens shall have the right to vote under the conditions prescribed by law.

    The Constitution provides for the right to vote for the President (Art. 67(1)), the members of the National Assembly (Art. 41(1)) and the members of local councils (Art. 118(2)).

    Article 8 of the Presidential Election Act provides that citizens who are twenty years of age or older shall have the right to vote.

304. The political rights, such as the right to vote, the right to be elected, and the right to hold a public office are accorded only to Korean nationals in accordance with the principle of sovereignty of the Korean people.

RIGHT TO HOLD A PUBLIC OFFICE

305. Article 25 of the Constitution states that all citizens shall have the right to hold a public office under the conditions prescribed by law.

The right to hold a public office includes the right to perform public duty as a member of the executive, the legislature, the judiciary and the local governments.

In this regard, the right to hold a public office is broader than the right to be elected. However, in order to hold certain public offices, citizens must be qualified for the office as prescribed by law. This practice is in conformity with Article 25, Paragraph (c) of the Covenant.

The National Assembly Members Election Act (Art. 9) and the Local Council Members Election Act (Art. 9) stipulate that citizens who are twenty-five years of age or more, shall have the right to be elected. However, a person who has been declared incompetent does not have the right to be elected to the National Assembly or the local council. (Arts, 11, 12 of the said Acts)

The Presidential Election Act provides that citizens, who are forty years of age or more, shall be eligible to be elected as the President (Art. 9). However, a person who is declared incompetent shall not have the right to be elected to the Presidency. (Arts. 11, 12)

UNIVERSAL, EQUAL, DIRECT AND SECRET VOTING

306. With respect to the voting system, the Constitution upholds the principal of universal, equal, direct and secret voting. (Art. 41(1), Art. 67(1))

Under the constitutional principle, the election acts stipulate that the vote shall be cast directly or by mail, that there shall be one vote per person and that the name of the voter shall not be indicated on the vote. (Presidential Election Act, Art. 94, National Assembly Members Election Act, Art. 100, Local Council Members Election Act, Art. 97)

In addition, the secrecy of the ballot shall be guaranteed. (Presidential Election Act, Art. 111, National Assembly Members Election Act, Art. 117, Local Council Members Election Act, Art. 114)

RESTRICTIONS ON POLITICAL RIGHTS

307. Under Article 13(2) of the Constitution, no restriction shall be imposed upon the political rights of any citizens by means of retroactive legislation.

The Political Party Act provides that citizens under twenty years of age, public officials, certain teachers and journalists are prohibited from becoming founders or members of a political party. (Arts. 6, 17)

Under Article 42 of the Political Party Act, when a political party is dissolved by a decision of the Constitution Court, any representative or executive member of the dissolved party shall not establish a political party with the same or similar party platform (or basic policy) as that of the dissolved party.

ARTICLE 26

308. All citizens shall be guaranteed human worth and
dignity and shall be equal before the law.
(Constitution, Art. 11(1)) All citizens shall have
the right to pursue happiness and it shall be the
duty of the State to confirm and guarantee the
fundamental and inviolable human rights of
individuals. (Constitution, Art. 10)

In connection with these provisions, Article 31 of
the Constitution provides that the citizens shall
have the right to receive an education corresponding
to their abilities and a compulsory education, which
is free of charge. Under Articles 32 and 33 of the
Constitution, the right to work is guaranteed.

309. In accordance with the above-mentioned provisions of
the Constitution, the Korean Government has been
doing its utmost to ensure equal and effective
protection of all citizens by improving social
security and the social welfare system.

In particular, as has been explained in this report
in the description of Article 2 of the Covenant, the
Korean Government has been concentrating its efforts
on persons who are in socially weak positions, such
as persons with disabilities, children and the aged.
(See para. 30)

310. The constitutional principle of equality before the
law and the principle of equal protection of the law
- referred to several times in this report - reflect
the general percepts of Article 26 of the Covenant.

ARTICLE 27

311. In Korea, no person is denied the right to enjoy his/her own culture, to profess and practice his/her own religion or to use his/her own language.

312. However, ethnic, religious, linguistic or cultural minorities do not exist in the Republic of Korea.

0186

주 제 네 바 대 표 부

제네(정) 2031-658   1991. 7. 26

수 신 : 외무부장관

참 조 : 국제기구조약국장

제 목 : 인권보고서

          대 : 국연 2031-24962, WGV - 0944

          대호, 유엔 인권사무국에 제출할 아국인권 보고서 최종본을

별첨 송부합니다.

     첨부 : 동 보고서 1부. 끝.

              주 제 네 바 대 사

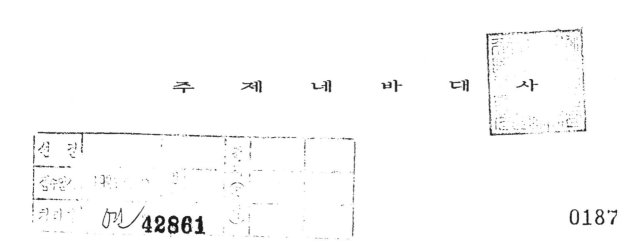

예/42861   0187

발 신 전 보

번 호 : WTH－1151   910730 1913 FO   종별 지 급

수 신 : 주 장 관   대사. 총영사   (주태국대사 경유)
(국연)

발 신 : 차 관

제 목 : 인권보고서 제출

　　　1.　아국이 90.7월 국제인권규약에 가입함에 따라 동규약

규정에 의거 시민적.정치적 권리에 관한 최초 인권보고서를 가입후

1년이내에 제출하여야 하는바, 관련부처는 가급적 아국의 최초보고서를
7.31 한 유엔에 제출하는것이 바람직하다라는 의견을 따라주해봄.

　　　2.　동 아국의 인권보고서는 법무부에서 관련부처의 의견을

취합하여 국문을 작성하고 당부가 이를 번역한 후 상부 및 관련부처의

검토의견을 종합하여 음7.30. 최종 번역문을 확정한 바, 동 인권보고서를

7.31(수) 유엔인권국에 제출토록 주제네바대사에게 지시코자 하니 장관님

방침 하시바람.

　　　　　　　　　　　　　　　지난
　　　　　　　　　　　구안임 6월중하순

　　　3.　아국 인권보고서(영문)는 7.22. 주제네바대표부에 송부하여　　등록 조치
동 ~~2개부처에서 제조치하여 장도아 조치하였음, 최종 번역문을 외부에~~

~~하였음.~~ 끝.

한 ~~것이~~ 으며, 최종번역문을 7.22 대표부에 송부하였음. (안)

(국제기구조약국장   문동석)

일반문서로재분류(.99 / .12 .31.)

	보 안 통 제	My.

앙 고 재	91 년 7 월 30 일	기안자 성 명	송명란 UN 과	과 장	심의관	국 장		차 관	장 관		외신과통제
				My.		정고철			ん		

발 신 전 보

	분류번호	보존기간

번 호 : WGV-0979 910731 1443 FO 종별 : 암호송신 /지급

수 신 : 주 제네바 대사. ♧♧♧♧

발 신 : 장 관 (국연)

제 목 : 인권보고서 제출

   연 : WGV-0944

   연호, 인권보고서를 7.31.중 유엔사무국에 제출하고 결과

보고바람. 끝.

(국제기구조약국장 문동석)

보 안 통 제				씨

앙고재	91년 7월 30일 과	기안자 성명 홍○○	과 장 씨	심의관 20결	국 장	차 관	장 관 ㅅ	외신과통제

0189

관리	91
번호	—813

외 무 부

종 별 : 긴 급

번 호 : THW-1582

일 시 : 91 0731 1040

수 신 : 장 관대리(국연)

발 신 : 장관(주태국 경유)

제 목 : 인권보고서 제출

대 : WTH-1151

표제건 대호 2항대로 조치바람

예고:91.12.31.까지

로 덕분류 (991 .12. 31.

국기국   차관

분류기호 문서번호	국연 2031-35752 (전화:)	시 행 상 특별취급	
보존기간	영구·준영구· 10. 5. 3. 1	장　　　　관	
수 신 처 보존기간			
시행일자	1991. 7. 31.		
보 조 기 관	국　장　전결 심의관 과　장	협 조 기 관	
기안책임자	송영완		
경　유		발 신 명 의	
수　신	수신처참조		
참　조			
제　목	국제인권규약보고서 (영문 번역문) 송부		

1. 국연 2031-30126(91.6.26) 관련입니다.

2. 국제인권규약 보고서 영문번역문 초안에 대한

관련부처 검토의견을 종합, 별첨 최종 번역문을 작성하였는 바,

귀업무에 참고하시기 바랍니다.

3. 상기 인권보고서 영문본은 주제네바대사를 통하여

제네바소재 유엔인권사무국애 91.7.31. 제출 예정이며, 급년

하반기 또는 내년초에 유엔문서로서 발간되어 유엔회원국 및

국제민간인권단체에 배포될 것으로 예상됨을 참고하시기바랍니다.

0191

첨 부 : 표제 보고서(영문) 1부. 끝.

수신처 : 법무부(인권과장), 내무부(치안본부수사과장),

국방부(법무관리관), 교육부(교직과장),

문화부(종무실장), 보사부(법무담당관),

노동부(노정과장), 체신부(법무담당관),

공보처(법무담당관), 정무 제2장관실(제2조정관),

안기부(대공수사국장)

0192

협조문용지			결	담 당	과 장	국 장
분류기호 문서번호	국연 2031- 317	(2179-80)	재			
시행일자	1991. 7. 31.					(서명)
수 신	수신처 참조	발신	국제기구조약국장			
제 목	국제인권규약 보고서(국.영문) 송부					

　　1. 90.7. 아국이 시민적.정치적 권리에 관한 국제규약

(B규약)에 가입함에 따라 동 규약 제 40조에 의거, 아국의 최초

인권보고서를 유엔인권사무국에 제출하게 되어 있습니다.

　　2. 이에 따라, 법무부가 관계부처 의견을 취합하여

작성한 아국의 최초 인권보고서 국문본 및 당국이 이를 번역

하여 작성한 영문본 각 1부를 별첨 송부하오니 업무에 참고

하시기 바랍니다.

　　3. 상기 아국 인권보고서는 7.31. 주제네바대사를

통하여 유엔 인권사무국에 제출할 예정임을 참고하시기 바랍니다.

　　첨 부 : 아국 인권보고서 국.영문 각 1부. 끝.

　　수신처 : 외교정책기획실장, 미주국장, 구주국장

0193

28013

기 안 용 지

분류기호 문서번호	국연 2031-	(전화:)	시 행 상 특별취급		
보존기간	영구·준영구· 10. 5. 3. 1	장		관	
수 신 처 보존기간					
시행일자	1991. 7. 31.				

보조기관	국 장	전결	협조기관		문서통제 1991. 8. 05
	심의관				
	과 장				발 송 인
기안책임자		송영완			

경 유		발신명의	
수 신	수신처 참조		
참 조			
제 목	국제인권규약보고서(국.영문) 송부		

1.   90.7. 아국이 시민적.정치적 권리에 관한 국제규약

(B규약)에 가입함에 따라 동 규약 제40조에 의거, 아국의 최초

인권보고서를 유엔인권사무국에 제출하여야 합니다.

2.   이에 따라, 법무부가 관계부처 의견을 취합하여

작성한 아국의 ░░ 인권보고서 국문본 및 당부가 이를 번역하여

작성한 영문본 각 1부를 별첨 송부하오니 업무에 참고하시기

바랍니다.

0194 / 계속 /

3.   상기 아국인권보고서는 7.31.■ 주제네바 대사를

통하여 유엔 인권사무국에 제출할 예정이며 금년 하반기 또는

내년초에 유엔문서로 발간될 예정인 바, 동 아국 보고서가

유엔문서로 발간.배포될때까지는 보고서가 민간인권단체등에 대해

배포되지 않도록 유의하여 주시기 바랍니다.

첨 부 : 아국 인권보고서 (국.영문) 각   부. 끝.

수신처 : 주미 , 영 , 독일 , 호주 , 카나다 , 스웨덴 , 화란 ,

노르웨이 , 덴마크 , 유엔 , EC , UNESCO 대사 ,

주뉴욕 , 시카고 , 마이애미 , 상항 , 라성 , 휴스톤 ,

아블란다 , 시애틀 , 보스톤 , 토론토 , 뱅쿠버 , 몬트리올

총영사

Africa, 中東 지역 송 관련직 대북면공사

규일, 팔리핀, ~~~~~~~, ~~~~~~, 멀리곤, 인서, 뉴질랜드, ~~~~

~~부르네이~~, ~~화란~~, 싱가폴, 인도, ~~~~~~, 파키스탄, 대국, 방글라데시,

~~화란~~, ~~~~, 매시코, ~~~~~~, ~~~~~~~, ~~~~, 페루, 베네쥬엘라,

~~~~~~~, ~~~~~~~, ~~~~~~, ~~~~~, 에쿠아돌, ~~~~~~~, 화이티,

~~~~~~, ~~~~~~~, 브라질, ~~~~, 알젠틴, ~~~~~~, 아일랜드,

핀랜드, 스위드, 터키, 뜨랑스, 이태리, 교황청, ~~~~~~, 오스트리아,

유고, 헝가리, 스페인, 노련, 벨기에, 희납, 포투논, 폴란드, ~~~~,

체로 ~~~~, 이집트, 세네꼴, 니이게리아, 사우디, 모로코대사

국제인권규약보고서 요지

규 약	요 지
일반적 사항	**A. 시민적 및 정치적 권리에 관한 헌법상의 보장** o 규약에 규정된 모든 권리는 대한민국 헌법에 의하여 보장된다 **B. 규약과 국내법과의 관계** o 규약은 비준, 공포됨으로써 별도의 국내 입법없이 국내법과 같은 효력을 갖는다 **C. 인권침해를 주장하는 개인이 취할 수 있는 조치** 가. 국가기관에 의해 침해된 경우 　　o 청 원 　　o 행정심판 　　o 행정소송 　　o 명령, 규칙 심사제도 　　o 헌법재판소에 의한 구제 　　o 손해배상청구권, 형사보상청구권

0196

규 약	요 지
	나. 개인에 의해 침해된 경우 ○ 고소, 고발 ○ 민사상 손해배상청구권 ○ 범죄피해자구조청구권 D. 시민적 및 정치적 권리에 관한 국제규약의 중요성 ○ 규약에 가입함으로써 대외적으로 인권존중 국가로서의 이미지 개선 ○ 규약가입 사실을 적극적으로 홍보 ○ 주요국가 인권보고서 및 인권규약사례집 발간 ○ 검찰, 경찰 등 인권관련업무 담당직원에게 직무교육 실시

0197

규 약	요 지
개별적 사항 제 1 조	**민족자결주의 원칙** ○ 중동문제 (팔래스타인 문제) ○ 쿠르드족 난민구호기금 제공 ○ 남아프리카 아파타이트정책 문제

제 2 조	**차별금지원칙**
	
	○ 헌법에 의하여 정치적, 경제적, 문화적, 사회적 생활영역
	  등 모든 생활영역에서 차별금지원칙이 보장된다
	○ 장애인의 평등한 권리보장 및 복지제도, 장애인복지법
	  등에 의한 장애인 보호 강조
	
	법앞에 평등
	
	○ 입법, 사법 및 행정의 모든 국가작용에 있어 적용되는
	  행위준칙
	○ 헌법재판소에 의한 위헌법률심판 및 헌법소원심판 사례

0198

규 약	요 지
	외국인의 권리 o 원칙적으로 내국인과 평등하게 보장 권리침해에 대한 구제수단 o 행정기관에 의한 구제 　- 청 원 　- 행정심판 　- 형사보상 o 법원에 의한 구제 　- 행정소송 　- 명령, 규칙 심사 　- 행정상 손해배상 o 헌법재판소에 의한 구제 　- 위헌법률심사 　- 헌법소원 o 특별한 인권옹호기관에 의한 구제 　- 대한법률구조공단 　- 대한변호사협회

0199

규 약	요 지
	o 고소, 고발 o 범죄피해자구조청구
제 3 조	남녀차별금지 o 헌법적 보장 - 헌법전문, 제10조, 제11조, 제32조, 제34조, 제36조 o 여성지위의 향상 - 헌법의 평등원칙에 따라 정부가 취한 여러가지 조치에 따라 여성지위는 비약적으로 향상되었다 o 1984.12.27. 여성에 대한 모든 형태의 차별철폐에 관한 협약을 비준 o 노동현장 여성의 지위 - 근로기준법 제5조, 노동조합법 제11조, 남녀고용평등법 o 형법상 여성의 지위 - 형사법상 여성에 대한 차별적 규정은 없다

0200

규 약	요 지

	○ 여성문제 담당기관
	- 정무제2장관실
	  브건사외부 부녀복지과, 노봉부 부녀소년과 등
	  1983.12.8. 여성정책심의위원회 설치
	
	○ 보육지원사업 확대
	- 1991.1.14. 시행된 영유아보육법을 중심으로 취업
	  기혼여성의 자녀양육 지원
	
	○ 모자보건보호
	- 모자보건법에 의거하여 모자보건증진 도모
	
	○ 여성에 대한 성적착취 금지
	- 매춘 등 성적착취로부터 여성을 보호
	
	○ 여성의 사회적 참여
	- 국회, 어론계, 교육계, 공무원직 등에 여성참여도가
	  크게 증가
	
	○ 여성의 교육
	- 남녀 평등교육 실시
	
	○ 혼인 및 가족관계에서의 여성의 평등
	- 민법개정으로 실질적 남녀평동보장

0201

규 약	요 지

제 4 조	대통령의 비상적. 긴급권적 권한
	
	○ 긴급사태시 헌법 제76조, 제77조에 의해 허용되는
	  대통령의 긴급권적 권한
	
	○ 긴급권적 권한행사에 대한 통제
	  - 국회에 의한 통제 : 국회승인을 요함
	  - 법원에 의한 통제 : 헌법재판소에 의한 심판재청
	  - 헌법재판소에 의한 통제 : 위헌여부 심판
	
	○ 6공화국 헌법시행 이후 비상적 권한이 행사되지 않았다

제 5 조	대한민국은 규약에 인정된 권리 및 자유를 파괴하거나 또는 규약에 규정된 제한의 범위를 넘어 자유를 제한하는 식으로 규약의 규정을 해석하지 아니한다
제 6 조	생 명 권 ○ 최고의 권리 ○ 국가권력 및 개인에 의한 자의적 생명박탈을 철저히 금지

0202

규 약	요 지
	○ 사형제도
	- 법감정상 사형제도 존치주장 우세
	- 가정파괴사범 등 중대한 범죄로 제한
	- 형법 개정작업 : 사형선고 신중조항 신설 등 추진
	- 형사특별법 개정 : 15개 조문에서 사형 폐지
	○ 낙태죄
	- 법감정상 낙태죄 존치주장 우세
	○ 사형선고를 받은 자의 사면, 감형청구권
	○ 18세 미만 소년, 임산부에 대한 사형 금지
	○ 사형집행대기자와 일반수형자의 취급상 차이
	- 형 집행 대기자로서 특수한 법적지위
	- 미결수용자에 대한 규정 준용
	○ 모자보건법을 위한 조치
	- 모자보건법 제7조, 제16조
	- 정부의 적극적 영유아보호정책 추진으로 영아사망율이
	크게 감소
	○ 장기이식
	- 선량한 풍속 기타 사회질서에 위반된 장기이식은 불허

0203

규 약	요 지
	○ 뇌사환자의 장기이식 　- 형법상 금지되나 뇌사인정에 관하여 활발한 논의가 　　진행중 ○ 전염병을 없애기 위한 조치와 관행 　- 전염병예방법 ○ 후천성면역결핍증 (AIDS) 관리 　- 에이즈 감염자의 인권보호 및 전염예방 ○ 집단살해죄의 방지 및 처벌에 관한 협약에 가입 　- 1951.1.12. 발효
제 7 조	고문 또는 비인도적 처우 금지 ○ 헌법 제12조, 제12조 제2항, 제7항에 의하여 고문 또는 　비인도적 처우금지가 보장된다 ○ 공무원의 독직폭행 등 처벌규정 　- 형법 제123조, 제124조, 제125조, 제383조 제2항, 　　특정범죄가중처벌등에관한법률 제4조의 2 (가중처벌), 　　형사소송법 제198조의 2 (검사의 구속장소 감찰), 　　제389조 (위법하게 수집된 증거의 증거능력 제한) 등

0204

규 약	요 지

	○ 재판상 준기소절차
	
	  - 복직폭행사건에 관하여 법원에 재정신청,
	    법원결정에 의해 공소재기된 것으로 간주
	
	○ 공무수행중의 고문 또는 가혹행위 금지
	
	  - 경찰관 등 사법경찰관리에게 직무교육 실시
	  - 민사상 손해배상 이외에 국가에 대한 손해배상청구 허용
	  - 대법원 판례 : 강요된 자백에 대한 증거능력 부인

제 8 조	**노예제도 금지**
	
	○ 헌법상 명문규정은 없으나 이에 관한 제18조에 규정된
	  일반원칙에 비추어 노예제도 금지가 인정된다
	
	강제노동 금지
	
	○ 헌법 제12조 제1항에 명시적으로 규정
	  근로기준법, 윤락행위등방지법, 직업안정및고용촉진에관한
	  법률, 아동복지법 등에 의해 금지
	
	○ 양심적 병역거부
	  헌법 제39조 제1항에 의해 불허, 대법원 판례도 같은 취지

규 약	요 지
제 9 조	**신체의 자유, 자의적 체포, 억류금지** ㅇ 헌법 제12조 제1항, 제3항에 의하여 보장 ㅇ 형사소송법 제78조, 제73조, 제75조, 제85조, 제201조, 제286조 등에 의하여 실질적으로 보장 ㅇ 1988.12.31. 경찰관직무집행법 개정 **체포이유 및 혐의사실 통보** ㅇ 헌법 제12조 제5항에 의하여 보장 ㅇ 형사소송법 제72조, 제87조, 제88조, 제209조 **신속한 재판, 미결수의 구금억제** ㅇ 헌법 제27조 제3항, 제12조 제7항에 의하여 보장 ㅇ ~~형사소송법 제102조 등~~ ㅇ 보석제도 활용 **구속적부심사** ㅇ 헌법 제12조 제6항에 의하여 보장 ㅇ 1987.11.28. 개정 형사소송법 모든 범죄에 대하여 구속적부심사청구를 할 수 있도록 개정

0206

규 약	요 지
제 10조	**형사보상** ㅇ 헌법 제28조에 의하여 보장 ㅇ 형사보상법 　수사기관에서 무혐의 석방된 피의자에게도 형사보상청구권 　허용하여 보상범위 확대 **피구금자의 인도적 처우** ㅇ 교도소 등 수용시설에 구금된 사람은 인간의 존엄성을 　존중하여 인도적 처우를 받는다 ㅇ 재소자에 대한 기본적 처우 　- 건강유지를 위한 충분한 영양 공급 　- 보건위생, 건강관리에 관한 배려 **분리수용** ㅇ 기결과 미결, 성년과 소년, 남자와 여자등 엄격히 분리수용 **교정제도** ㅇ 수형자의 사회복귀에 중점을 두어 교정교화 ㅇ 교화교육 　- 초.중.고등학교 수준의 학과교육과정 개설

0207

규 약	요 지
	○ 종교생활 허용
	○ 귀휴제도
	○ 사회인 교정참여제도
	○ 직업기술훈련
	○ 개방교도소
	○ 정서교육
	재소자의 교통권
	○ 행형법 제18조, 제46조에 의하여 재소자의 친지 접견권, 변호인 접견권 등 허용
	○ 도서열독, 서신왕래, 신문구독도 허용하여 정보수취의 자유 인정
	미성년 범죄자 교화
	○ 단계, 분류처우 등 미성년 범죄자를 특별보호
	교도소 등 교정시설에 대한 통제
	○ 법무부장관이 지정하는 순열공무원에 의한 순열 (행형법 제5조 제1항)
	○ 감사원의 감사 (감사원법 제28조)
	○ 판사, 검사의 시찰 (행형법 제5조 제2항)

0208

규 약	요 지

	권리구제
	
	○ 수형자의 청원권 허용 (행형법 제6조)
	    청원의 비밀보장, 기타 인권침해에 대한 고소.고발,
	    민사상.행정상 손해배상청구, 헌법소원을 제기할 수 있다
	
	피구금자처우최저기준규칙
	
	○ 대한민국의 행형관계 법규는 국제연합에서 채택한 피구금자
	    처우최저기준규칙의 규정내용 대부분을 반영하고 있다

제 11조	대한민국 법체계하에서는 계약상 의무의 불이행은 민사책임 만을 발생시킬 뿐 그 자체만으로는 범죄를 구성하지 않는다
제 12조	<u>거주.이전의 자유</u> ○ 헌법 제14조에 의해 보장된다
제 13조	**외국인 강제퇴거** ○ 출입국관리법 제45조에 규정된 사유에 의해서만 외국인을 대한민국 밖으로 강제퇴거 시킬 수 있다 ○ 강제퇴거명령에 대하여 이의신청 허용

0209

규 약	요 지
제 14조	재판의 평등, 법률에 의하여 설치된 독립·공평한 법원의 재판을 받을 권리, 공개재판의 원칙

○ 헌법 제11조, 제27조 제1항, 제101조-제118조 등에 의해 보장

○ 법원조직법, 형사소송법 등에 의해 실질적 보장

무죄추정의 원칙

○ 1988.2.25. 시행된 제6공화국 헌법은 새로이 무죄추정의 원칙을 명시적으로 규정 (제27조 제4항)

○ 형사소송법 제275조의 2

○ 1989.9.1. 시행된 형사소송규칙 제118조 제2항 예단배제의 원칙을 실질적 보장

형사피고인의 재판상 권리

○ 자신의 혐의에 관하여 즉시 상세하게 통고받을 권리 (형사소송법 제72조, 제266조, 제298조 등)

○ 변호준비를 위한 충분한 시간과 편의를 부여받을 권리 및 변호인과 연락을 취할 권리 (헌법 제12조 제4항, 제5항, 형사소송법 제34조) |

0210

규 약	요 지
	신속한 재판을 받을 권리 o 헌법 제27조 제3항에 의하여 보장 **피고인의 출석권과 무료변호를 받을 권리** o 피고인은 공판기일에 출석하여 이익되는 사실을 진술할 권리를 가진다 (형사소송법 제276조) o 국선변호인제도 (헌법 제12조 제4항 단서, 형사소송법 제33조) **피고인의 증인신청 및 신문권** o 형사소송법 제293조, 제294조 등 **묵비권과 자백강요의 금지** o 헌법 제12조 제2항, 제7항, 형사소송법 제389조, 제318조

0211

규 약	요 지
	소년에 대한 특별배려 ○ 소년법에 의하여 소년의 건전한 성장을 확보 상소권의 보장 ○ 헌법 제101조 제1항, 제2항, 형사소송법 제3편(상소) 등 ○ 군사법원법 제534조 　비상계엄하에서 일정한 범죄에 대하여 단심 　규약비준시 제5항을 유보하였음 사면 및 형사보상 ○ 규약 제9조 제5항 부분과 동일함 일사부재리 또는 이중처벌의 금지 ○ 헌법 제13조 제1항 ○ 외국에서 받은 형의 집행을 형의 임의적 감면사유로 규정 　(형법 제7조) 　위 조항을 이유로 규약비준시 제7항을 유보하였음

0212

규 약	요 지
제 15조	**형벌불소급의 원칙** ㅇ 헌법 제13조 제1항, 형법 제1조 **위헌결정의 소급효** ㅇ 형벌법규에 대하여만 예외적으로 위헌결정의 소급효를 인정 (헌법재판소법 제47조 제2항)하여 피고인의 권익보호
제 16조	**인간으로서의 존엄과 가치** ㅇ 헌법 제10조, 제37조에 의하여 보장 ㅇ 유죄판결을 받은 자에 대한 자격정지, 자격상실 (형법 제43조) ㅇ 미성년자, 한정치산자, 금치산자의 행위능력 제한
제 17조	**주거의 자유** ㅇ 헌법 제16조에 의하여 보장 (형법 제319조-제322조) **사생활의 비밀과 자유** ㅇ 헌법 제17조에 의하여 보장 (형법 제317조, 형사소송법 제149조, 민사소송법 제286조)

0213

규 약	요 지
	통신의 자유 ○ 헌법 제18조에 대하여 통신비밀의 자유 보장
제 18조	사상의 자유 ○ 헌법 제19조, 제20조에 의하여 양심,종교의 자유를 보장 ○ 국교는 인정되지 아니하며 종교와 정치는 분리 　(헌법 제20조 제2항) ○ 교정시설에 수형된 수형자에게도 종교의 자유 보장 　(행형법 제31조)
제 19조	표현의 자유에 대한 권리 ○ 헌법 제19조, 제21조 제1항, 제22조 제1항에 의하여 보장 　언론,출판에 대한 허가 및 검열제 금지조항 신설 ○ 헌법 제21조 제4항 　언론,출판의 권리 행사에 따른 특별한 의무와 책임을 　명백히 규정

규 약	요 지
	<u>라디오, TV 등 방송매체</u> ㅇ 방송의 자유 보장 ㅇ 정치.사회적 중립인사에 의한 공영방송의 운영 ㅇ 헌법 제37조 제2항의 일반적 원칙에 의한 제한이 가능 <u>알 권리</u> ㅇ 1989.9.4. 헌법재판소는 공공기관과 사회집단에 대하여 정보를 공개하도록 청구할 수 있는 개인의 알 권리를 인정
제 20조	<u>전쟁선전 금지</u> ㅇ 국제평화주의, 침략적 전쟁 부인 (헌법 전문, 제5조 제1항) <u>민족적, 인종적, 종교적 증오를 부추기는 선전 금지</u> ㅇ 형법 제181조 제2항(선동.선전죄), 제111조(외국에 대한 사전죄)에 의하여 처벌

0215

규 약	요 지

제 21조	## 집회. 결사의 자유
	
	o 헌법 제21조에 의하여 보장
	
	o 집회및시위에관한법률 제3조 제1항
	  사인에 의하여 집회의 자유가 침해되는 경우까지 보호
	
	o 집회및시위에관한법률 개정
	  집회 및 시위의 금지사유를 축소, 개정
	  - 추상적 내용의 5개항목 -> 헌법재판소의 결정에 의하여
	    해산된 정당의 목적을 달성하기 위한 집회 또는 시위 및
	    집단적인 폭행 등으로 공공의 안녕질서에 직접적인
	    위협을 가할 것이 명백한 집회 또는 시위로 제한
	
	## 집회의 자유의 제한
	
	o 사전허가제 금지 (헌법 제21조 제2항)
	  행정상의 참고를 위한 신고제
	
	## 옥외집회 및 시위의 신고
	
	o 경찰서장에게 신고서 제출 -> 금지통고 -> 시장.도지사
	  등에게 이의신청 -> 불허재결에 대하여 관할 고등법원에
	  행정소송을 제기할 수 있다

0216

규 약	요 지
제 22조	시간, 장소상 및 공중보건상 금지되는 집회 ㅇ 일출시간전, 일몰시간후 또는 주요도시, 주요도로에서의 집회 및 제1종 전염병 예방상 필요에 의해 집회 및 시위를 제한할 수 있다 결사의 자유 ㅇ 헌법 제21조 (일반적 결사의 자유) 등에 의해 보장 결사의 자유에 대한 제한 ㅇ 사전허가제 금지 (헌법 제21조 제2항) ㅇ 기본권 제한에 관한 일반원칙에 따라 최소한 제한 ㅇ 결사의 자유의 내재적 한계상 범죄단체 등 불법적 결사를 보호하지 아니함 공무원 노조설립 및 활동 ㅇ 헌법 제33조 제2항, 국가공무원법 제66조 등에 의해 사실상 노무에 종사하는 공무원을 제외한 나머지 공무원의 노동3권을 제한 ㅇ 위 이유로 규약 가입당시 규약 제22조를 유보하였음

0217

규 약	요 지
	정당의 복권 ㅇ 헌법재판소의 심판에 의해 해산되는 경우 이외에는 해산 되지 아니하고 (헌법 제8조 제4항), 국가는 운영자금을 보조 (본조 제3항) ㅇ 정치자금에 관한 법률 제4조, 제5조-제18조 등 **노동조합의 해산** ㅇ 회사의 폐업, 노조자체 결의에 의한 해산이 대표적 노동조합법 제31조 : 해산사유를 제한적으로 규정 **노동쟁의행위의 한계** ㅇ 입법례 독일의 경우 단체협약법은 있으나 단체행동(쟁의행위)을 규율하는 실정법은 없고 학설, 판례를 통하여 쟁의행위의 정당성의 판단기준이 확립되어 있다 ㅇ 아국에서는 집단적 노사관계법(쟁의행위)에 관한 판례가 축적되어 있지 않기 때문에 해석상 다툼이 있는 경우 노,사가 서로 자기측에서 유리한 논리만을 강변하므로 분쟁해결이 어렵다

0218

규 약	요 지
	노동쟁의조정법상의 직권중재제도 o 공익사업에 있어서 공공성이 강조되어야 할 사업체의 쟁의행위가 노사자치의 한계를 넘어 남용될 경우에 대비한 제도적 장치로서 헌법상 노동3권의 보장취지에 배치되지 아니한다 o 2차례 법개정을 통해 직권중재 대상사업을 대폭 감소 o 대법원은 1989.3.16. 발생한 서울지하철공사 파업과 관련하여 합헌결정
제 23조	**가정의 보호** o 헌법 제36조 제1항에 의하여 보장 o 성차별적 민법 개정 **혼인연령** o 남자 만 18세, 여자 만 16세 이상은 혼인할 수 있다 (민법 제887조) **혼인제도** o 일부일처제, 축첩, 중혼제도 배척

0219

규 약	요 지
	배우자의 권리
	○ 성차별적 요소 수정하여 1991.3.15자로 규약 제23조 제4항에 대한 유보를 철회하였음
	○ 혼인중 ... 부부협조의무, 생활비공동부담, 미성년자의 자에 대한 부모의 공동친권행사 혼인해소시 ... 자녀양육에 관한 사항 협의, 자녀면접 교섭권 신설, 이혼 배우자의 재산분할청구 제도를 신설
제 24조	**아동에 대한 차별금지** ○ 헌법 제11조 제1항에 의하여 보장 **아동보호에 관한 제도적 장치** ○ 아동복지법 제정 　아동이 건전하게 출생하여 행복하고 건강하게 육성되도록 복지를 보장 ○ 5.5을 어린이날로 제정 　범국민적 아동애호사상 함양 ○ 대한민국 어린이헌장 제정, 선포

0220

규 약	요 지
	아동복지담당기관 ㅇ 보건사회부 아동복지과, 각 시.도에 가정복지과 설치 **요보호아동에 대한 보호조치** ㅇ 보호자로부터 유기된 경우 등 아동복지법에 의하여 　보호를 받을 아동에 대한 생계보호 등 특별한 보호조치 **아동의 교육** ㅇ 헌법 제31조 제2항, 교육법 제8조에 의해 6년의 무상초등 　교육과 3년의 중등교육을 받을 권리 보장 **아동의 근로관계** ㅇ 18세 미만자는 도덕상 또는 보건상 유해, 위험한 사업에 　사용하지 못하는 등 (근로기준법 제51조) 특별한 보호 **사생아의 지위** ㅇ 혼인외의 출생자도 호주상속순위를 제외하고는 혼인중 　출생자와 동등하게 취급

0221

규 약	요 지
제 25조	**미성년자의 입양** o 미성년자의 실질적 보호를 위하여 반드시 가정법원의 허가를 얻도록 민법 개정 **아동의 국적 취득** o 모든 어린이는 국적법 제2조에 따라 출생에 의하여 국적취득 **국민주권의 원리** o 헌법 제1조 제2항에서 국민주권의 원리 선언 **선거권** o 헌법 제24조 대통령, 국회의원, 지방의회의원 선거권 보장 **공무담임권** o 헌법 제25조에 의하여 공무담임권 보장 대통령, 국회의원, 지방의회의원 선거법에 의하여 피선거권 규정

0222

규 약	요 지
	보통, 평등, 직접, 비밀투표 O 헌법상 보장 **참정권의 제한** O 소급입법에 의한 참정권제한 금지 (헌법 제13조 제2항)
제 26조	**인간으로서의 존엄과 가치** O 헌법 제10조, 제11조 제1항 등에 의하여 보장
제 27조	대한민국에는 규약에서 언급하고 있는 종류의 소수민족 즉 민족적, 종교적, 언어적 소수자는 존재하지 아니한다

보 도 자 료
외 무 부

제91-*183*호　　　문의전화 : 720-2408-10　　　보도일시 : 1991.7.31.　15:00

제 목 : 시민적.정치적 권리에 관한 인권보고서 제출

o　정부는 91.7.31. 시민적.정치적 권리에 관한 최초 인권보고서를 유엔
　　인권국(제네바 소재)에 제출하였다.

o　시민적.정치적 권리에 관한 최초 인권보고서는 법무부, 내무부,
　　노동부, 보건사회부등 11개 관련부처가 우리나라의 인권보장에 관한
　　제반사항을 담당분야별로 작성(법무부 종합, 외무부 번역)한 것으로서,
　　금번 유엔인권국에 제출한 영문 인권보고서는 총 312개항, 141페이지로
　　구성되어 전반부는 우리나라의 시민적.정치적 권리 보장에 관한 일반적
　　법률체계를, 후반부는 시민적.정치적 권리에 관한 국제규약(B규약)상의
　　각조항(27개 조항)의 권리를 보장하기 위하여 우리나라에서 시행되고
　　있는 사법적.행정적 조치등을 기술하고 있다.

o　우리나라는 90.7월 경제적.사회적 및 문화적 권리에 관한 국제규약
　　(A규약), 시민적.정치적 권리에 관한 국제규약(B규약) 및 B규약 선택
　　의정서에 가입하였는 바, B규약 제40조에 따르면 B규약 가입국은
　　가입후 1년이내에 시민적.정치적 권리에 관한 최초 인권보고서를 제출
　　하여야 하며, 최초 인권보고서 제출후 매 5년마다 정기적으로 추가
　　보고서를 제출토록 규정하고 있다.

o　현재 시민적.정치적 권리에 관한 국제규약(B규약) 가입국은
　　남북한을 포함하여 91개국이다.　끝.

0224

외 무 부

종   별 :

번   호 : GVW-1448   일   시 : 91 0731 1700

수   신 : 장관(국연,법무부)

발   신 : 주 제네바 대사

제   목 : 인권보고서 제출

대: WGV-0979

1. 대호, 금 7.31 인권 보고서를 유엔 인권 사무국 KLEIN 규약 담당관에게 제출함.

2. 아국 보고서 심의 시기와 관련, 동 담당관에 따르면 현재 인권 이사회에는 12 개 보고서가 심의 계류중인바, 동 이사회에서는 최초 보고서를 우선적으로심의하는 경향이 있음을 고려할때, 아국 보고서는 92.3 월(뉴욕), 또는 92.7 월(제네바) 회의시 심의될 가능성이 있다고 함. 인권이사회는 매 회기말 차기회의 심의대상 보고서를 결정하는바, 92.3 월 심의 보고서는 91.10 월 회의시 결정됨. 끝

(대사 박수길-국장)

국기국   법무부

PAGE 1

정부, 유엔에 人權보고

加入 1년만에…3백12개항

정부는 지난달 31일 시민적, 정치적 권리에 관한 첫 유엔인권보고서를 제네바소재 유엔인권국에 제출했다고 1일 외무부가 밝혔다.

인권보고서는 법무 내무 노동 보사등 11개 관련부처가 우리나라의 인권관련 제반사항을 담아 작성한 이 최초인권보고서를 제…

우리나라는 작년 7월경 시민적 정치적권리에 관한 국제규약 (B규약)및 경제적 사회적및 문화적권리에 관한 국제규약 (A규약)에 가입했으며, 가입국은 가입후 1년이내에 …

첫 人權보고서 정부, 유엔제출

정부는 지난31일 시민적, 정치적 권리에 관한 첫 인권보고서를 제네바에 있는 유엔 인권국에 제출했다고 1일 외무부가 밝혔다.

이 인권보고서는 법무 내무 노동 보사 등 11개 관련 부처가 우리나라의 인권보장에 관한 제반사항을 담아 작성, 종합한 것으로 총 3백12개항에 시민적, 정치적 권리보장과 관련한 일반적 법률체계와 사법적, 행정적 조치들이 포함되어있다.

부처가 우리나라의 인권보장에 관한 제반사항을 담아 작성, 종합 해야 한다. 시민적 정치적권리에 관한 국제규약에는 남북한을 포함해 모두 91개국이 가입해있다.

정부가 우리나라의 인권보장을 적으로 추가 보고서를 제출해야하며, 5년마다 정기적으로 …로 총 3백12개항으로 구성돼 있으며, 시민적 정치적 권리에 관한 일반적 법률체계와 사법적, 행정적 조치들이 기술되어 있다.

韓國 人權보고서 유엔에 처음제출

정부는 지난달31일 시민적, 정치적권리에 관한 인권보고서를 최초로 유엔인권국에 제출했다고 외무부가 1일 발표했다.

법무·내무·노동부등 11개관련부처가 우리나라의 인권보장을 위한 법률체계와 사법·행정적 조치들등 제반사항을 분야별로 작성한 이 보고서는 총3백12개항에 1백41쪽으로 구성돼있다.

0226

The Korea Herald ,
1991. 8. 2. 금, page 2

Korea submits report on rights to U.N.

The government handed in a report on civil and political rights of Koreans to the Department of Human Rights of the U.N. Secretariat in Geneva Wednesday, the Foreign Ministry said yesterday.

The report is the first of its kind Korea ever made to the United Nations since it joined the International Covenant on Civil and Political Rights in July last year.

Signatories of the covenant are required to submit a report on civil and human rights situations in the country within one year after they sign the accord and additional reports every five years.

김

주 제 네 바 대 표 부

제네(정) 2035-♧♂   1991. 10. 14

수 신 : 장 관

참 조 : 국제기구국장

제 목 : 시민적 정치적 권리에 관한 규약

　　　　표제 규약 가입에 따른 최초 보고서 및 정기 보고서 작성 요령을
별첨 송부합니다.

　　첨부 : 상기 자료 · 끝 ·

주 제 네 바 대  사 .

2의59535   0228

UNITED
NATIONS

International covenant
on civil and
political rights

Distr.
GENERAL

CCPR/C/5/Rev.1
30 September 1991

Original: ENGLISH

HUMAN RIGHTS COMMITTEE

GUIDELINES REGARDING THE FORM AND CONTENTS OF INITIAL REPORTS
FROM STATES PARTIES

Adopted by the Committee at its 44th meeting (second session),
on 29 August 1977, and embodying amendments adopted by the
Committee at its 1002nd meeting (thirty-ninth session), on
24 July 1990, and 1089th meeting (forty-second session), on
25 July 1991

GE.91-17594/1767H

0229

GUIDELINES REGARDING THE FORM AND CONTENTS OF INITIAL
REPORTS FROM STATES PARTIES

1. Under article 40 of the International Covenant on Civil and Political Rights each State party has undertaken to submit, within one year of the entry into force of the Covenant in regard to it and thereafter whenever the Human Rights Committee established under the Covenant so requests, reports on the measures which it has adopted to give effect to rights recognized in the Covenant and on the progress made in the enjoyment of those rights. Article 40 also provides that the reports shall indicate the factors and difficulties, if any, affecting the implementation of the Covenant.

2. In order to assist it in fulfilling the tasks entrusted to it pursuant to article 40 of the Covenant, the Committee has decided that it would be useful to inform States parties of its wishes regarding the form and contents of reports. Compliance with the following guidelines will help to ensure that reports are presented in a uniform manner and enable the Committee and States parties to obtain a complete picture of the situation in each State as regards the implementation of the rights referred to in the Covenant. This will also reduce the need for the Committee to request additional information under its rules of procedure.

3. The general part of the report should be prepared in accordance with the consolidated guidelines for the initial part of the reports of States parties to be submitted under the various international human rights instruments, including the Covenant, as contained in document HRI/1991/1.

4. The part of the report relating specifically to parts I, II and III of the Covenant should describe in relation to the provisions of each article:

    (a) The legislative, administrative or other measures in force in regard to each right;

    (b) Any restrictions or limitations, even of a temporary nature, imposed by law or practice or any other manner on the enjoyment of the right;

    (c) Any other factors or difficulties affecting the enjoyment of the right by persons within the jurisdiction of the State;

    (d) Any other information on the progress made in the enjoyment of the right.

5. When a State party to the Covenant is also a party to the Optional Protocol, and if in the period under review the Committee has issued views finding that the State party has violated provisions of the Covenant, the report should include a section explaining what action has been taken relating to the communication concerned. In particular, the State party should indicate what remedy it has afforded the author of the communication whose rights the Committee found to have been violated.

6. The report should be accompanied by copies of the principal legislative and other texts referred to in the report. These will be made available to members of the Committee. It should be noted, however, that, for reasons of

0230

expense, they will not normally be reproduced for general distribution with the report except to the extent that the reporting State specifically so requests. It is desirable therefore that when a text is not actually quoted in or annexed to the report itself, the report should contain sufficient information to be understood without reference to it.

7. The Committee will welcome at any time information on any significant new development in regard to the rights referred to in the Covenant, but in any event it intends, after the completion of its study of each State's initial report and of any additional information submitted, to call for subsequent reports under article 40 (1) (b) of the Covenant. The aim of such further reports will be to bring the situation up to date in respect of each State.

8. On the basis of reports prepared according to the above guidelines, the Committee is confident that it will be enabled to develop a constructive dialogue with each State party in regard to the implementation of the Covenant and thereby contribute to mutual understanding and peaceful and friendly relations among nations in accordance with the Charter of the United Nations.

0231

UNITED
NATIONS

**International covenant
on civil and
political rights**

Distr.
GENERAL

CCPR/C/20/Rev.1
30 September 1991

Original: ENGLISH

HUMAN RIGHTS COMMITTEE

GUIDELINES REGARDING THE FORM AND CONTENTS OF PERIODIC REPORTS
FROM STATES PARTIES

Adopted by the Committee at its 308th meeting (thirteenth session),
on 27 July 1981, and embodying amendments adopted by the Committee
at its 1002nd meeting (thirty-ninth session), on 24 July 1990, and
1089th meeting (forty-second session), on 25 July 1991

GE.91-17599/1775H

0232

GUIDELINES REGARDING THE FORM AND CONTENTS OF PERIODIC
REPORTS FROM STATES PARTIES

1.   Under paragraph 1 of article 40 of the Covenant every State party has
undertaken to submit reports to the Human Rights Committee on the
implementation of the Covenant

     (a) Within one year of the entry into force of the Covenant for the
State party concerned,

     (b) Thereafter whenever the Committee so requests.

2.   At its second session, in August 1977, the Committee adopted guidelines
for the submission of reports by States parties under article 40*.   In drawing
up these guidelines the Committee had in mind in particular the initial
reports to be submitted by States parties under paragraph 1 (a) of
article 40.   These guidelines have been followed by the great majority of
States parties that have submitted reports subsequent to their issuance and
they have proved helpful both to the reporting States and to the Committee.

3.   In paragraph 5 of those guidelines, the Committee indicated that it
intended, after the completion of its study of each State's initial report and
of any subsequent information submitted, to call for subsequent reports under
article 40, paragraph 1 (b), of the Covenant.

4.   At its eleventh session, in October 1980, the Committee adopted by
consensus a statement concerning the subsequent stages of its future work
under article 40.   It confirmed its aim of engaging in a constructive dialogue
with each reporting State and determined that the dialogue should be conducted
on the basis of periodic reports from States parties to the Covenant
(para. (d)).   It also decided that in the light of its experience in the
consideration of initial reports, it should develop guidelines for the purpose
of subsequent reports.   Pursuant to this decision and to the decision taken by
the Committee at its thirteenth session to request States parties to submit
reports under article 40, paragraph 1 (b), on a periodic basis, the Committee
has drawn up the following guidelines regarding the form and contents of such
reports, which are designed to complete and to bring up to date the
information required by the Committee under the Covenant.

5.   General information should be prepared in accordance with the
consolidated guidelines for the initial part of reports of States parties to
be submitted under the various international human rights instruments,
including the Covenant, as contained in document HRI/1991/1.

6.   Information relating to each of the articles in parts I, II and III of
the Covenant should concentrate especially on:

     (a) The completion of the information before the Committee as to the
measures adopted to give effect to rights recognized in the Covenant, taking
account of questions raised in the Committee on the examination of any
previous report and including in particular additional information as to
questions not previously answered or not fully answered;

----

     * See Official Records of the General Assembly, Thirty-second Session,
Supplement No. 44, (A/32/44) annex IV.

(b) Information taking into account general comments which the Committee may have made under article 40, paragraph 4, of the Covenant;

(c) Changes made or proposed to be made in the laws and practices relevant to the Covenant;

(d) Action taken as a result of experience gained in cooperation with the Committee;

(e) Factors affecting and difficulties experienced in the implementation of the Covenant;

(f) The progress made since the last report in the enjoyment of rights recognized in the Covenant.

7. When a State party to the Covenant is also a party to the Optional Protocol and if, in the period under review, the Committee has issued views finding that the State party has violated provisions of the Covenant, the report should include a section explaining what action has been taken relating to the communication concerned. In particular, the State party should indicate what remedy it has afforded the author of the communication whose rights the Committee found to have been violated.

8. It should be noted that the reporting obligation extends not only to the relevant laws and other norms, but also to the practices of the courts and administrative organs of the State party and other relevant facts likely to show the degree of actual enjoyment of rights recognized by the Covenant.

9. The report should be accompanied by copies of the principal legislative and other texts referred to in it.

10. It is the desire of the Committee to assist States parties in promoting the enjoyment of rights under the Covenant. To this end, the Committee wishes to continue the dialogue which it has begun with reporting States in the most constructive manner possible and reiterates its confidence that it will thereby contribute to mutual understanding and peaceful and friendly relations among nations in accordance with the Charter of the United Nations.

0234

외 무 부

종   별 :

번   호 : GVW-2274   일   시 : 91 1107 1800

수   신 : 장관(연이, 법무부)

발   신 : 주 제네바 대사

제   목 : 아국 인권 보고서 심의 일정

1. 당지 유엔 인권 사무국의 KLEIN 규약 담당관은 11.6 인권 이사회에 참관중인 김응기 검사와, 위성락 서기관에게 아국의 B 규약 보고서가 92.3.23-4.10 간 뉴욕에서 개최되는(인권 이사회는 뉴욕과 당지에서 교대 개최) 44 차 인권 이사회의 심의 대상으로 이제 막 결정되었음을 통보하였으며, 인쇄 완료된 아국 보고서를 전달하였음. (동 보고서 파편 송부)

2. 동 담당관은 추후 공한으로 공식 통보가 있을 것이나, 아측 참고로 미리 알린다고 하였으며, 아국 보고서 심의 일자는 미정이나, 관례상 첫보고서 심의가 첫째주에 있고 1 국 심의에 1.5 일 또는 2 일이 소요됨을 참고로 할수 있을 것이라고 하였음.

또한 동인은 니제, 알제리가 아국과 함께 첫 보고서 심의 대상국임도 언급하였음.

3. 기타 회의 진행 방식, 대표단 구성, 요준비 사항, 동시 통역 문제중에 관해서도 일차 의견을 교환한바, 이에 관해서는 추가로 상세 파악 한후 당관 의견과 함께 별도 건의 예정임. 끝

(대사 박수길-차관)

예고 91.12.31. 까지

일반문서로 재분류 (1991 .12. 31.

국기국   장관   차관   1차보   외정실   분석관   청와대   안기부   법무부

ㄱㄴ

주 제 네 바 대 표 부

제네(정) 2031-950·   1991. 11. 8.

수신 : 장   관

참조 : 국제기구국장

제목 : 인권보고서

        연 : GVW- 2274

        연호 인권사부국 문서로 인쇄된 아국의 시민적 정치적 권리에 관한

협약 제 40조에 의거한 아국의 인권 보고서(CCPR/C/68/Add. 1)을 별첨 송부합니다.

        첨부 : 상기 문서 1부.   끝.

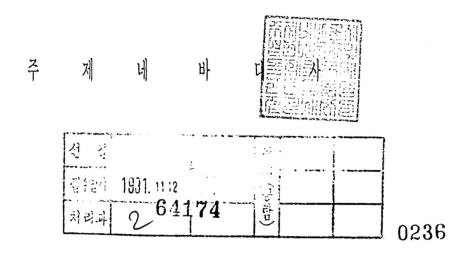

주 제 네 바 대 사

0236

UNITED
NATIONS

CCPR

**International covenant
on civil and
political rights**

Distr.
GENERAL

CCPR/C/68/Add.1
20 September 1991

Original: ENGLISH

HUMAN RIGHTS COMMITTEE

CONSIDERATION OF REPORTS SUBMITTED BY STATES PARTIES
UNDER ARTICLE 40 OF THE COVENANT

<u>Initial reports of States parties due in 1991</u>

<u>Addendum</u>

REPUBLIC OF KOREA

[31 July 1991]

GE.91–17520/3747B

0237

CONTENTS

0238

INTRODUCTION

1.   The Government of the Republic of Korea submits the following initial
report, which relates to the progress made in the guarantees of the
fundamental human rights provided for in the International Covenant on Civil
and Political Rights, and in the enjoyment of these rights, to the
Secretary-General of the United Nations in accordance with article 40 of the
said Covenant.

I.   GENERAL COMMENTS

A.   Constitutional protection of civil and political rights

2.   The first Constitution of the Republic of Korea was proclaimed
on 17 July 1948 and there were several amendments to the Constitution until
February 1988 when the present Constitution of the Sixth Republic (hereinafter
referred to as "the Constitution") was proclaimed. As the supreme law of the
State, the Constitution, which was adopted upon the desire and consensus of
the Korean people, has enormously contributed to the political, economic and
social development of the Republic of Korea, and to the protection of human
rights of the Korean people.

3.   The Constitution guarantees all the rights provided for in the
International Covenant on Civil and Political Rights (hereinafter referred to
as "the Covenant"). Article 10 of the Constitution provides, "All citizens
shall be assured of human worth and dignity and have the right to pursue
happiness. It shall be the duty of the State to confirm and guarantee the
fundamental and inviolable human rights of individuals." In addition,
Article 37(1) of the Constitution guarantees the fundamental human rights in
an explicit and comprehensive manner stating that "Freedoms and rights of
citizens shall not be neglected on the grounds that they are not enumerated in
the Constitution." In compliance with these provisions of the Constitution,
the laws and regulations contain more detailed provisions in order to
guarantee the rights which are recognized by the Covenant.

4.   Generally, the fundamental human rights protected by the Constitution are
equally guaranteed to all foreigners in the Republic of Korea. All rights
under the Covenant, with the exception of the rights which require Korean
nationality as a condition for enjoyment, such as the right to vote or to hold
public office, are equally guaranteed to all foreigners residing or
temporarily staying in the Republic of Korea. The Constitution provides that
the fundamental human rights may be restricted by law only when necessary "for
national security, the maintenance of law and order, or for public welfare"
(Art. 37(2), para. 1). Concepts such as "national security, the maintenance
of law and order or public welfare" imply limited cases where restrictions on
the rights are inevitable in order to resolve conflicts among individuals in
the enjoyment of those rights and to guarantee the human rights of each
individual to the fullest extent. With regard to restrictions on the
fundamental human rights, the Constitution prescribes strict limitations on
the exercise of the Government's power, in order to prevent an abuse of power,
by providing that "any such restrictions may not infringe upon the essential
aspects of the fundamental human rights" (Art. 37(2), para. 2).

0239

B. Relationship between the Covenant and the domestic laws of the Republic of Korea

5.   Since Article 6(1) of the Constitution provides that "Treaties duly concluded and promulgated under the Constitution and the generally recognized rules of international law shall have the same effect as the domestic laws of the Republic of Korea," the Covenant, which was ratified and promulgated by the Government with the consent of the National Assembly, has the same effect as domestic laws without the enactment of separate domestic legislation.

6.   The Korean Government has concluded that the Constitution does not conflict with the Covenant. However, the Government has made reservations on articles 14, paragraph 5, 22 and 23, paragraph 4, of the Covenant which were considered to be incompatible with traditional Korean customs, and the statutory framework and practice based upon the crucial policy objectives of the Republic of Korea. (The reservation on article 23, paragraph 4, was withdrawn on 15 March 1991 when the relevant domestic law was amended to conform with the Covenant.)

C. Authorities having jurisdiction over human rights

7.   The Constitution guarantees all citizens the right of access to the courts (Arts. 27 and 101). The judicial power is vested in the Supreme Court, the highest court of the State, and in other lower courts (Art. 101(2)). In order to secure independent and just trials, the Constitution provides that "the judges shall rule independently under their own conscience and in accordance with the Constitution and law" (Art. 103).

8.   In addition, the Constitution has a provision relating to the organization and competence of the Constitution Court (Arts. 111 to 113) which has jurisdiction over the following matters:

    (a) Upon a request by the courts, the adjudication of the constitutionality of a law;

    (b) Impeachment;

    (c) Dissolution of a political party;

    (d) Dispute between State agencies, between State agencies and local governments and between local governments;

    (e) Petitions prescribed by law relating to the Constitution.

    In adjudicating the above matters, the Constitution Court has been performing an important and effective role in checking the abusive acts of the Government, securing the independence of the Judiciary and protecting fundamental rights.

9.   The Government of the Republic of Korea has a "Human Rights Division" in the Ministry of Justice. The Division has full competence over human rights matters. The Human Rights Division is responsible for, inter alia, "the protection of human rights, legal aid, enhancement of the respect for law and.

0240

order, and affairs relating to private human rights organizations". The Ministry of Justice is planning to reinforce the Division in order to handle more effectively human rights matters which are presently handled by several Government authorities.

10. In the Republic of Korea, the prosecutor has a duty to protect human rights. As a part of the measures to protect and enhance the fundamental human rights of citizens, the prosecutor establishes a human rights consultation centre in every district attorney's office and its branch offices. The prosecutor also designates a prosecutor in charge of human rights matters to gather information on the instances of human rights violations, and to handle the criminal cases, petitions or secret investigations relating to human rights violations.

11. The Government of the Republic of Korea has several legal aid programmes which provide free legal advice, aid for legal costs and an attorney to those who are unable to obtain legal remedies because they are ignorant of the law or cannot afford the legal costs. The Korea Legal Aid Corporation, established on 1 September 1987 and subsidized by the Government, had dealt with 782,684 cases of legal consultation and 64,328 cases of legal aid by the end of 1990.

12. In the Republic of Korea, there are numerous private organizations for the protection of human rights. The Korean Federal Bar Association is the most prominent of these organizations.

D. Remedies available to an individual who claims an infringement of his rights

13. The Constitution and other relevant laws provide numerous remedies to an individual who claims an infringement of his/her fundamental human rights by Government agencies or by an individual.

14. Remedies available in case of an infringement of the rights by Government agencies are as follows:

   (a) Petition: Generally, an individual who claims an infringement of his fundamental rights may obtain remedies by petitioning for the annulment or nullification of the administrative actions, or for the dismissal of the relevant officials under Article 26 of the Constitution. Matters for which petitions are available are prescribed in Article 4 of the Petition Act, and the petitioning method and procedure are prescribed in Articles 6 to 8 of the said Act.

   (b) Appeals: An individual, whose rights or interests have been violated by an illegal or unjust administrative action, or by the exercise or non-exercise of Government power by administrative agencies, may use the administrative appeals procedure in order to achieve the proper operation of the administration. (Administrative Appeals Act, Art. 1.)

   (c) Litigation: Article 107(2) of the Constitution provides that the courts shall adjudicate the constitutionality or legality of administrative actions. The details of the litigation procedure are prescribed in the Administrative Litigation Act.

0241

CCPR/C/68/Add.1
page 4

(d) Review of administrative decrees and regulations: In order to
ensure that administrative decrees and regulations do not violate the
fundamental rights of the citizens, Article 107(2) of the Constitution
provides courts with the power to review administrative decrees and
regulations. The review may be conducted by the courts when their
constitutionality or legality is at issue in a trial. The Supreme Court has
the power to make a final review.

(e) Remedies of the Constitution Court: In case of an infringement of
fundamental rights by an unconstitutional administrative action, an individual
may obtain remedies through a petition to the Constitution Court (see
para. 8 (e)).

(f) Remedies available in case of an infringement of fundamental human
rights and compensation for damages: An individual, whose fundamental human
rights have been infringed by the unlawful action of a public official in the
course of his official duties, may claim compensation for damages from the
State under the procedures prescribed by the National Compensation Act
(Constitution, Art. 29(1)). In case an arrested criminal suspect is not
indicted due to lack of evidence, or an accused person placed under detention
is acquitted by the court, such persons may claim compensation from the State
(under the procedures prescribed by the Criminal Compensation Act
(Constitution, Art. 28)).

15. Remedies available in case of an infringement of fundamental human rights
by an individual are as follows:

(a) Complaint or accusation: In case of an infringement of fundamental
rights by an individual, the person claiming the infringement is entitled to
seek the withdrawal of the illegal act from the criminal investigation
authorities, i.e., the prosecutor's office and the police. For example,
through a complaint or accusation with respect to an unlawful detention or an
infringement of property rights, an individual can initiate an investigation
or prosecution of the above unlawful acts. In addition to a complaint or
accusation, the laws of the Republic of Korea provide for other procedures for
requesting an adjudication (Code of Criminal Procedure, Arts. 260-262), the
details of which will be explained later (see para. 135).

(b) Civil lawsuit for compensation: An individual, who claims an
infringement of his fundamental rights by another person, can also file a
lawsuit to seek compensation for damages.

(c) Remedies available to the victims of a crime: The Constitution
provides for State aid to the victims of a crime, by stipulating that
"Citizens, who have suffered bodily injury or death due to criminal acts of
others, may receive aid from the State under the conditions as prescribed by
law" (Art. 30). The State Aid for Victims of Crime Act, promulgated
on 1 July 1988, sets forth detailed methods and procedures for the payment
of State aid.

16. Further explanations of the above-mentioned measures to protect human rights, and numerous remedies for the infringements of the rights, will be provided in "Information concerning the application of articles 1 to 27 of the Covenant".

E. Other measures to ensure the implementation
of the provisions of the Covenant

17. By acceding to the Covenant, the Republic of Korea has expressed its will to participate actively in the concerted international efforts for the protection of human rights. Korea's accession will also contribute to the promotion of respect for human rights in Korea. The Republic of Korea has acceded to the Optional Protocol with a view to enabling its citizens to submit a complaint to the Human Rights Committee. This clearly demonstrates the commitment of the Government of the Republic of Korea to promote respect for and observance of human rights.

18. The Government of the Republic of Korea has made every effort to make the contents of the Covenant fully understood by the Korean people. Before Korea's accession to the Covenant, the Ministry of Justice held a symposium on the Covenant where people from academic and legal circles participated in a fruitful discussion of the conflicts between the Covenant and domestic laws. The symposium enhanced public awareness of the Covenant and accelerated the process of accession. With the accession to the Covenant, the Ministry of Justice has translated into Korean the Covenant, several initial reports submitted by the States Parties to the Covenant, in accordance with article 40 thereof, and selected decisions of the Human Rights Committee. With the publication and distribution of these translated materials, education on human rights was provided to all levels of public officials - the prosecutors, police, and other law enforcement officers - in order to protect human rights in accordance with the spirit of the Covenant.

19. Every year, the Government of the Republic of Korea designates the week which includes "Human Rights Day" (10 December) as "Human Rights Week" and holds numerous events such as a commemorative ceremony and symposiums to promote the respect for human rights.

20. The Government will do its utmost to inform every Korean of the provisions and spirit of the Covenant so that human rights are respected by all individuals. In this respect, there is a positive trend for lawyers as well as agencies such as the Supreme Court and the Constitution Court, to solve legal problems by applying the Covenant in litigation.

II. INFORMATION CONCERNING THE APPLICATION
OF ARTICLES 1 TO 27 OF THE COVENANT

Article 1

21. The Preamble and Article 5(1) of the Constitution state that the Republic of Korea shall contribute to a lasting world peace and the common prosperity of mankind and shall renounce all aggressive wars.

22. Under the principle of international peace as embodied in its Constitution, the Republic of Korea accepts the principles and the provisions of the Charter of the United Nations and recognizes that all nations have the right of self-determination and to pursue freely their political, economic, social and cultural development. The Republic of Korea has based its foreign policy on the principles enshrined in the Constitution and the Charter of the United Nations and has made every effort for the complete realization of these principles.

23. With respect to situations where the right of self-determination has not yet been respected or where racial discrimination still persists, the position of the Republic of Korea may be summarized in the following paragraphs.

The Middle East and the question of Palestine

24. The Republic of Korea believes that the question of Palestine should be settled in a peaceful manner by respecting the legitimate rights of the Palestinians and supports a prompt resolution of the question of Palestine in accordance with Security Council resolutions 242 (1967) and 388 (1973).

25. Since 1950, the Republic of Korea has made, and continues to make, voluntary contributions to the United Nations Relief and Works Agency for Palestine Refugees in the Near East (UNRWA). The Republic of Korea also contributed to the Arab Student Aid International (ASAI) from 1981-1988. In addition, since 1978, the Korean Government has participated in activities held under the auspices of the United Nations such as the commemoration of the International Day of Solidarity with the Palestinian People.

26. In response to United Nations Security Council resolution 688 (1991), the Republic of Korea also made a voluntary contribution of $US 300,000 on 17 April 1991 to the United Nations Relief Activities for Kurdish and other Iraqi Refugees.

Apartheid in South Africa

27. The Republic of Korea, in the firm belief that apartheid constitutes a crime against the conscience and dignity of mankind, reaffirms its support for the efforts of the South African people and the international society to establish, through peaceful means, a united, non-racial and democratic society in South Africa in which all people, irrespective of race, colour, sex or creed, will enjoy the same fundamental human rights. In this regard, the Government of the Republic of Korea welcomes recent developments in South Africa which will foster a climate fully conducive to a peaceful settlement of the problems through negotiation. The Korean Government

0244

believes that these developments are positive steps toward the elimination of all forms of racial discrimination and the establishment of a united, democratic and non-racial society in South Africa. The Korean Government, as an expression of its support for and solidarity with the peoples of South Africa, has provided, since 1978, financial assistance to the United Nations Trust Funds and Programmes for Southern Africa and is fulfilling its pledge of $US 1 million, pledged in 1987, to the Action for Resisting Invasion, Colonialism and Apartheid Fund. The Republic of Korea fully supports the noble and untiring efforts of the Special Committee against Apartheid and other relevant organs of the United Nations to achieve the lofty goal of eliminating all forms of racial discrimination and apartheid.

28. The Republic of Korea established full diplomatic relations with Namibia at ambassadorial level on 21 March 1990 and opened its embassy in Windhoek on 18 June 1990.

Article 2

29. Respect for the dignity of an individual and non-discrimination are fully reflected in the Constitution. The Preamble of the Constitution states, "... to afford equal opportunities to every person in all fields" and Article 11(1) states, "All citizens shall be equal before the law and there shall be no discrimination in political, economic, social or cultural life on account of sex, religion or social status." Non-discrimination is guaranteed in all aspects of the citizens' lives (Constitution, Art. 11(1)).

Political sphere

30. All citizens shall enjoy, without any discrimination, the equal right to vote and to hold public office (Constitution, Arts. 41(1), 67(1) and 116(1)).

Economic sphere

31. Unequal treatment in employment, wages and taxation is prohibited. The right of women to work is guaranteed and they shall not be subjected to unjust discrimination in employment, wages or working conditions (Constitution, Art. 32(4)).

32. Article 5 of the Labour Standard Act provides, "An employer shall not discriminate against the employees on account of sex and shall not discriminate with respect to the terms of employment on the basis of nationality, religion or social status."

33. Article 1-2 of the Employment Security and Promotion Act provides that "No person shall be discriminated against with respect to employment assistance, occupational guidance and relations for reasons of sex, religion, social status or marital status." Under Article 17-3 of the said Act, the Minister of Labour is responsible for the enforcement of the non-discrimination principle. The Minister shall endeavour to increase the availability of occupational and employment opportunities for women, shall assist in developing occupations suitable for middle-aged, elderly or disabled persons and shall assist them in finding employment in the above occupations.

34. Articles 4(3) and (4) of the Basic Vocational Training Act states, "... vocational training for women, the middle-aged, the elderly and the disabled shall be considered as important", and Article 11 of the Labour Union Act provides, "A member of a union shall not be discriminated against under any circumstances on account of race, religion, sex, political party or social status."

Cultural sphere

35. All citizens shall have an equal right to receive an education corresponding to their abilities (Constitution, Art. 31(1)). However, reasonable discrimination on the basis of their abilities is not prohibited.

Social sphere

36. Any discrimination with respect to residence, travel or access to public facilities is prohibited. Any discrimination between legitimate and illegitimate children, or between men and women in marriage or family life is also prohibited (Constitution, Art. 36(1)).

Equal treatment and welfare policy for disabled persons

37. The Government of the Republic of Korea has enacted the "Welfare Law for Persons with Disabilities" in order to guarantee equal treatment of disabled persons. The said law prohibits any discrimination against persons with disabilities in employment, education, the grant of a licence, residence, access to public facilities, transportation and in all other social activities.

38. In order to ensure that disabled persons enjoy equal opportunities in political, economic, social and cultural activities, the Korean Government has developed and carried out numerous welfare programmes, including: the grant of a monthly living allowance to persons with severe disabilities who are considered incapable of earning a certain level of income; tax exemptions on automobiles or rehabilitation appliances; and income tax deduction for persons with disabilities.

39. Article 38 of the Welfare Law for Persons with Disabilities provides that national or local governments may establish welfare institutions for disabled persons who suffer difficulties in coping with everyday life. As of the end of 1990, 156 welfare institutions had been established and have been supporting such persons in need. Furthermore, the 12 welfare centres for rehabilitation and vocational training of the disabled have been modernized to provide more opportunities for participation in leisure and social activities.

40. The Minister of Health and Social Affairs, mayors and governors may instruct the relevant public officials to inspect the operational condition, records and other documents of the welfare institutions, or may require the founders and managers of the welfare institutions to submit reports concerning the managements of the institutions to the relevant authorities (The Welfare Law for Persons with Disabilities, Arts. 41-42).

Problems with the implementation of the policy on persons with disabilities

41. Due to Confucian tradition and customs, there are some Koreans who consider it a dishonour to have a disabled family member and thus tend to conceal that fact. This tendency creates an obstacle in establishing and implementing the policy on the disabled. It can however be overcome by the expansion of welfare programmes and by the enhancement of public awareness of this Korean tendency. The Government of the Republic of Korea is determined to guarantee fully the enjoyment of fundamental human rights by the disabled.

Equal protection of the law

42. The principle of equal protection of the law is observed in all legislative, judicial and administrative activities of the State. Under Articles 107(1) and 111(1) of the Constitution, the Constitution Court adjudicates whether a law violates the Constitution and, also whether a law violates the principle of equal protection of the law.

43. Laws and administrative actions which were held unconstitutional by the Constitution Court due to the violation of the equal protection principle are as follows:

    (a) Laws which were held unconstitutional:

        (i) The Bond Provision of the "Special Measures Act Relating to Overdue Loans of Financial Institutions" (89-HUNGA-37, 96 of 24 May 1989). Article 5-2 of the Special Measures Act was held unconstitutional because it unlawfully restricts, in favour of the financial institutions, the right to appeal the decision to allow a public auction in the case of a financial institution applying for an auction.

        (ii) Deposit Money Provision of the "National Assembly Members Election Act" (88-HUNGA-6 of 8 September 1989). Articles 33 and 34 of the National Assembly Members Election Act were declared to be unconstitutional since they discriminate against non-party candidates in favour of party candidates in violation of the principle of equal protection of the law.

        (iii) Restrictions on the place of practice in the "Lawyers Act" (89-HUNGA-102 of 28 November 1989). Article 10(2) and (3) of the Lawyers Act, which contain certain restrictions with respect to the place of practice of lawyers who have practised law for less than 15 years, violates the "equal protection principle" and "the right to choose jobs" provided for in the Constitution.

        (iv) Special Corporate Liquidation Provision of the "Special Measures Act Relating to Overdue Loans of Financial Institutions" (89-HUNGA-98, 101, 105 of 25 June 1990). Article 7-3 of the Special Measures Act violates the equal protection principle and was thus held to be unconstitutional because, notwithstanding the provisions of the Corporate Liquidation Act, it allows financial institutions to sell the property of a bankrupt company by auction for collection of the debt.

0247

(v)   Preference of the National Tax in the "Basic National Tax Act"
        (89-HUNGA-95 of 3 September 1990). Article 35(1) item 3 of the
        Basic National Tax Act was held unconstitutional because it provides
        that national tax shall have priority over any security rights
        established less than one year after the tax payment due date.

(b)   Constitutional petitions:

   (i)   Non-prosecution (89-HUNMA-10 of 14 July 1989). In case a
          prosecutor decides not to prosecute a criminal case due to his
          poor investigation, the decision must be revoked because it
          constitutes a violation of the victim's right of equal
          protection.

   (ii)   Military prosecutor's decision to suspend the indictment
          (89-HUNMA-56 of 27 October 1989). Rightful resistance to a
          superior officer's unjust harsh actions does not constitute the
          offence of resisting a lawful order. Therefore, the military
          prosecutor's decision to suspend, in violation of the right of
          equal protection, the indictment of the petitioner was held
          unconstitutional.

   (iii) Preference in the employment of teachers in the Educational
          Public Official Act (89-HUNMA-89 of 8 October 1990).
          Article 11(1) of the Educational Public Official Act, which
          gives preference to graduates from national teachers colleges
          over graduates from private teachers colleges in the employment
          of teachers, violates the equal protection principle and is
          thus unconstitutional.

   (iv)   Provision relating to the legal clerk examination of the
          "Enforcement Regulation of the Legal Clerk Act" (89-HUNMA-178
          of 15 October 1990). Article 3(1) of the Enforcement
          Regulation of the Legal Clerk Act violates the equal protection
          principle because it prescribes that the legal clerk
          examination shall be held only when the administrative director
          of the court determines that additional legal clerks are needed.

   (v)   Prohibition of local councilmen from having an additional job
          in the Local Councilmen Election Act and the Local Autonomy Act
          (90-HUNMA-28 of 11 March 1991). Article 28(1) item 7 of the
          Local Councilmen Election Act and Article 33(1) item 6 of the
          Local Autonomy Act, which prohibit the directors and officers
          of the Agricultural Cooperative, Fisheries Cooperative and
          Livestock Cooperative from concurrently holding the office of
          local councilmen, violate the right to hold public office and
          the equal protection principle and were thus held
          unconstitutional.

   (vi)   Deposit Money System in the Local Councilmen Election Act
          (91-HUNMA-21 of 11 March 1991). The deposit money system
          contained in Article 36 of the Local Councilmen Election Act
          infringes upon the right to hold public office and the right of
          equality.

0248

44. Fundamental human rights, with the exception of the rights which require Korean nationality as a precondition of enjoyment, such as the right to vote or to hold public office, are equally guaranteed to foreigners in the Republic of Korea regardless of their nationality. The Republic of Korea ratified the International Convention on the Elimination of All Forms of Racial Discrimination on 5 December 1978 and has submitted reports six times in accordance with Article 9 of the Convention.

Remedies available in case of an infringement of rights

45. The laws of the Republic of Korea provide effective remedies to an individual whose rights and freedoms have been infringed by Government agencies or by individuals.

Infringement of the rights by Government agencies

46. Administrative remedies

(a) Petition: In the case of an infringement of fundamental rights by Government agencies, under Article 26 of the Constitution an individual may obtain remedies by petitioning for the nullification or annulment of the relevant administrative actions, or for the removal or punishment of the relevant officials. Article 4 of the Petition Act enumerates the matters for which petitions are available, and the petitioning procedures are provided for in Articles 6 through 8 of the said Act. No person shall be discriminated against or shall suffer any disadvantages on the grounds that the person has filed a petition (Petition Act, Art. 11).

(b) Administrative adjudication: an individual, whose rights or interests have been violated by an illegal or unreasonable administrative action or an exercise or a non-exercise of the Government power by the administrative agencies, may obtain remedies by applying for an administrative adjudication (Administrative Adjudication Act, Art. 1). Article 107(3) of the Constitution provides, "An administrative appeal may be conducted as a procedure prior to a judicial trial. The procedure of administrative appeals shall be determined by law and shall be in conformity with the principles of judicial procedures."

(c) Criminal compensation: In cases where a criminal suspect or an accused person, who has been placed under detention is not indicted or acquitted by a court, the person is entitled to claim compensation from the State under the conditions prescribed by law (Constitution, Art. 28). The Criminal Compensation Act prescribes detailed rules on the compensation for victims of unlawful detention.

47. Court remedies

(a) Administrative litigation: The Supreme Court shall have the power to make a final review of the constitutionality or legality of administrative decrees, regulations or actions (Constitution, Art. 107(2)). The Administrative Litigation Act provides remedies to an individual whose rights or interests have been violated by an illegal administrative action or an exercise or non-exercise of Government power by administrative agencies.

(b) Review of administrative decrees and regulations: Article 107(2) of the Constitution protects fundamental rights by providing the Supreme Court with the power to review the constitutionality or legality of administrative decrees and regulations.

(c) Compensation: In cases where a person has sustained damages due to an unlawful act committed by a public official in the course of his official duties, such a person may claim compensation from the State under the National Compensation Act, which was enacted in accordance with Article 29(1) of the Constitution.

48. Remedies provided by the Constitution Court

(a) Review of the constitutionality of a law: The Constitution Court shall adjudicate the constitutionality of a law upon the request of a court (Constitution, Art. 111(1) item 1). If the constitutionality of a law is at issue in a trial, the court in charge of the trial (including the military court) shall request the Constitution Court to adjudicate the constitutionality of the law. In cases where a party to a trial requests an adjudication of the constitutionality of a law, the court shall request, upon its decision, an adjudication by the Constitution Court (Constitution Court Act, Art. 41(1)). Any law or provisions thereof held unconstitutional shall be null and void from the date of the decision. However, any unconstitutional law or provisions thereof relating to punishment shall be null and void retroactively (Constitution Court Act, Art. 47(2)). One may apply for a retrial in cases where a conviction was based upon the law or provision thereof as held unconstitutional.

(b) Petitions relating to the Constitution: The Constitution Court shall adjudicate the petitions relating to the Constitution (Constitution, Art. 111(1) item 5). Any person whose fundamental rights guaranteed by the Constitution have been infringed by the exercise or non-exercise of Government power, may request the Constitution Court to adjudicate a constitutional petition (Constitution Court Act, Art. 68(1)). A ruling in favour of the constitutional petition shall bind all the agencies of the State and the local governments (Constitution Court Act, Art. 75(1)). In cases where the Constitution Court rules in favour of the constitutional petition against non-exercise of Government power, the relevant administrative agencies shall take new action in accordance with the decision (Constitution Court Act, Art. 75(4)). In addition, the Constitution Court may nullify the exercise of Government power by which fundamental rights were infringed (Constitution Court Act, Art. 75(3)).

49. Remedies provided by special human rights protection institutions

In addition to the above-mentioned remedies through legal procedures, an individual may seek remedies through human rights consultation or legal aid provided by special human rights protection institutions.

(a) Korean Legal Aid Corportion: was established under the Legal Aid Act in order to protect fundamental human rights and to contribute to the promotion of legal welfare by providing legal aid to those who are either in economic difficulty or ignorant of the law (Legal Aid Act, Art. 1).

0250

(b) The Korean Federal Bar Association: has been providing legal aid since June 1985 through the establishment of the Legal Aid Committee and the Legal Aid Fund (Lawyers Act, Art. 67).

Infringement of rights by an individual

50. Complaint and accusation

(a) A person who has been injured in consequence of an offence, and the legal representative, spouse or relatives of the said person many file a complaint in order to seek the prosecution of the offender (Code of Criminal Procedure, Arts. 223, 225(1) and (2), 226). Any person other than the offender and those with the right to file a complaint, who believes that an offence has been committed, may file an accusation (Code of Criminal Procedure, Art. 234(1)).

(b) A complaint or an accusation shall be filed with a prosecutor or a police officer in writing or orally (Code of Criminal Procedure, Art. 237(1)).

(c) Investigation period: In order to provide prompt remedies, Article 257 of the Code of Criminal Procedure prescribes that if a prosecutor investigates a crime on a complaint or an accusation, he shall determine whether or not to indict the case within three months of the filing of the complaint or accusation.

(d) Notice to complainant, accuser or suspect: In cases where a prosecutor decides not to file an indictment with respect to a case based on a complaint or accusation, or to withdraw the indictment or to send the case to another prosecutor's office, the prosecutor shall inform the complainant or accuser of such a decision in writing within seven days after such a disposition has been made (Code of Criminal Procedure, Art. 258(1). In cases where a prosecutor decides not to file an indictment or to send the case to another prosecutor's office, the prosecutor shall promptly inform the suspect of such a decision (Code of Criminal Procedure, Art. 258(2)).

(e) Notice of the reasons for the decision not to file an indictment: In cases where a prosecutor decides not to file an indictment with respect to a case based upon a complaint or accusation, the prosecutor, upon the request of the complainant or accuser, shall inform the complainant or accuser of the reasons therefore in writing within seven days after the decision (Code of Criminal Procedure, Art. 259).

(f) Appeal and reappeal: Any complainant or accuser, who is dissatisfied with a prosecutor's decision not to file an indictment, may appeal the decision to the chief prosecutor of the competent High Prosecutor's Office (Prosecutor's Office Act, Art. 10(1)). Any appellant who is dissatisfied with a decision to reject the appeal referred to in Article 10(1) of the Prosecutor's Office Act, may reappeal the decision to the Attorney General. In cases where the chief prosecutor or the Attorney General determines that the appeal or reappeal is well-founded, the decision shall be rectified (Prosecutor's Office Act, Art. 10(2)).

0251

Remedies available to a victim of a crime

51. Under Article 30 of the Consititution, any citizen who has suffered a
bodily injury or death due to criminal acts of others may receive aid from the
State under the conditions prescribed by law. In accordance with the
provision of the Consititution, the State Aid Act for Victims of Crime
prescribes detailed rules for the payment of State aid. In cases where a
victim of a felony, such as murder or robbery, is unable to obtain
compensation because the criminal is missing or is unable to compensate for
the damages, the State protects the interests of the victim by paying State
aid to the victim or the bereaved family.

Article 3

Enhancement of Women's Status

52. Until the establishment of the Government of the Republic of Korea in
1948, women had to endure sexual discrimination due to prevalent Confucian
tradition. However, the Constitution which was proclaimed on 17 July 1948,
guarantees the equality of men and women and thus allows for women to
participate equally in social activities. In accordance with the equal
protection principle of the Constitution, the Government of the Republic of
Korea has implemented various measures in order to eliminate the
discrimination against women and as a result, the status of women experienced
a revolutionary change in political, economic, social and cultural areas.

53. As a result of strenuous efforts over 30 years, women have achieved the
revision of the discriminatory family law (December 1989), the enactment of
the Gender-equal Opportunity Employment Act, which came into force in April
1988, and the establishment of the Vocational Training Centre for Women, which
has been accepting applicants since March 1991. The Government and the
competent authorities continue to search for measures to stimultate women's
participation in the major public vocational training courses.

Constitutional Guarantees

54. Since its promulgation in 1948, the Constitution has upheld the equality
of men and women as a supreme principle of the State, and this is reflected in
various provisions of the Constitution. The preamble to the Constitution
states, "... to destroy all social vices and injustice, ... and to afford
equal opportunities to every person and to provide for the fullest development
of the individual capabilities in all fields, including political, economic,
social and cultural life by further strengthening the basic free and
democratic order..." and thus emphasizes equal treatment and equal opportunity
for all citizens.

    (a) All citizens shall be assured of human worth and dignity and shall
have the right to pursue happiness (Constitution, Art. 10).

    (b) All citizens shall have the right to equal protection of the laws
and there shall be no discrimination in political, economic, social or
cultural life on account of sex, religion or social status (Constitution,
Art. 11).

(c) Women shall not be subjected to unjust discrimination in terms of employment, wages of working conditions (Constitution, Art. 32) and the State shall endeavour to promote the welfare and rights of women (Constitution, Art. 34).

(d) In addition, the Government shall endeavour to promote equality between men and women in marriage and family life (Constitution, Art. 36).

55. The Government of the Republic of Korea has exerted every effort to enact or modify the relevant laws so as to guarantee the equality of men and women and to enhance women's status, and ratified the Convention on the Elimination of All Forms of Discrimination against Women on 27 December 1984.

Status of women under labour laws

56. In accordance with the equal protection principle of the Constitution, Article 5 of the Labour Standards Act provides "an employer shall not discriminate against employees with regard to the conditions of employment on the basis of sex". In addition, Article 11 of the Labour Union Act provides, "a member of a labour union shall not be discriminated against under any circumstances on account of sex". The Equal Opportunity Employment Act is designed to rectify discriminatory practices in employment between men and women and to enhance the social stutus of women.

The status of women under the criminal law

57. The sole provision relating to the equality of men and women under the criminal law is Article 241 (adultery) of the Criminal Code, which renders equal punishment to the offenders regardless of their sex.

Authorities in charge of women's affairs

58. On 25 February 1988, the office of the Minister of Political Affairs (2) was created and a women was appointed as the Minister. The office devises and implements policies relating to women.

59. The Women's Welfare Division in the Ministry of Health and Social Affairs, and the Women's and Minor's Labour Division in the Ministry of Labour are also in charge of matters relating to women. The Women's Welfare Division devises an overall plan for the social welfare of women and the Women's and Minors' Labour Division is in charge of improving the employment conditions of working women. In addition, the Ministry of Labour has a Women's Affairs Guidance Officer for the special protection of working women.

60. Family welfare Bureaux were established in 15 local administrations in 1988 and women were appointed as directors. In order to promote the social welfare of women, these bureaux maintain close relationship with the Women's Welfare Division in the Ministry of Health and Social Affairs.

61. The National Committee on Women's Policies was established under the control of the Prime Minister on 8 December 1983. As the supreme Government Committee concerned with policies relating to women, it devises the basic policy and supervises the activities of other related Government authorities.

This Committee has up to 25 members who are experts on women's issues and the relevant Ministers. The Prime Minister is the chairman of the Committee.

62. Other Government committees concerned with policies relating to women are the Committee on Working Women, the Committee to Provide Guidance to Women in Prostitution and the Council on Guidance to Women.

Increase of childcare subsidies

63. The Government, realizing that childcare usually prevents married women from working, has established 360 national and public childcare facilities subsidized by the Government, 39 private childcare facilities, 20 office childcare facilities, 1,500 home placement facilities, which between them take care of approximately 48,000 children.

64. The Government enacted the Childcare Act on 14 January 1991. The important provisions of the said Act are as follows:

(a) The State and local governments shall be responsible for the protection of children who are less than six years old (Art. 3).

(b) The owner of a workplace greater than the prescribed size shall establish an office childcare facility. If the facility cannot be established for unavoidable reasons, it must be jointly established with another workplace or the owner shall pay a childcare allowance to the employees (Art. 7(3)).

(c) The State or local governments may subsidize the costs of childcare, such as the cost of establishing and operating the childcare facilities (Art. 22).

(d) There shall be a reduction and/or exemption of taxes from the legal guardian's cost of childcare for children less than six years of age and for the cost incurred by an owner of a workplace for the establishment and operation of the childcare facility.

65. The Government is planning to establish 1,440 childcare facilities for 17,000 children from low-income families as prescribed by law by 1992 and childcare facilities that can accommodate 1,025,000 children by 1995.

Mother-child health protection

66. Under the provisions of the Maternal and Child Health Act the government has improved the maternity protection services and the childcare system by establishing 81 maternal and child health centres and the Mother-Child Health Committee was established in the Ministry of Health and Social Affairs in 1987.

Sexual exploitation

67. Prostitution or other forms of sexual exploitation is prohibited by law in the Republic of Korea. Article 303 of the Criminal Code provides "a person who, through fradulent means or the power of authority, has sexual intercourse with a women under his protection or supervision by reason of business, employment or other relationship, shall be punished...". In order to

eliminate prostitution, the Government enacted the Anti-Prostitution Act in 1961 and its enforcement decree in 1969. The Act prohibits prostitution (Art. 4) and the intermediation of prostitution (Art. 6) and provides that the Government shall establish guidance centres for women in prostitution (Art. 7) and vocational training and employment guidance centres to support such women in building a new life. Prostitution is a crime under the Criminal Code.

68. The Government has established 105 consultation centres in the major cities for women in need of protection; 22 employment guidance centres offer vocational training and guidance to women in prostitution in order to support their return to a normal social life.

Social Participation of Women

69. Since the establishment of the Korean Government, women have enjoyed equal political rights with men. The Constitution provides that "all citizens shall have the right to vote under the conditions prescribed by law" (Art. 24). In addition, Article 25 of the Constitution states "all citizens shall have the right to hold public offices under the conditions as prescribed by law".

70. Women's participation in the State's policy decisions has increase, but the level of participation is still unsatisfactory. There have been 61 women n in the National Assembly so far; 16 members from "the local constituency" and the other 45 members from "the national constituency". Currently, there are 6 women out of a total 299 members in the National Assembly.

71. As of December 1989, there were 181,083 female public officials (23.7 per cent) out of a total of 764,563 officials, 111,831 of the female officials (61.5 per cent) were teachers. The Public Official Employment Regulation, amended by Presidential Decree No. 12730, has deleted the previous provision, which required a separate testing system for men and women, and thus prohibits sexual discrimination in the employment of public officials. Furthermore, since 1991 "education on the equality of men and Women" has been adopted as a required subject in the training programme for public officials.

72. The field of education is the dominant centre of women's social participation. As of April 1990, there were 159,003 female teachers which is 41.33 per cent of all teachers, and the number of female teachers continues to rise.

73. With the increase of members in the political parties, the number of female members has also increased. With regard to the composition of the executive committee of the main political parties, the ruling Democratic Liberal Party has 1 female consultant and 73 female committee members out of 1,698 standing committee members. The opposition New Democratic Pararty, has 2 female members out of 70 members of the executive committee, and the People's Party has 2 female members out of 20 members of the standing committee.

74. The Government guarantees equal treatment of men and women in the eligibility for and score evaluation of the Korean Bar Examination, which confers the licence to practise law in the Republic of Korea. However, the Confucian custom of sexual discrimination has hindered women from entering the

legal field. With the social changes arising out of modernization and industrialization, women's participation in the legal field has gradually increased. As of 31 March 1991, there were 35 female judges, 2 female prosecutors and 21 female lawyers.

75. There are 2,694 female workers in the press which constitutes 12 per cent of all workers in the mass media. They work as reporters, directors, scriptwriters and administrators.

76. Article 21 of the Constitution, along with other provisions, guarantees that all citizens shall enjoy freedom of assembly and association. Many Korean women participate in the activities of private associations.

Education of Women

77. According to Article 31(1) of the Constitution, all citizens shall have an equal right to receive an education corresponding to their abilities. Furthermore, all citizens who have children shall be responsible for their elementary education, at least, and other education as provided by law (Constitution, Art. 31(2)).

78. During the course of industrialization, the percentage of school attendance for women and the percentage of enrolment at the institutions of higher education for women have increased tremendously.

79. Since primary school education was made compulsory in 1948, over 99 per cent of children have attended primary school. As of 1990, the percentage of female students entering high school was 94.96 per cent and the percentage of male students was 96.34 per cent. The percentage of high school female graduates entering college was 32.36 per cent and the the percentage for male students was 33.89 per cent in 1990. In 1988, female students constituted 35.56 per cent of all enrolled college students.

80. Since 1989, the discriminatory descriptions and subjects in the textbooks have been corrected in accordance with the principle of equality between men and women. In addition, efforts have been made to eliminate sexual discrimination in education.

Status of Women in Labour Matters

81. The laws of the Republic of Korea guarantee the equality of men and women with respect to employment. The Constitution provides that all citizens shall have the right and duty to work (Art. 32(1) and (2)) and that all citizens shall have the freedom to choose their occupations (Art. 15). The State shall enact laws to guarantee that the standards of employment protect the dignity of the workers and to guarantee reasonable wages for workers (Constitution, Art. 32(1)). Article 6-2 of the Equal Opportunity Employment Act, amended on 1 April 1989, provides that equal wages shall be paid for equal work, irrespective of sex.

82. Due to rapid industrialization since the 1960s, the number of working women has greatly increased. As of 1990, 7,474,000 women out of 15,897,000 women over 15 years of age were working, making the percentage of working women 47 per ccent. Most of the 8,423,000 women who were not working were housewives or students.

83. There are many opportunities for Korean women to receive vocational training. The Government enacted the Basic Vocational Training Act to promote vocational training for women. As of 1989, 63,429 trainees have received vocational training in 167 subjects, such as electronics and industrial arts, in 295 institutions, i.e, national and local training centres and in-office training centres. To improve the training for women, the Government is planning to establish a vocational training centre for women by 1991.

Status of women in other fields

84. The Constitution guarantees the equality of men and women in accordance with the equal protection principle. Thus, men and women enjoy equal rights with respect to family allowances, bank loans, mortgages and financial credit evaluations. Moreover, women have the right to participate in all cultural activities including sports.

85. Article 23(1) of the Constitution guarantees the right of property to all citizens, and under the relevent laws of the Republic of Korea men and women have equal legal competence concerning property.

Status of women in marriage and family life

86. The Constitution states that individual dignity and equality of the sexes shall be the basis of marriage and family life (Art.36(1)).

Revision of the Discriminatory Family Law

87. As a result of the struggle of Korean Women over three decades, the revision of the discriminatory Family Law was passed by the National Assembly in December 1989. The amendments to the Family Law are considered fairly satisfactory because they reflect most women's requests. The amendments may be summarized as follows:

(a) Adjustment of the Confucian family head system in order to eliminate the discrimination against women under the grand family regime. (The deletion of Arts. 797-799 of the old Civil Code).

(b) Equality in the scope of relatives through extension of the scope of relatives to blood relatives within eighth degree of relationship of both husband and wife (Civil Code, Art. 777).

(c) Improvement of the inheritance system to allow the successors to inherit equal shares irrespective of sex, age and marital status (Civil Code, Art. 1009).

(d) Establishment of the right of both husband or wife to seek a division of the joint property on the basis of his or her contribution to the formation of the property (Civil Code, Art. 839-2).

(e) Establishment of equal parental rights of husband and wife (Civil Code, Art. 909) and the revision of the previous law, which granted fostering and education of a child to his or her father in case an agreement on fostering and education has not been reached, in order to require that the Family Court decide the fostering and education issue (Civil Code, Art. 837).

<u>Article 4</u>

88. In case of an emergency that threatens the existence of the State, the President, in order to cope with the emergency situation, may issue emergency orders, may take financial and economic emergency actions and orders, and may proclaim martial law (Constitution, Arts. 76-77). These emergency powers of the President derive from the duty and responsibility of the President, under Article 66(2) and (3) of the Constitution, to safeguard the independence, territorial integrity and continuity of the State, to protect the Constitution, to pursue the peaceful unification of the homeland and to overcome the crisis of the State.

89. The current Constitution has deleted the emergency powers of the President under the former Constitution, and has vested the President with only the power to issue emergency orders, to take financial and economic emergency actions and orders, and to proclaim martial law (Constitution, Art. 76). Article 37(2) of the Constitution provides that the freedom and rights of citizens may be restricted by law only when absolutely necessary for national security, the maintenance of law and order, or public welfare, and that such restriction may not infringe upon the essential aspects of fundamental rights. This provision also applies to any restrictions on fundamental rights under the emergency powers of the President. Therefore, Articles 76 and 77 of the Constitution are consistent with the derogating measures in case of public emergencies pursuant to article 4, paragraph 1 of the Covenant.

90. The detailed descriptions of the President's emergency powers are as follows:

(a) <u>Constitution, Article 76</u>

(i) Paragraph 1: In time of internal turmoil, external menace, natural calamity or a grave financial or economic crisis, the President may take in respect to them the minimum necessary financial and economic actions or issue orders having the effect of law, only when it is required to take urgent measures for the maintenance of national security or public peace and order, and there is no time to await the convocation of the National Assembly.

(ii) Paragraph 2: In case of major hostilities affecting national security, the President may issue orders having the effect of law, only when it is required to preserve the integrity of the nation, and it is impossible to convene the National Assembly.

(b) **Constitution, Article 77, paragraph 1:** When it is required to cope with a military necessity or to maintain the public safety and order by mobilization of the military forces in time of war, armed conflict or similar national emergency, the President may proclaim martial law under the conditions prescribed by law.

91. Restrictions on fundamental rights under the emergency orders are allowed only by measures designed for the maintenance of national security. Restrictions under the financial or economic emergency orders are allowed only on the financial or economic emergency measures, and the restrictions under martial law are allowed only on certain fundamental rights or powers prescribed in Article 77(3) of the Constitution – the necessity for warrants, freedom of speech, press, assembly and association or the powers of the Executive or Judiciary.

92. Restrictions on fundamental rights are subject to the limitation imposed by Article 37(2) of the Constitution. In addition, the emergency measures are effective only during the period when the survival of the State is at stake.

Control on the exercise of emergency powers

93. The National Assembly, the Courts, and the Constitution Court control the exercise of emergency powers.

    (a) Financial and economic emergency actions and orders

        (i) The National Assembly: The President shall promptly notify the National Assembly of any emergency orders or financial and economic emergency actions or orders issued or taken by him and shall obtain its approval (Constitution, Art. 76(3)).

        (ii) The Court: Even if the emergency orders or the financial and economic orders have been approved by the National Assembly, the Court may still request a decision of the Constitution Court when the constitutionality of these measures is at issue in a trial (Constitution, Art. 107(1)); the Court still has the power to review the constitutionality or legality of these measures (Constitution, Art. 107(2)).

        (iii) The Constitution Court: In cases where the emergency orders or the financial and economic emergency orders have legal effect due to the approval of the National Assembly, the Constitution Court may still adjudicate the constitutionality of these orders upon the request of the courts (Constitution, Art. 111(1) item 1). In addition, the Constitution Court may adjudicate the constitutionality of the financial and economic emergency actions, which were approved by the National Assembly, in the case of a Constitutional petition relating thereto (Constitution, Art. 111(1) item 5).

0259

(b)   Martial law: the President shall notify the National Assembly of a proclamation of martial law without delay (Constitution, Art. 77(4)). In the case that the majority of the members of the National Assembly request the lifting of martial law, the President shall comply (Constitution, Art. 77(5)).

94. The above provisions relating to restrictions on fundamental rights in the case of an emergency do not explicitly refer to the absolute fundamental rights of article 4 of the Covenant. In terms of Korean legal context, it is understood that absolute fundamental rights fall under "the essential aspect of the freedom or right" referred to in Article 37(2) of the Constitution, and thus cannot be restricted under any circumstances.

95. In the case of an exercise of these emergency powers, the Secretary-General of the United Nations shall be notified of the steps and grounds for the exercise. Similar notice shall be rendered when the emergency situation ends. Since the promulgation of the current Constitution, these emergency powers have never been exercised in the Republic of Korea.

Article 5

96. The Government of the Republic of Korea does not interpret the Covenant so as to destroy the rights and freedoms recognized by the Covenant or to restrict the rights more severely than as provided for in the Covenant. On this point, the Constitution states that "All citizens shall be assured of human worth and dignity ... and it shall be the duty of the State to confirm and guarantee the fundamental and inviolable human rights of individuals" (Art. 10) and that "the freedoms and rights of citizens shall not be neglected on the ground that they were not enumerated in the Constitution (Art. 37(2))."

97. No derogation or limitation of fundamental human rights recognized by the Constitution, but not referred to in the Covenant, is allowed on the grounds that they are not stated in the Covenant. For instance, Article 13(3) of the Constitution provides that no citizen shall suffer unfavourable treatment on account of an act committed by a relative.

Article 6

Paragraph 1: the right to life

98. The right to life provided for in article 6, paragraph 1 of the Covenant is not subject to any restrictions even during a State emergency since it is the supreme fundamental human right. Although the right to life is not explicitly stated in the Constitution, it is implicitly guaranteed by Article 10 of the Constitution which provides for the respect of human dignity and by Article 12(1) which provides for personal liberty.

99. With respect to the right to life, the Supreme Court has stated that "Life once lost is never restored. It is absolute and cannot be exchanged for anything in the world. The life of a man is more precious and solemn than the entire world. It is the basis of the solemn existence of mankind". Thus the Court has clearly indicated that the right to life is the supreme fundamental right (Supreme Court Decision, 1969.9.19, 67 Do 988).

0260

100. Every individual, regardless of citizenship, has this inherent right to life. Not only life after birth, but also life of a foetus is protected under the laws of the Republic of Korea (Criminal Code, Chap. 27, the crimes of abortion, Arts. 269-270).

Paragraph 2: death penalty

101. In the Republic of Korea, criminal punishment, including the death penalty, is enforced in accordance with the following provisions and a decision of a competent court:

(a) Constitution, Article 13(1): "No citizen shall be prosecuted for an act which does not constitute a crime under the law in force at the time it was committed.".

(b) Constitution, Article 27(1): the right to be tried in conformity with the law by judges qualified under law.

(c) Criminal Code, Article 1(1): "The criminality and punishability of an act shall be determined by the law prevailing at the time of the commission of that act.".

(d) Criminal Code, Article 41: types of punishment i.e., death penalty, penal servitude, imprisonment, deprivation of qualification, suspension of qualification, fine, detention, minor fine, confiscation.

(e) Code of Criminal Procedure, Art. 321(1): pronouncement of punishment.

(f) Code of Criminal procedure, Art. 459: "Except as otherwise provided in this Code, a decision shall be executed after it has become final.".

As a result of the above rules and procedures, any arbitrary deprivation of life by the State is strictly prohibited.

102. Articles 250-256 of the Criminal Code provides for the punishment of murderers and thus strictly prohibits any arbitrary deprivation of life by an individual.

103. The Korean laws provide for the death penalty in the Criminal Code and the other related regulations. Crimes subject to the death penalty are strictly limited to crimes that threaten the very existence of the State such as an insurrection, heinous crimes such as a murder and other designated felonies. Even with respect to crimes subject to the death penalty, a fair trial by an independent, competent court, the presumption of innocence of the accused, representation by a lawyer, the right of appeal and the right of retrial are fully guaranteed under the following provisions, and due process of law are strictly observed:

(a) The right to be tried by a judge designated by law (Constitution, Art. 27(1));

(b) The right to a prompt trial (Constitution, Art. 27(3));

(c) The presumption of the innocence of the accused (Constitution, Art. 27(4));

(d) The right to receive assistance from a counsel or a counsel assigned by the State (Constitution, Art. 12(4));

(e) The right to appeal (Code of Criminal Procedure, Art. 338 para. 1);

(f) The right to a retrial (Code of Criminal Procedure, Art. 429);

(g) Execution of the death penalty (Code of Criminal Procedure, Art. 465).

104. The Special Deliberation Council on the Revision of the Criminal Law, established 21 June 1985, has studied the issue of abolishing the death penalty. The Council has come to the conclusion that it is premature to eliminate the death penalty in view of the criminal situation in Korea where heinous crimes are being committed, such as the recent incident of a gang of burglars breaking into a peaceful home and raping a woman in the presence of her husband and family. However, the Council also concluded that it would be better to limit the crimes that are subject to the death penalty in consideration of the spirit of the Constitution to respect human dignity and worth, and the international trend toward the abolition of death penalty.

105. Revisions to the Criminal Code are being made in order to limit the crimes which are subject to the death penalty. A new provision, which requires careful consideration when pronouncing the death penalty, has been added to the Criminal Code. In addition, a proposal to eliminate the death penalty for five crimes for which punishment is augmented for certain results, such as causing the death of or injury to a person by setting fire to a dwelling structure, is under consideration.

106. The death penalty was eliminated from 15 provisions of the Special Criminal Act, i.e., the Act Concerning Additional Punishment for Specified Crimes and the Act Concerning Additional Punishment for Specified Financial Crimes.

107. The average period of time between the final death penalty sentence and execution from 1981 to 1990 was as follows:

(a) Total: 82 cases;

(b) Shorter than 1 year: 9 cases (11.0 per cent);

(c) 1-2 years: 31 cases (37.8 per cent);

(d) 2-3 years: 20 cases (24.4 per cent);

(e) 3-4 years: 13 cases (15.8 per cent);

(f) Longer than 4 years: 9 cases (11.0 per cent).

108. A retrial of a death sentence judgement was held three times in 1986 and twice in 1987 and 1988. There was no retrial in 1989 and 1990. In none of these cases was the death sentence judgement reversed.

109. There is a Constitutional petition case pending in the Constitution Court, which contends that Article 338 of the Criminal Code (death penalty for robbers) and Article 57 of the Penal Administration Act (execution of death sentence) are unconstitutional because they violate human worth, dignity and personal liberty.

Abortion

110. Under chapter 27 of the Criminal Code, it is a crime to have or commit an abortion. However, the Maternal and Child Health Act allows abortions for medical, eugenic and moral reasons (Art. 14). With regard to the abolition of crimes of abortion, the Special Deliberation Council on the Revision of the Criminal Law has concluded overwhelmingly to sustain those provisions criminalizing abortion.

Paragraph 4

111. Under Article 26 of the Constitution, and Articles 4, 6 and 7 of the Petition Act, a person who has been sentenced to death may petition for an amnesty or commutation. The President may grant an amnesty or commutation under Article 79 of the Constitution and Articles 2, 3, 5 and 8 of the Amnesty Act. However, a general amnesty can be granted only with the consent of the National Assembly. Of all criminals sentenced to death between 1951 and 1990, one was granted an amnesty and 35 had their sentences commuted.

Paragraph 5

112. The minimum age for the death sentence was raised from 16 to 18 on 31 December 1988 through the revision of the Juvenile Act in conformity with article 6 of the Covenant. Under Article 59 of the Juvenile Act, the death sentence of a juvenile who is less than 18 years of age when the crime is committed, shall be changed to 15 years of penal servitude. Furthermore, Article 469 of the Code of Criminal Procedure provides that the execution of a pregnant woman who is condemned to death shall be stayed until delivery.

Differential treatment of the convicted persons under the death sentence

113. Article 13 of the Penal Administration Act provides that a person sentenced to death shall be committed to a detention place for unconvicted detainees. The detention of persons sentenced to death is to secure the execution of the death penalty, and thus it differs from the detention of unconvicted persons and the execution of the imprisonment of the convicted persons.

114. Article 170 of the Enforcement Decree of the Penal Administration Act prescribes that the provisions relating to the unconvicted detainees shall apply equally to the convicts who received the death sentence. According to this provision, convicts under the death sentence enjoy equal humanitarian treatment as provided to the unconvicted detainees based on respect for human

dignity. In case of request by a convict under the death sentence, various services to relieve the agony and anguish arising from the death sentence are rendered through enlightenment by religious workers and benevolent volunteers.

Maternal and child health care (MCH)

115. In accordance with Article 7 of the Maternal and Child Health Act, the State and local governments have established maternal and child health institutions, (12 Comprehensive Maternal and Child Health Centres, 81 Maternal and Child Health Centres and Child Health Clinics). Under Article 10 of the said Act, maternal and child health institutions have been providing regular medical examinations and immunizations to pregnant women, new-born babies and infants or, when deemed necessary, arranging health worker home visits and health treatment for them.

116. For the proper health care of pregnant women, regular medical examinations (at least 7 times) are provided and the maternal and child health institutions take care of them during delivery. In addition, mothers and new-born babies are properly taken care of by the maternal and child health institutions.

117. The Korean Government has been issuing a Maternal and Child Health Handbook to pregnant women, which explains the MCH programme and records of MCH services provided by the State.

118. The Government has established 81 MCH Centres as of December 1990, in secluded areas and the Offices provide medical care, i.e., delivery assistance, first-aid treatment and family planning.

119. To cut down the infant mortality rate, the Korean Government is implementing various MCH programmes such as regular medical examination, nutritional guidance and health education for pregnant women. In addition, medical examinations and proper treatment for infants between six months and one to two years of age are being provided.

120. The Korean Government has been providing health care services to 1,323,000 children under five years of age (U5's) namely 33 per cent of all the U5's in the Republic of Korea. Under Article 8 of the Maternal and Child Health Act, the Government provides free health care service to pregnant women, usually from low-income families, if the pregnant woman or her guardian so wishes. Vaccination is not covered by the medical insurance to which all Korean people have been entitled since July 1989. Thus, the Government provides, without charge, the cost of vaccination for 70 per cent of all children. In the Republic of Korea, children are vaccinated against tuberculosis (94 per cent), diphtheria, polio and tetanus (97 per cent), polio (96 per cent) and measles, mumps and rubella (89 per cent).

0264

121. With these efforts by the Government, the U5 mortality rate has decreased as follows:

U5 mortality rate

Year	1970	1984	1986	1989
U5 mortality rate (per thousand U5s)	51.0	15.7	12.5	11.0

Organ transplants

122. Article 103 of the Civil Code prohibits any organ transplants that violate good morals and social order. With advances in medical technology, some organ transplants have been performed after the formal and complete consent of the donor or his family. According to a Korean Medical Association report, 2,040 kidney transplants were performed from 1969 to 1989.

Transplantation of an organ from a patient in a state of brain-death

123. According to the Supreme Court precedent in terms of "the heart and lung cease theory", the transplantation of an organ from a patient in a state of brain-death and whose heart and/or lungs still function constitutes a murder under Article 250 of the Criminal Code. Even an organ transplant with the consent of the patient or his family constitutes the crime of murder upon request or with consent (Criminal Code, Art. 252).

124. However, the recognition of brain-death as legal death may contribute to saving another life by means of an organ transplant and to mitigating the mental and economic burdens of the patient and the family by terminating the meaningless treatment. Therefore, some people are seeking the recongition of brain-death as legal death.

Measures and practices to prevent and control communicable diseases

125. In order to prevent and control communicable diseases and protect human rights of patients, communicable diseases are classified as first, second and third class communicable diseases. The Communicable Diseases Prevention Act provides the following:

    (a) State and local authorities establish medical treatment facilities specialized in communicable diseases and pay the costs of preventing communicable diseases and of treating first class communicable diseases;

    (b) People infected with first class communicable diseases or some of the third class diseases shall be treated in isolation (Communicable Diseases Prevention Act, Art. 29, its Enforcement Decree, Art. 5, Enforcement Regulation, Art. 16);

   (c) Patients with first or third class communicable diseases may be
temporarily prohibited from working in restaurants, bars, hotels, etc.
(Communicable Diseases Prevention Act, Art. 30, Enforcement Regulation,
Art. 17);

   (d) Patients with communicable diseases shall not enter public
gatherings or other places where they may transmit the disease (Communicable
Diseases Prevention Act, Art. 31).

126. The isolation of patients with communicable diseases is intended to
facilitate treatment of the patients in an efficient and effective manner. In
practice, the consent of the patient, or his family is required before the
patient is isolated. The clause that prevents patients from entering public
places has never been applied.

AIDS prevention and control

127. The Government has maintained the minimum regulations relating to AIDS
prevention and control in order to protect the human rights of persons with
AIDS/HIV and to prevent further transmission.

   Those who fall under the following categories are subject to the
protective measures by the Government upon a strict evaluation for the public
interests by the Protection Review Committee (AIDS Prevention Act, Art. 14 and
its Enforcement Decree, Art. 15):

   (a) Person with HIV who works or is likely to work at a place, the
employees of which are required to take a sexually transmitted disease
examination;

   (b) Person with HIV with a risk of spreading the infection;

   (c) Person with HIV who has no one to depend on and who is deemed to be
in need of protection, or person with HIV who requires protection in the
protection facilities.

   Since the first person with HIV was discovered in 1985, no protective
measures have been applied to the 138 persons with HIV.

   Article 18 of the AIDS Prevention Act prohibits the person with HIV from
working in restaurants, bars, hotels, etc. Employees of these establishments
areas, under the provisions of the relevant laws, are obliged to have a
periodic sexually transmitted disease check-up. The Government has been
granting subsidies to those infected people who have difficulty in earning a
living.

Convention on the Prevention and Punishment of the Crime of Genocide

128. On 14 October 1950, the Republic of Korea acceded to the Convention on
the Prevention and Punishment of the Crime of Genocide, which entered into
force on 12 January 1951.

0266

Article 7

Prohibition of torture and other inhumane treatments

129. The provisions in the first sentence of article 7 of the Covenant are also reflected in the domestic laws, such as the Constitution and the Criminal Code. The above Korean laws use a variety of expressions, such as torture, intimidation and other harsh treatment. Taken as a whole, these terms correspond to the same kind of treatment expressed in the Covenant.

130. Under the Constitution, all citizens shall be assured of human worth and dignity (Art. 10) and no citizen shall be tortured or be compelled to testify against himself in a criminal case (Art. 12(2)). In cases where a confession is deemed to have been made against the defendant's will due to torture, violence, intimidation, unjustifiably prolonged arrest, or deceit etc., such a confession shall not be admitted as evidence of guilt, nor shall the defendant be punished by reason of such a confession (Art. 12(7)). The above provisions prohibit torture and harsh treatment, and ensure that suspects will not be subject to such inhumane treatment by prohibiting the admission of confession derived from torture and other harsh treatment.

131. There are numerous laws in the Republic of Korea prohibiting any kind of torture and inhumane treatment by the police and public officials. Article 123 of the Criminal Code prohibits a public official from abusing his official authority in order to cause a person to perform an act which the person has no duty to do, or to obstruct the person from exercising his rights. Article 124 of the said Code provides that a person who performs or assists in activities concerning judgement, prosecution, law enforcement or other functions involving restraint of the human body, shall be punished in the case that the person commits the arrest or detention of an individual by abusing his official authority. Article 125 provides that a person, described in Article 124, shall be punished in the case that he commits an act of violence or cruelty against a suspect or any other person in the performance of his official duties.

132. A person who has sexual intercourse with a female held in his custody according to law shall be punished more severely than in the case of normal maltreatment (Criminal Code, Art. 303, para. (2)). Article 4-2 of the Act Concerning Additional Punishment for Specified Crimes prescribes increased punishment for a person who causes injuries or death to an individual in consequence of committing the crimes stipulated in Articles 124 or 125 of the Criminal Code.

133. The prosecutor must inspect the detention places more than once every month in order to investigate whether an illegal detention has been made or not (Code of Criminal Procedure, Art. 198-2). In accordance with the spirit of the above provision, and in order to eliminate cruelty against a person during the course of an investigation, the prosecution strictly guides and supervises the police and the investigators to ensure that they follow the relevant legal procedures.

134. Article 309 of the Code of Criminal Procedure provides that any confession extracted by torture, violence, threat, unjustifiably prolonged detention or which is suspected to have been made involuntarily, shall not be admitted as evidence of guilt.

Request for ruling

135. In the case that the prosecutor decides not to prosecute a case based on a complaint or an accusation with respect to the crimes prescribed in Articles 123 through 125 of the Criminal Code, the person who filed the complaint or accusation may apply to the competent High Court for a ruling on the prosecutor's decision in accordance with the procedures prescribed in Articles 260 through 265 of the Code of Criminal Procedure which are designed to ensure the actual enforcement of the above provisions of the Criminal Code. In the case that the High Court decides that the case shall be committed to the competent district court for a trial, public prosecution shall be deemed to have been instituted in the case and a special prosecutor appointed by the competent district court shall be in charge of prosecuting the case.

Prohibition of torture and cruelty committed in the performance of official duties

136. Law enforcement officers are strictly educated never to inflict torture in the performance of their official duties and a Constitution course is a compulsory subject of the educational programme for all Government officials. As the Prosecutor General instructed, 9,303 law enforcement officers and 5,059 members of the prosecutor's office staff have been educated on the above subject in 222 and 410 courses respectively from 1 January to 31 December 1990.

137. The detainees are equally entitled to file a complaint or an accusation with respect to any incidence of torture, violence or cruelty. In the case that they are victims of the above-mentioned unlawful acts, they may obtain compensation in accordance with the relevant provisions of the Civil Code and if any unlawful acts were committed in the performance of official duties, they shall be entitled to claim just compensation from the State. Twenty-nine public officials have been prosecuted for inflicting torture: nine police officers in 1986, five police officers and four prison officers in 1987, four police officers in 1988, five police officers in 1989, and two police officers in 1990. In the case that prosecution of public officials is accompanied by a claim for damage compensation from the State or a claim based on the Civil Code, a guilty verdict may be accompanied by a court's decision to grant compensation for damages.

138. By denying the admissibility of a confession made against a defendant's will due to torture in the following instance, the Supreme Court has actually prohibited torture, violence, intimidation and unduly prolonged arrest which are committed in order to obtain a confession from a suspect or the accused. In case the accused had made a confession against his will due to torture during investigation by police and the accused made the same confession under coerced state of mental oppression during investigation by the prosecutor, the fact that no torture was committed during the investigation by the prosecutor does not preclude the conclusion that confessions were involuntary and thus inadmissible (Supreme Court decision, 13 October 1981, 81-TO-2160).

0268

139. Article 10 of the Constitution protects the right of an individual to not be subjected to a medical or scientific experiment without his consent. This right is provided for in the second sentence of article 7 of the Covenant. A medical or scientific experiment carried out without the individual's consent constitutes the crime of bodily injury and the crime of violence (Criminal Code, Arts. 257, 260). In the spirit of international efforts to protect human rights, the Government is seriously considering the accession to the Convention against Torture and Other Cruel, Inhuman or Degrading Treatment or Punishment. In addition, from 1988 to 1990, the Government contributed $US 15,000 to the United Nations Voluntary Fund for Victims of Torture, to participate in the concerted efforts of the international community to fight against torture and other harsh treatment or punishment.

Article 8

140. The Constitution does not explicitly prohibit slavery. However, according to Article 10 of the Constitution, there is no doubt that slavery is unlawful. Article 10 of the Constitution protects human dignity, fundamental human rights and the right to pursue the free development of oneself.

141. In accordance with the above provision, the Criminal Code provides that a person, who forces, through violence or intimidation, another to perform an act which the latter does not have a duty to do, or who kidnaps another, or buys or sells another for the purpose of transporting him out of the Republic of Korea, shall be subject to penal servitude (Arts. 324, 288, 289, 292, 293). Furthermore, if the kidnapper under the above provisions kills or causes the death or the injury of the kidnapped, the person shall be subject to increased punishment (Act Concerning the Additional Punishment for Specified Crimes, Art. 5-2).

142. Article 12(1) of the Constitution provides that no person shall be subject to involuntary labour except as provided by law and through lawful procedures. In accordance with this provision, the Labour Standards Act prohibits forced labour and excessive work (Arts. 6, 55-57) and the Anti-Prostitution Act prohibits prostitution and enticement or intermediation thereof and provides for penal servitude or penalty for those who violate the provisions of the said Act (Arts. 4-6, 14-17).

143. The Employment Security and Promotion Act provides that a person, who engages in a placement service or the recruitment of employees using violence, threat, illegal confinement etc., shall be subject to penal servitude or a fine (Art. 29).

144. Under the Child Welfare Act, a provincial governor who finds that a person with parental authority abuses that authority, commits misconduct or cannot exercise the authority for a significant reason whatsoever, may request from a court, the forfeiture of the parent authorities. And a person, who makes his child beg for food or who begs for food by using the child, shall be subject to penal servitude or a fine (Arts. 15, 18, 34). In addition, any legal act for the purpose of committing slavery shall be void under Article 103 of the Civil Code.

145. With respect to imprisonment with hard labour set forth in paragraph 3(b) of the Covenant, the Criminal Code provides for penal servitude with a certain amount of labour (Art. 41) and a substitute term of lock-up at a place of hard labour in the case that a fine is not paid in full (Art. 70).

146. With respect to labour that is not compulsory labour under paragraph 3(c) of the Covenant, or alternative service for conscientious objectors to military duty, the Constitution provides that all citizens shall have the duty of national defense under the conditions prescribed by law (Art. 39(1)). The Supreme Court has decided that a Jehovah's Witness, who refuses the duty of national defense is subject to the punishment prescribed in the Military Service Act, and the so-called "conscientious decision" is not included in the freedom of conscience protected by Article 19 of the Constitution (Supreme Court decision, 22 July 1969, 69-TO-934).

Article 9

Right to liberty and prohibition of arbitrary arrest and detention

Paragraph 1

147. Article 12(1) of the Constitution provides "All citizens shall enjoy personal liberty. No person shall be arrested, detained, searched, seized or interrogated except as provided by law. No person shall be punished or placed under preventive restrictions except as provided by law and through lawful procedures". In addition, Article 12(3) provides that a warrant issued by a judge upon the request of a prosecutor shall be presented in the case of an arrest, detention, seizure or search.

148. In accordance with these provisions of the Constitution, the Code of Criminal Procedure prescribes strict requirements for arrest and detention. The Court may detain the accused when there are resonsable grounds to suspect that the person has committed a crime and he has no fixed dwelling or there are reasonable grounds to suspect that the person may destroy evidence or that he may escape (Code of Criminal Procedure, Art. 70). In order to place the accused under detention, a warrant containing the following items must be issued and presented to the accused: the name and address of the accused, description of the crime, essential facts of the charge, the place of detention, the date of issue, the effective period of the warrant, a statement that after the lapse of the effective period the warrant may not be executed and must be returned to the court of issuance, and the name and seal of the judge issuing the warrant (Code of Criminal Procedure, Arts. 73, 75, 85).

149. Under the Code of Criminal Procedure, a prosecutor or a police officer may detain a suspect with a warrant issued by a competent court upon a request by the prosecutor (Art. 201). However, in the case that there is reasonable ground to suspect that the suspect committed a crime punishable by death, imprisonment for life or imprisonment of three or more years, and there are reasonable grounds to believe that the suspect may destroy evidence or escape, and it is not possible to obtain a warrant due to the urgent situation (Art. 206), or in the case that the suspect committed a crime in the presence of a police officer (Arts. 211-214), the suspect may be detained without a warrant. In case of detention without a warrant, the prosecutor or police

officer must obtain a warrant within 48 hours or 72 hours from the time of arrest (Art. 207). In case the warrant is not obtained within the time period, the suspect shall be released immediately (Arts. 207 and 213-2).

150. Although the Code of Criminal Procedure strictly requires a warrant for arrest, it contains no provisions requiring a warrant for the temporary detention of a suspect. Therefore, it has been pointed out that there is a discrepancy between the norms of the Code of Criminal Porcedure and the actual practices of investigatory agencies, in that the agencies sometimes detain a suspect who is willing to accompany the officer to the police station, and request the issuance of a warrant for detention after conducting an investigation. In response to the above criticism, the Government is exerting efforts to improve the situation by the following:

(a) The Police Officers' Duty Performance Act has been amended twice, on 31 December 1988 and 8 March 1991. By strictly regulating the procedures for the suspect's voluntary submission into police custody in the following way, the amended Act prevents the abuse of the suspect's voluntary submission into police custody and the human rights violations resulting therefrom: "A suspect may refuse a police officer's request for a voluntary submission into custody". (Art. 3(2)). "In the case of a suspect's voluntary submission into police custody, the police shall notify the family or close relatives of the suspect of the identity of the officer who took the suspect into custody, the place of custody and the reasons for custody, or shall allow the suspect to contact them and shall notify the suspect that he has the right to the assistance of a defence counsel." (Art. 3(5)). "In case of a voluntary submission into police custody, the police may not detain the suspect for more than six hours." (Art. 3(6)).

(b) The Government continues to search for ways to improve the entire arrest and detention system. In addition, the Government is making efforts to ensure that suspects are arrested pursuant to a warrant based upon sufficient evidence, or are arrested without a warrant only in the case of an urgent situation prescribed in the Code of Criminal Procedure.

Notification of the charge and the reasons for arrest

Paragraph 2

151. No person shall be arrested or detained without being informed of the reasons therefore and of his right to the assistance of a defence counsel. The family of a person arrested or detained, and other individuals designated by law, shall be notified without delay of the reasons for and the time and place of the arrest or detention. (Constitution, Art. 12(5)). In accordance with this provision, Article 72 of the Code of Criminal Procedure provides that the accused shall not be placed under detention unless the court has informed the accused of the facts of the alleged crime, the reasons for detention and the fact that the accused may select a defence counsel, and unless the court has given the accused the opportunity to defend himself. In addition, Article 88 of the Code of Criminal Procedure provides that the accused shall be informed of the facts concerning the charge against him and the fact that the accused may select a defence counsel.

152. The right of the accused to defend himself was reinforced by Article 87 of the Code of Criminal Procedure, as amended on 28 November 1987, which provides that in the case that the accused is detained, his defence counsel shall be notified immediately, in writing, of the reasons for the detention. (Prior to the amendment, the defence counsel was not informed of the reasons for detention and the notice was made in writing within three days from the time of detention.) The Supreme Prosecutor's Office Regulation No. 172 (3 May 1988) prescribes that the detention notification form shall contain the statement of the facts of the alleged crime, and that a copy of the warrant shall be given to the defence counsel upon the counsel's request. In the case of an urgent arrest without a warrant, the reason why it was impossible to obtain the warrant shall also be given (Code of Criminal Procedure, Art. 206(1)).

Speedy trial and restrictions on detention of the accused

153. All citizens shall have the right to a speedy trial. The accused shall have the right to a public trial without delay in the absence of any justifiable reasons (Constitution, Art. 27(3)). If a confession is deemed to have been made against the defendant's will due to an unduly prolonged detention, such a confession shall not be admitted as evidence of guilt, nor shall a defendant be punished by reason of such a confession (Constitution, Art. 12(7)). Under the above-mentioned provisions, the right of an arrested offender to a speedy trial is ensured.

154. The Code of Criminal Procedure contains provisions to limit the period of detention reasonably and to allow the suspect to be released at each step of the criminal procedure as follows:

(a) The period of detention by a police officer and a prosecutor is limited to 10 days each, i.e., if a police officer arrests a suspect, the suspect shall be released if he or she is not transferred to the prosecutor within 10 days, and the suspect shall also be released if the prosecutor does not file an indictment within 10 days (Code of Criminal Procedure, Arts. 202, 203). However, detention by a prosecutor may be extended at his request only once for no longer than 10 days. In the request, the grounds for such an extension shall be stated (Code of Criminal Procedure, Art. 205). However, since violations of the National Security Law require prolonged investigation and information gathering, the detention period may be extended for a total of 50 days upon the request of a police officer (once) or a prosecutor (twice) (National Security Law, Art. 19).

(b) The period of detention and trial by a court shall not exceed two months. In the case that continuation of the detention is especially necessary, the period of detention may be extended twice by a ruling of the court and the extended period of detention shall not exceed two months (Code of Criminal Procedure, Art. 92(1) and (2)). If the trial does not come to an end during the period of detention, the accused must be released and the trial shall proceed without the detention of the accused.

(c) After the indictment, the accused in detention or the defence counsel may request release on bail (Code of Criminal Procedure, Art. 94). When request for release on bail has been made, it must be allowed except for

0272

certain cases (Art. 95) and if a court deems it proper, it may permit release on bail _ex officio_ (Art. 96). Recent figures on the operation of bail system are as follows:

(number of persons)

Kind Year	Request	Permitted	Not Permitted	Bail ex officio
1989	29 801	17 664	12 137	110
1990	37 585	22 701	14 884	114

Review of the legality of detention

Paragraph 4

155. Article 12(6) of the Constitution provides that any person who is arrested or detained shall have the right to request the court to review the legality of the arrest or detention. Furthermore, Article 214(2) (Review of the Legality of Detention) and Article 214(3) (Restrictions on Re-arrest) of the Code of Criminal Procedure provide for the right to request the review of the legality of all crimes.

Criminal compensation

Paragraph 5

156. Article 28 of the Constitution provides that in case a criminal suspect or an accused person who has been placed under detention is not indicted as provided by law or is acquitted by a court, such a person shall be entitled to claim just compensation from the State under the conditions prescribed by law. The Criminal Compensation Act has been enacted in accordance with this provision. The Criminal Compensation Act, amended on 28 November 1987, has expanded the types of people who may seek compensation from the State by providing that suspects released for lack of evidence are also entitled to compensation. (Prior to the amendment, only the accused persons who had been acquitted could seek compensation from the State.) Through the revision of the Enforcement Decree of the Criminal Compensation Act, compensation of 8,000 won per day was increased to 15,000 won per day.

Article 10

Humane treatment of detained persons

Paragraph 1

157. In accordance with Article 10 of the Constitution, which guarantees respect for human rights, any person placed under detention in a prison or other detention place is accorded humane treatment based on respect for human dignity.

0273

Treatment of the inmates

158. In accordance with the menu determined by the inmates Meal Regulation Committee composed of nutrition specialists, inmates are provided with meals of 3,150 Kcal per day (Penal Administration Act, Art. 21, its Enforcement Decree, Arts. 78-82).

159. For sanitary reasons, sufficient clothes and bedsheets, which are appropriate for the season, are supplied to and are regularly changed for the inmates (Penal Administration Act, Art. 20, its Enforcement Decree, Arts. 73, 75, 76).

160. In order to take care of the inmates, two to five doctors, who reside at detention places, provide medical treatment, regular check-ups and epidemic prevention. An inmate may also receive medical attention at his own expense upon request of a family member or defence counsel (Penal Administration Act, Arts. 25, 26, 28, 29 and its Enforcement Decree, Art. 97-105).

Segregation

Paragraph 2

161. All persons in the detention places are segregated according to their status, such as whether the person is convicted, adult or juvenile, male or female. Even within the same detention place, they are accorded separate treatment and accommodation based on the number of times the person has committed a crime, the type of crime, etc.

162. Unconvicted detainees are committed to detention houses whereas convicted detainees are committed to prisons. Even when a prison and a detention house are built in one place, unconvicted and convicted detainees are accorded separated accommodation (Penal Administration Act, Art. 2(4) and (5)). As unconvicted detainees are presumed innocent until proven guilty (Constitution, Art. 27(4)), they are entitled to prepare and submit trial documents, to communicate with their defence counsels, to have access to general information including the newspapers. Aside from the minimum duty imposed on them so as to secure order at the detention institution, they receive the same treatment as is rendered to civilians (Penal Administration Act, Arts. 45, 65).

163. Convicted persons who are 20 or more years of age shall be committed to the prisons, while convicted persons who are under 20 years of age shall be committed to juvenile correction centres. In addition, unconvicted detainees who are under 20 years of age shall be separately accommodated within detention places for unconvicted detainees (Penal Administration Act, Arts. 2-4, Art. 11, Regulation on the Separate Accommodation of Juvenile Detainees). Basically, juvenile convicts with similar problems are accommodated in the same detention places. Therefore, the juvenile correction centre located in Cheonan city accommodates first offenders and the juvenile correction centre in Kimcheon city accommodates repeat offenders.

164. Female convicts are accommodated in female prisons and unconvicted female detainees are in segregated accommodation in detention places. Female detainees are treated in a manner that is appropriate for their physical characteristics (Penal Administration Act, Arts. 4, 30).

Penitentiary system

Paragraph 3

165. The purpose of the Penal Administration Act is to reform and rehabilitate convicted persons through vocational training and the cultivation of a sound spirit and work ethic.

166. In order to return convicted persons to a normal life in society, the following education programmes are carried out in the correction facilities:

(a) Restoration of morals through education;

(b) Access to social information and intellectual education;

(c) Promotion of self-improvement through technical education and vocational training.

Education

167. Courses equivalent to elementary, middle and high school education are offered to convicted persons. Juvenile convicts may obtain education from the correspondence high school and exemplary convicts who graduated from high school may enter the correspondence university. There are also study groups for the convicts in order to enable them to pass the qualifying examination to enter schools of higher education. In addition, in order to correct the criminal tendencies of the convicts, renowned people are invited for moral education (2 weeks per year) and social education (1 week per year) (Penal Administration Act, Arts. 32, 34, its Enforcement Decree, Arts. 112, 113, Cumulative Correction Treatment Regulation, Art. 63, Regulation on the Education of the Convicts). In 1990, 9 convicts passed the qualifying examination for middle school, 177 convicts passed the qualifying examination for high school and 361 convicts obtained the certificate for high school graduation by passing the qualifying examination.

Convicts' right to communicate

168. According to Article 18 of the Penal Administration Act, an inmate may see his relatives and is permitted to see other persons when deemed necessary. However, in the interests of inmates, an inmate may see other persons except in limited cases where the meeting is deemed harmful for the rehabilitation of the inmate. An unconvicted person may be restricted from communicating with other persons by an order of the court, due to the possibility that necessary evidence may be destroyed. An inmate who has violated prison regulations and is thus under a disciplinary punishment, is prohibited from communciating with other persons (Penal Administration Act. Art. 46). Even in this case, the convict may communicate with his family members if deemed necessary. However, the right to communciate with the defence counsel is never restricted.

169. Inmates may send and receive letters without any restrictions, except in limited cases where there is a possibility that the relevant evidence may be

0275

destroyed or where the order at the prison may be disturbed (Penal
Administration Act, Art. 18, its Enforcement Decree, Arts. 54, 56, 61,
Cumulative Correction Treatment Regulation, Arts. 45, 56).

170. Inmates are allowed to enjoy radio and television programmes which
contribute to the restoration of their morals and self-improvement (Cumulative
Correction Treatment Regulation, Art. 55). Furthermore, inmates are permitted
to read newspapers and books and other publications that are not inappropriate
or that do not encourage crimes (Penal Administration Act, Art. 33).

Religion

171. Inmates are free to worship according to their own religion and religious
workers are permitted to enter the prison in order to perform religious
activities for inmates.

Home leave

172. Programmes of home leave and adaptation to social life have been
implemented in order to assist inmates in returning to a normal life in
society. These programmes are linked with the programme of release on parole
for exemplary inmates (Penal Administration Act, Arts. 44, 49-52, its
Enforcement Decree, Art. 139, Cumulative Correction Treatment Regulation,
Art. 88 and Home Leave Enforcement Regulation).

Civilians' participation in inmates' rehabilitation

173. Renowned people from the community, such as social workers, lawyers and
businessmen assist in rehabilitating inmates through religious lectures and
mediation of job opportunities. The Religious Guidance Committee which is
composed of pastors, monks and priests, provides religious guidance to inmates
through religious education and counselling, etc.

Technical and vocational training

174. In order to enable inmates to make a living after their release from
prison, they are offered vocational training on 54 subjects such as computers,
carpentry, etc. As a result, almost all inmates have acquired technician
certificates and many have won awards in technical skills competitions. In
addition, the inmates are provided with vocational training according to their
work experience, interests and age and are provided with compensation of up to
3,000 won per day for their work in order to assist them to make a living
after they return to society (Penal Administration Act, Art. 39). In 1990,
3,329 inmates acquired the technician certificate.

Open correction facilities

175. Exemplary inmates in open correction facilities and general correction
facilities are permitted to commute to companies in order to receive technical
training. After their release from prison, these inmates are guaranteed a job
in these companies.

0276

Cultivation of a sound and stable personality

176. Juvenile inmates are permitted to participate in sports, singing and speech contests, to watch movies and television and listen to the radio so that they may cultivate a sound and stable personality.

Parole

177. Since a long period of detention and the environment of places of detention significantly affect the character of juvenile inmates, Article 65 of the Juvenile Act provides for more lenient standard of parole for juveniles than adults. Accordingly, a juvenile inmate who has served the following period may be released on parole:

    (a) 5 years in case of a life sentence;

    (b) 3 years in case of a 15 year sentence;

    (c) One third of the minimum term of an indeterminate sentence.

Rehabilitation of juvenile offenders

178. Juvenile offenders between 14 and 19 years of age, who were transferred to a juvenile reformatory in accordance with Article 32(1) No. 6 and 7 of the Juvenile Act (protected juveniles), are treated in a humane manner that provides an appropriate environment for the further development of stable and disciplined character (Juvenile Reformatory Act, Art. 5).

Upgraded treatment

179. The treatment of protected juveniles is upgraded step-by-step according to improvements in their character and behaviour (Juvenile Reformatory Act, Art. 6, its Enforcement Decree, Arts. 5, 6).

Separate treatment

180. (a) Review

    The place and period of detention and educational courses for new juvenile inmates are determined by the Protected Juvenile Treatment Committee after 10 days of review (Enforcement Decree of the Juvenile Reformatory Act, Arts. 4, 11, 14 and 15).

    (b) Separate detention

    Juvenile reformatories are classified and operated according to the following categories: four educational reformatories, three vocational training reformatories, one female reformatory, one special reformatory and two general reformatories. The place of detention for the juvenile inmates is determined by such factors as their sex, age, number of times of entering the reformatory, crime, sentence and the educational course they are required to take, etc. (Juvenile Reformatory Act, Art. 8 and its Enforcement Decree, Arts. 4, 11, 15 and 16).

0277

Detention period

181. The detention period for juveniles is flexible and depends on their behaviour at the detention place. The period of detention is as follows:

    (a) Six months or less for a juvenile inmate under the minimum sentence;

    (b) Thirteen months or more but less than 18 months for a juvenile inmate whose rehabilitation is deemed difficult;

    (c) Eighteen months or more for a juvenile inmate whose rehabilitation is deemed extremely difficult.

In all cases, the maximum period of detention cannot exceed two years (Juvenile Act, Art. 32, para. 1, No. 6 and 7, Juvenile Reformatory Act, Arts. 43 and 44, Protection and Supervision Act, Art. 28(1), Juvenile Reformatory Manual, Art. 21(2)).

Detention facilities

182. In the juvenile reformatories, each inmate has three square metres of space. The educational programmes for juvenile inmates are generally identical with that of regular schools in society. Inmates are permitted to watch television, read newspapers and participate in sports activities during their leisure time.

183. Protected juvenile inmates are provided with everything they need for their life and education in the detention places. In every juvenile reformatory, there are doctors and nurses to treat the juvenile inmates and if a proper treatment is not possible within the reformatory, the inmates are taken to an outside hospital.

184. A juvenile inmate is permitted, without any restriction, to meet people other than those who are deemed to be harmful to him (Juvenile Reformatory Act, Art. 18, its Enforcement Decree Arts. 48, 50).

Petitions

185. In every reformatory, there are boxes for petitions by the juvenile inmates and the petitioning inmate is notified of the relevant decision promptly. At least once every month, a poll is conducted on the conditions of detention and the results of the poll are taken into account in operating the reformatory (Juvenile Reformatory Act, Arts. 10, 11 and its Enforcement Decree, Arts. 19, 20).

Control of correction facilities

186. In order to protect the human rights of convicts in the correction facilities and to ensure that they receive appropriate treatment, strict controls are imposed on every correction facility.

    (a) A public official designated by the Minister of Justice inspects correction facilities such as prisons, juvenile reformatories and detention places at least once a year (Penal Administration Act, Art. 5(1)).

0278

(b) The Board of Audit and Inspection inspects correction facilities in order to supervise and improve their operation and management (Board of Audit and Inspection Act, Art. 20).

(c) Judges and prosecutors may inspect the correction facilities in order to ensure just execution of criminal penalties and to check the conditions of the detention of unconvicted persons (Penal Administrations Act, Art. 5(2)).

Remedies

187. In case an inmate has any complaints regarding treatment at the prison, he may petition the Minister of Justice in writing or the public official who is making the inspection rounds, either in writing or orally (Penal Administration Act, Art. 6). He may also petition the prison chief by requesting an interview (Enforcement Decree of the Penal Administration Act, Art. 9). In any case, the confidentiality of the petition is guaranteed (Enforcement Decree of the Penal Administration Act, Art. 4, 6). In the case of an infringement of human rights, a complaint, accusation, claim for compensation from the State and administrative petition are available in addition to the above-mentioned measures. In case a remedy for an infringement of fundamental rights guaranteed by the Constitution is not available through the legal procedures, a constitutional petition may be made to the Constitution Court (Constitution Court Act, Art. 68).

Standard minimum rules for the treatment of prisoners

188. As has been explained in detail in the preceding paragraphs, the penal administration laws and regulations of the Republic of Korea reflect most of the "Standard Minimum Rules for the Treatment of Prisoners" adopted by the United Nations.

Article 11

189. Under the Korean legal system, failure to perform contractual obligations may incur civil liability but does not constitute a crime. Thus, no person may be arrested or detained on the grounds that he failed to perform contractual obligations.

190. The Special Deliberation Council on the Revision of the Criminal Law in the Ministry of Justice has once considered criminalizing the failure to perform contractual duties in order to punish debtors who can afford to meet their obligations but evade doing so. However, it was concluded that such criminalization is not in accordance with the spirit of the Covenant.

191. The Code of Civil Procedure, amended on 13 January 1990, provides that a court, at the request of a creditor, may order a debtor to submit an affidavit describing his property and punish the debtor who refuses to submit the affidavit or presents a false one (Art. 524(8)).

Article 12

192. Article 14 of the Constitution provides that "all citizens shall enjoy freedom of residence and the right to move at will". Therefore, all citizens are free to move, to emigrate and to travel in and out of the Republic of Korea. Although the Constitution does not contain an explicit provision, it fully guarantees the right of a citizen to enter his own country provided for in article 12, paragraph 4 of the Covenant.

193. The right stated in this Article may be restricted in accordance with the following provisions only when it is necessary for national security, public order or public welfare:

(a) Restriction on the residence of an accused person when execution of his detention was suspended (Code of Criminal Procedure, Art. 101(1));

(b) Restriction on leaving Korea for a person who is under criminal investigation (Immigration Law, Art. 4) and restriction on the area of activity for those who were granted permission to land (Immigration Law, Arts. 12(2), 13(2), 14(2));

(c) Temporary isolation of a patient with an infectious disease (Communicable Disease Prevention Act, Art. 37);

(d) Restriction by special measures of the martial law commander (Martial Law Act, Art. 9).

Article 13

194. A foreigner, who violates the provisions of the Immigration Law, may be expelled from the Republic of Korea (Immigration Law, Art. 45).

195. The persons who may be expelled under the Immigration Law are those who threaten the national security or public order, such as:

(a) A person who entered the Republic of Korea without an entry visa (Art. 45(1) and (3));

(b) A person who is not permitted to enter the Republic of Korea (Art. 45(2));

(c) A person who has landed without permission (Art. 45(4));

(d) A person who has violated the conditions set forth in the landing permission (Art. 45(5));

(e) A person who is in Korea after the expiration of a visa (Art. 45(6));

(f) A person who has been released after having been sentenced to imprisonment or a more severe punishment (Art. 45(10)).

196. A foreigner may be expelled in accordance with the procedures provided for in Articles 46 to 64 of the Immigration Law. Any foreigner under

0280

investigation for expulsion is guaranteed the right to submit pleadings against his expulsion to the competent authority. When an expulsion order is issued, the foreigner shall be informed by the Immigration Office and is guaranteed the right to appeal to the Minister of Justice.

197. In addition, a foreigner under an expulsion order may institute an administrative litigation with respect to the order. If the defendant has complaints about the judgement of the administrative litigation, he may appeal to the Supreme Court.

Article 14

Equality before the courts, right to a fair, open and independent trial

Paragraph 1

198. Article 11 of the Constitution states that "All citizens shall be equal before the law". Furthermore, right to a fair, open and independent trial is guaranteed by Article 27(1) and (3) and Chapter 5 (Arts. 101-110) of the Constitution.

199. Article 27(1) of the Constitution states that "all citizens shall have the right to be tried in conformity with the law by judges qualified under the Constitution and the law". The provisions of the Constitution and the Court Organization Act concerning the qualification of the judges are as follows:

　　(a) Article 42 of the Court Organization Act, which was promulgated in accordance with Article 101(3) of the Constitution, prescribes the qualification of the judges.

　　(b) Article 104 of the Constitution provides:

　　　　(i) That the Chief Justice of the Supreme Court shall be appointed by the President with the consent of the National Assembly;

　　　　(ii) That the Supreme Court Justices shall be appointed by the President on the recommendation of the Chief Justice and with the consent of the National Assembly;

　　　　(iii) That judges other than the Chief Justice and the Supreme Court Justices shall be appointed by the Chief Justice with the consent of the Conference of the Supreme Court Justices.

　　(c) In order to ensure the independence of the court, the Constitution prescribes the term of office and the retirement age of the judges (Art. 105) and further guarantees the independence of the judges by stating that "no judge shall be removed from office except by impeachment or by a sentence of imprisonment or heavier punishment ..." (Art. 106).

0281

(d) The Constitution also provides that "Judges shall rule independently according to their conscience and in conformity with the Constitution and law".

(e) Judges may be precluded from adjudicating a case for reasons prescribed by law.

200. Article 27(3) of the Constitution provides that "All citizens shall have the right to a prompt trial" and that "The accused shall have the right to a public trial without delay in the absence of justifiable reasons to the contrary".

201. Article 109 of the Constitution also provides that "Trials and decisions of the courts shall be open to the public. Provided, however, that when there is a danger that such trials may undermine the national security, or disturb public safety and order or may be harmful to public morals, trials may be closed to the public by a court decision".

202. The Court Organization Act and the Code of Criminal Procedure contain detailed provisions to enforce the principle of open trials. Article 57 of the Court Organization Act provides that if a court decides to close a trial to the public because an open trial might endanger national security, public peace and order or good public morals, the court must indicate the reasons therefor and may admit to the trial those it deems appropriate. The record of the trial shall state whether or not the trial was open to the public and if it was not open to the public, the reasons why it was held in closed session (Code of Criminal Procedure, Art. 51(2), item 5). When the principle of open trials is violated, this may be the subject of an appeal (Code of Civil Procedure, Art. 394(1), Code of Criminal Procedure, Art. 361-5, item 9). However, Article 13 of the Non-Contentious Cases Act states that "Trials of non-contentious cases shall not be open. However, the court may permit anyone whom it deems appropriate to attend the trial" and the Code of Civil Reconciliation Procedure provides that "Reconciliatory procedures shall not be open. However, the judge in charge of the reconciliation may permit anyone whom he/she deems appropriate to attend the hearing."

Presumption of innocence

Paragraph 2

203. While the presumption of innocence was not explicitly provided for in the earlier Constitutions, Article 27(4) of the current Constitution provides that an accused person shall be presumed innocent until proven guilty.
Article 275-2 of the Code of Criminal Procedure also provides for the presumption of innocence. Article 118(2) of the Rules of Criminal Procedure also states that documents or any other articles, which may cause the court to have a presupposition on the case, shall not be attached to the indictment. Under the above-mentioned provisions, presumption of innocence is the resolute principle of criminal procedure.

0282

Right of the accused in a trial

Paragraph 3

204. Regarding the right of the accused in a trial, Korean laws provide for the following safeguards:

    (a) Right to be promptly notified the details of the crime the accused is suspected to have committed:

        (i) When a suspect or an accused is arrested or detained, he shall be immediately notified of the reasons for the arrest or detention (Code of Criminal Procedure, Arts. 72, 88, 209). In the case of a public trial, the court shall send, at least five days prior to the first trial date, a copy of the indictment to the accused or his defence counsel (Code of Criminal Procedure, Art. 266).

        (ii) In the case that there is a change in the charges during a trial, the court shall promptly notify to the accused or his defence counsel of the reasons thereof. In the case that the change is deemed to place the accused at a further disadvantage, the court may, ex officio or upon the request of the accused or his defence counsel, grant a recess for a period necessary for the accused to prepare his defence (Code of Criminal Procedure, Art. 298(3) and (4)). Such provisions ensure that the accused and his defence counsel are informed of the facts concerning the charges against the accused in advance and prepare their defence against the charges.

    (b) Right to have sufficient time and appropriate conveniences for the preparation of defence and the right to communicate with his defence counsel:

        (i) Article 12(4) of the Constitution provides that any person who is arrested or detained shall have the prompt assistance from a defence counsel and Article 12(5) further provides that no person shall be arrested or detained without being informed of the reasons therefor, and of his right to the assistance from defence counsel.

        (ii) In this connection, Article 34 of the Code of Criminal Procedure states that the defence counsel may interview the accused or suspect who is in detention, deliver to or receive from the accused or suspect any documents and other materials and have a doctor treat the accused or the suspect.

        (iii) The Supreme Court has recently decided that the right to communicate with the defence counsel may not be restricted (Supreme Court decision on 28 March 1991, 91-MO-24). The decision is consistent with the spirit of the Constitution and the Code of Criminal Procedure.

(c) Right to a speedy trial: Article 27(3) of the Constitution guarantees the right to a speedy trial. As has been stated in article 9, paragraph 3 of the Covenant in this report (see para. 154 (a)), the Code of Criminal Procedure strictly limits the detention period of the accused and the detention for a trial may not extend for more than six months, even for the trial of the most serious crime.

(d) Right to appear in the trial and right to a defence counsel appointed by the State:

(i) The accused has the right to appear in the trial and state facts favourable to his case. When the accused does not appear on the trial date, the trial cannot be commenced (Code of Criminal Procedure, Arts. 276, 286). However, the trial may be convened without the appearance of the accused in the following exceptional cases (Code of Criminal Procedure, Arts. 277, 306, 330, 365, Special Act for Speedy Proceedings, Art. 23):

a. Where the offence charged is a misdemeanour;

b. Where it is evident that the charged is to be dismissed;

c. Where an accused refuses to make a statement, leaves the court without permission or is ordered by the judge to leave the court for the maintenance of court order;

d. Where the accused does not appear in the court more than twice without a proper reason;

e. Where the accused cannot be located for more than six months. However, in the case that the offence charged is punishable by death or imprisonment or confinement of more than three years, public trials shall not be conducted without the presence of the accused.

(ii) In case a defendant in a criminal trial is unable to secure a defence counsel, the State shall assign a counsel, free of charge, for the defendant as prescribed by law (Constitution, Art. 12(4)). Article 33 of the Code of Criminal Procedure provides that the court shall, ex officio, appoint a counsel in the following cases:

a. Where the accused is a minor;

b. Where the accused is 70 years of age or more;

c. Where the accused is a deaf or a mute;

d. Where the accused is suspected of being mentally unsound;

e. Where the accused is unable to select a counsel because of poverty or any other reason.

(iii) Furthermore, in case the offence charged is punishable by death or imprisonment of more than three years, public trials shall not be conducted without defence counsel. In case a defendant in a military court has no counsel, the court shall appoint a counsel _ex officio_ (Code of Criminal Procedure, Arts. 282, 283, Military Court Act, Art. 62(1)).

(e) Right to examine evidence and witnesses:

(i) Under the Code of Criminal Procedure, the prosecutor, the accused or his defence counsel may apply for the examination of the evidence and the judges shall ask the accused for his opinion in the results of the examination and shall inform the accused of his right to apply for the examination of the evidence (Arts. 293, 294). The prosecutor, the accused or his defence counsel may raise objections regarding the examination of the evidence (Art. 296) and may be present during the examination of witnesses (Art. 163).

(ii) In the case that the judge recognizes that a witness cannot sufficiently testify in the presence of the accused, the accused may be ordered to leave the court (the defence counsel may remain at the court). However, the court shall inform the accused or his defence counsel of the witness' testimony if it contains unexpected and serious statements which are disadvantageous to the accused (Art. 164). Furthermore, Article 310-2 of the Code of Criminal Procedure strictly limits the probative value of hearsay evidence and provides that the accused shall have the right to cross-examine witnesses.

(f) Right to an interpreter: If a person is not versed in the Korean language, he shall be provided with an interpreter (Code of Criminal Procedure, Art. 180, Court Organization Act, Art. 62(2)). If a person required to make a statement is deaf or mute, any interpreter shall be provided and letters, signs or marks not in the Korean language shall be translated (Code of Criminal Procedure, Arts. 181, 182). The State pays for the cost of interpretation including travel and accommodation costs of the interpreter.

(g) Right to be silent and right not to be compelled to testify:

(i) Article 12(2) of the Constitution states that no citizen shall be tortured, or shall be compelled to testify against himself in criminal cases. Further, Article 12(7) provides that in the case that a confession is deemed to have been made against a defendant's will due to torture, violence, intimidation, unduly prolonged arrest or deceit, etc., such a confession shall not be admitted as evidence of guilt, nor shall a defendant be punished by reason of such a confession.

0285

(ii)   In criminal cases, confessions made against the defendant's
will and a disadvantageous confession without supporting
evidence cannot be taken as evidence of guilt (Code of Criminal
Procedure, Arts. 309, 310)).

(iii) Article 289 of the Code of Criminal Procedure provides that the
accused may refuse to answer questions and Article 200(2) of
the Code states that the prosecutor or the police officer shall
notify the suspect in advance he may refuse to answer questions.

Special treatment for juvenile offenders

Paragraph 4

205. The Juvenile Act contains special provisions that promote healthy and
sound upbringing of juveniles.

Juveniles to be protected

206. Protected juveniles are defined as follows (Juvenile Act. Art. 4(1)):

(a)   Juveniles between the ages of 14 and 19 who have committed a crime;

(b)   Juveniles between the ages of 12 and 13 who have committed acts
against the criminal laws and decrees;

(c)   Juveniles between the ages of 12 and 19 who may be prone to commit
acts against the criminal laws and decrees.

Investigation

207. In investigating juvenile cases, medical science, psychology, pedagogy,
sociology and other professional disciplines are used to examine the
character, personal records, family background, and other circumstances of the
juvenile (Juvenile Act, Art. 9). When the Juvenile Department (the Juvenile
Department of the Family Court or the Juvenile Department of a District Court)
or an investigator investigates a juvenile with respect to the facts of the
crime, the Juvenile Department or the investigator shall notify that he may
refuse to make any incriminating statement (Juvenile Act, Art. 10). In its
investigation or trial, the Juvenile Department or the investigator takes into
account diagnosis by psychiatrists, psychologists, social workers, educators
and other experts as well as classification results and opinions by the
Juvenile Classification Office (Juvenile Act, Art. 12).

208. When a criminal case involving a juvenile is related to another ordinary
case, the trial of the juvenile shall be conducted separately from the other
case if such separation does not cause any obstruction to the trial
proceedings of the juvenile case (Juvenile Act, Art. 57). The trial of the
juvenile case shall be conducted in a kind and gentle manner and particular
emphasis should be placed on the evaluation of the juvenile's physical and
mental condition, character, career, family background and other circumstances
(Juvenile Act, Art. 58). The judge and clerk shall be present during the

trial and the investigator, guardian and assistant of the juvenile may attend and state their opinions concerning the case (Juvenile Act, Arts. 23, 25). The trial shall not be made public. However, when deemed appropriate, the judge may permit certain persons to attend the trial (Juvenile Act, Arts. 23 to 25).

Prohibition of reporting

209. Regarding the cases involving protected juveniles and criminal cases under investigation or a trial in accordance with the Juvenile Act, facts or photographs which may identify the juveniles by means of their names, ages, occupations, appearances and other things shall not be published in newspapers or other publications nor shall they be broadcast. In case of violation of this provision, the authors, editors, publishers or broadcasters shall be punished by an imprisonment of less than one year or a fine not exceeding 3,000,000 won (Juvenile Act, Art. 68(1) and (2)).

Right to appeal

Paragraph 5

210. The judicial power is vested in the courts, and the courts are composed of the Supreme Court, which is the highest court of the State, and the other lower courts (Constitution, Art. 101(1) and (2)). In accordance with this provision, the Code of Criminal Procedure contains detailed provisions on the appeal to the High Court and the Supreme Court (Part III), and on the retrial and the extraordinary appeals (Part IV). Through those provisions the right of the accused to appeal or reappeal is fully guaranteed and when evidence which may prove the innocence of the convict is newly discovered after the end of a trial, the convict may request a retrial.

211. The Korean Government has made a reservation on paragraph 5 of article 14 of the Covenant, because Article 110(4) of the Constitution and Article 534 of the Military Court Act, which stipulate that military trials under extraordinary law may not be appealed except in case of death sentences, are not in conformity with the Covenant.

Amnesty and criminal compensation

Paragraph 6

212. With regard to amnesty and criminal compensation, explanations have already been given in the descriptive paragraph of article 9, paragraph 5 of the Covenant (see para. 156). In this connection, no criminal compensation is provided in the case of an amnesty in the Republic of Korea.

Double jeopardy

Paragraph 7

213. Article 13(1) of the Constitution clearly expresses the principle against double jeopardy (ne bis in idem) by providing that no citizen shall be prosecuted for an act which does not constitute a crime at the time the act was committed, nor shall he be placed under double jeopardy. Thus, a case

involving a retrial of the crime for which a final judgement of acquittal has
already been rendered, must be dismissed (Code of Criminal Procedure, Art. 326,
item 1). The principle against double jeopardy also applies to misdemeanour
cases where the accused has already been sentenced to confinement or a fine.

214. However, the principle against double jeopardy cannot be forced upon
another country as considerable differences might exist in legal systems and
laws from one country to another. Article 7 of the Criminal Code provides
that a sentence imposed abroad may be the basis for mitigating or eliminating
the sentence in the Republic of Korea for the same crime. It is for this
reason that the Korean Government has made a reservation on paragraph 7 of
article 14 of the Covenant.

Article 15

Nulla poena sine lege, nullum crimen sine lege

215. Article 13(1) of the Constitution stipulates that no citizen shall be
prosecuted for an act which does not constitute a crime under the law in force
at the time it was committed. The prohibition of ex post facto laws is
guaranteed by the provisions of the Criminal Code. Article 1 of the Criminal
Code reaffirms the principle and further provides that if a law is changed
after the commission of an act and such an act thereby no longer constitutes a
crime under the new law, or the punishment for the act under the new law is
less severe than under the previous law, the new law shall apply and that if a
law is changed after the sentence for a crime has become final and such act
thereby no longer constitutes a crime under the new law, the punishment shall
not be executed. Therefore, the accused are guaranteed the benefits of the
new law.

Retroactive effect of a decision of unconstitutionality

216. Article 47(2) of the Constitution Court Act provides that any law decided
to be unconstitutional shall lose its effect from the decision date and that
the law relating to any penalty shall lose its effect retroactively. Thus,
retroactive effect of a decision of unconstitutionality is acknowledged only
with respect to laws relating to criminal punishment. In accordance with this
provision, a retrial may be requested with respect to a conviction based on
the law which was held unconstitutional (Constitution Court Act, Art. 47(3)).

Article 16

217. Article 10 of the Constitution provides that, "All citizens shall be
assured of human worth and dignity and shall have the right to pursue
happiness and it shall be the duty of the State to confirm and guarantee the
fundamental and inviolable human rights of individuals".

218. Article 37 of the Constitution states, "Freedoms and rights of citizens
shall not be neglected on the grounds that they are not enumerated in the
Constitution and the freedoms and rights of citizens may be restricted by law
only when necessary for national security, the maintenance of law and order or
public welfare. Even when such restriction is imposed, no essential aspect of
the freedom or right shall be violated". These provisions of the Constitution

guarantee that human rights shall be respected in all the laws and regulations. In this connection, Article 3 of the Civil Code provides that "All persons can enjoy rights and assume duties during their lives".

219. All persons, irrespective of their nationality, are entitled to be treated as human beings. Therefore, human worth shall not be denied to criminals, patients of mental disease, embryos and deformed children.

Restrictions of the rights in exceptional cases

220. Article 16 of the Covenant should not be interpreted to prohibit any restrictions on the right of minors, mentally disabled persons and foreigners.

221. Article 43 of the Criminal Code prescribes restrictions on the rights of the persons who are convicted.

(a) A person who is sentenced to death or life imprisonment shall be deprived of the following:

(i)   Qualification to become a public official;

(ii) Right to vote and to be elected under public law;

(iii) Qualification concerning a business under public law, for which necessary conditions have been prescribed by law;

(iv) Qualification to become a director, auditor, manager, inspector or custodian of a juristic person.

(b) Qualifications (i) through (iii) shall be suspended for a person who is sentenced to an imprisonment for a limited term until the sentence is fully served or exempted.

222. (a) Capacity of a minor: The Civil Code prescribes restrictions on the legal capacity of a minor in Article 5 which states, "A minor shall obtain the consent of his/her legal guardian in order to perform any juristic act, except for an act to merely acquire a right or to be relieved of an obligation. Any act performed in violation of this provision is voidable".

(b) Capacity of a person with limited financial capacity: The Family Court must adjudge a person with a severe mental or physical disease or spendthrift who is liable to bring his family to bankruptcy as a person with limited financial capacity (Civil Code, Art. 9). The capacity of a person with a limited capacity shall be that of a minor.

(c) Capacity of an incompetent: The Family Court must adjudge a person with a mental disorder an incompetent. The judicial acts of an incompetent may be voidable (Civil Code, Arts. 12 and 13).

Article 17

223. Article 16 of the Constitution states "All citizens shall be free from intrusion into their place of residence. In the case of search or seizure in a residence, a warrant issued by a judge upon request of a prosecutor shall be presented". The Criminal Code also prohibits arbitrary entry by State agencies into the residence of citizens (Arts. 319-322). Any person who, without a justifiable reason, conceals himself in an uninhabited and unguarded house, shall be punished by Article 1, item 1 of the Minor Offence Punishment Act.

224. The rights to privacy of the citizens shall not be infringed upon (Constitution, Art. 17). A doctor, lawyer or any other person who discloses another person's secrets which have come to his knowledge in the course of practising his profession, shall be punished (Criminal Code, Art. 317, Code of Criminal Procedure, Art. 149, Code of Civil Procedure, Art. 286). The right to privacy, which includes the right to non-disclosure, without good reason, of the past events that may injure the honour and reputation of a person, is protected in Korea.

225. The honour and credibility of an individual are protected as follows:

    (a) A person who defames another by disclosing facts concerning the other person or defames a dead person by publicly alleging false facts shall be punished (Criminal Code, Arts. 307-309).

    (b) A person who injures the credibility of another person shall be punished (Criminal Code, Art. 313).

    (c) A person whose credibility or reputation is damaged may seek compensation for mental distress (Civil Code, Art. 751) and may also request the restoration to the original state (Civil Code, Art. 764).

226. Article 18 of the Constitution provides that the right to privacy of correspondence shall not be infringed upon. Under the Criminal Code, a person, who violates the right to privacy of another person by opening his letter, document or drawing sealed or protected in other ways, shall be punished (Art. 316). The Postal Act and the Korea Telecom Corporation Law also guarantees the secrecy of correspondence in accordance with the spirit of the Constitution. No one who engages or had engaged in the postal services or telecommunication services shall divulge any information obtained in the discharge of his duties. Offenders shall be subject to imprisonment or a fine (Postal Act, Arts. 3, 51, 51-2, Korea Telecom Corporation Law, Arts. 9, 20).

227. The Government is about to operate a nationwide administrative telecommunication network with a view to improving public administration. In this regard, the Enforcement Decree of the Resident Registration Law is being amended so that only a person, his family or representative is allowed to review the person's certificate of Resident Registration or request a copy thereof. At the same time, the Personal Information Protection Act is to be legislated, which will provide an individual with the rights to request information on himself and to seek compensation for the infringement of his rights.

228. The Telecommunication Privacy Act will soon be legislated, which will provide that the censorship of correspondence and wiretapping shall be prohibited "except in limited cases where they are inevitable for the purpose of investigating felonies and where the court grants permission to do so". Evidence acquired from illegal censorship or wiretapping shall not be admitted in a trial.

Article 18

229. The Constitution provides that all citizens shall enjoy freedom of conscience (Art. 19) and freedom of religion (Art. 20). The Constitution does not expressly provide for the freedom of thought. However, it is considered that the conscience stated in Article 19 of the Constitution, covers not only non-metaphysical thought (moral, ethical decision and perception of moral duty) but also metaphysical thought (creed and values). Thus, all the rights stated in article 18 of the Covenant are guaranteed by the Constitution.

230. Freedom of conscience includes the right not to be forced, coerced or interfered with in making conscientious decisions and the right to be silent on what has been decided in one's conscience. The right to be silent does not include the right not to testify on simple facts as a witness in a criminal trial (Code of Criminal Procedure, Art. 161). However, no citizen shall be compelled to testify himself in a criminal case (Constitution, Art. 12(2)) and, in certain cases, refusal to testify as a witness is allowed (Code of Criminal Procedure, Arts. 147-150).

231. The Constitution Court has held that a court's order to the press to make a public apology for damaging the honour and reputation of an individual violates the constitutional rights of conscience and is thus unconstitutional (89-HUNMA-160 of 1 April 1991).

232. Conscientious objection to the military service has been explained in the description of article 8, paragraph 3 of the Covenant (see para. 146).

233. Freedom of religion comprises the following rights:

   (a) Right to manifest one's religious creed;

   (b) Right to hold religious ceremonies, to preach and to worship;

   (c) Right to congregate and to assemble for religious purposes;

   (d) Right to engage in a missionary work;

   (e) Right to render religious education.

Freedom of speech in the course of religious activities is also guaranteed. Hence, religious groups are not discriminated against in their publication and distribution of religious literature (Constitution, Art. 21). In Korea, there are a variety of broadcasting institutions, newspapers and publications run by religious groups.

234. In accordance with Article 37(2) of the Constitution, the right to carry out religious activities may be restricted for the maintenance of public order. This restriction is consistent with paragraph 3 of article 18 of the Covenant.

235. Article 20(2) of the Constitution provides that "No State religion shall be recognized and church and State shall be separated". Therefore, religion is separated from the Government and the State shall not perform any religious education or engage in any religious activities. Article 5(2) of the Education Act provides that the public schools shall not conduct any religious education. The State is prohibited from rendering special economic and financial assistance in favour of a religion and from discriminating against a religion. However, the State may subsidize the costs for the management of cultural properties such as old churches or temples (Cultural Properties Protection Act, Art. 28).

236. Under paragraph 4 of article 18 of the Covenant, the parties undertake to respect the liberty of parents or legal guardians to ensure the religious and moral education of their children in conformity with their own convictions. No law which restricts the above liberty exists in Korea. Article 913 of the Civil Code states that a person with parental authority has the liberty to protect and educate a child. In accordance with this provision, parents or legal guardians are guaranteed the liberty to provide moral and religious education for their children according to their own conviction. In Korea, the religion of a parent is not automatically transferred to his child. In addition, a child who attends a private school established by a religious group is free to choose his own religion. Therefore, everyone is entitled to choose his own religion in accordance with his own conviction.

237. Inmates in the correctional facilities are also free to choose and change their religion. Article 31 of the Penal Administration Act provides that in the case that an inmate requests an admonition based on his religion, the prison authority shall allow it. In accordance with this provision, religious workers of various denominations, have requested membership to the Religious Guidance Committee and perform weekly religious ceremonies, jointly or individually, by denomination, and deliver lectures to those who are in detention.

Article 19

238. The right under paragraph 1 of article 19 of the Covenant is guaranteed under Article 19 of the Constitution which provides for freedom of conscience. Freedom of conscience is an absolute fundamental right which is not subject to any kind of restriction. No law which places restrictions on this right exists in Korea.

239. The rights referred to in paragraph 2 of article 19 of the Covenant are guaranteed under Article 21(1) of the Constitution which provides that all citizens shall enjoy freedom of speech, press, assembly and association and Article 22(1) which provides that all citizens shall enjoy freedom of education and arts. Article 21(2) of the Constitution provides that censorship of speech and the press shall not be recognized.

240. Freedom of expression is the essence of mental freedom and the cornerstone of democracy. However, it is not an absolute fundamental right. Thus, it is subject to restrictions. The duties and responsibilities in the exercise of this right are specified in Article 21(4) of the Constitution, which provides that the exercise of freedom of expression shall not violate the honour or rights of other persons or undermine public morals or social ethics and that, should the exercise of freedom of expression violate the honour or rights of other persons, claims may be made for the damage resulting therefrom. Under the Broadcast Act and the Act Relating to the Registration of Periodicals, correction of the report is available as a remedy for infringements committed by the press, publishing firms or broadcasting companies (Act Relating to the Registration of Periodicals, Arts. 16, 20, Broadcast Act, Arts. 41, 42).

241. The following provisions prohibit the abuse of freedom of expression by the press or the publishing firms:

    (a) Defamation through printed materials (Criminal Code, Art. 309);

    (b) Disclosure of others' occupational secrets (Criminal Code, Art. 317);

    (c) Distribution of obscene pictures, etc. (Criminal Code, Art. 243);

    (d) Incitement of crimes relating to insurrection and foreign aggression (Criminal Code, Arts. 90(2), 101(2), 120(2), National Security Law, Art. 4(1), item 6, 7);

    (e) Intrusion into another's privacy (Civil Code, Art. 751) etc.

Broadcasting companies

242. The purpose of the Broadcast Act is to help the formation of public opinion in a democratic manner, to improve national culture and to contribute to the promotion of public welfare by guaranteeing freedom of press and the public functions of broadcasting companies (Broadcast Act, Art. 1). Under the Act, freedom of broadcast is guaranteed and no person shall regulate or interfere with the making of a programme or the operation of a broadcasting company without complying with the conditions prescribed by law (Art. 3).

243. In Korea, there are three kinds of broadcasting companies, public, private and special. Public broadcasting companies are invested by the State or special public legal corporations but operate independently. Private broadcasting companies are corporations operated by an individual or a company. Special broadcasting companies are operated and subsidized by the State, local governments or religious groups for the limited purposes of education and transportation information, etc.

    The operators of public broadcasting companies must be socially and politically neutral figures. There are two public broadcasting companies in Korea, the Korea Broadcasting System (KBS) and the Munhwa Broadcasting Company (MBC):

0293

(a) The Executive Board of KBS is composed of 12 members who are appointed by the President of the Republic of Korea on the recommendation of the Broadcast Committee. The president of the KBS is appointed by the President of the Republic of Korea on the recommendation of the Executive Board. The Broadcast Committee is composed of nine members of whom the Executive, the National Assembly and the Judiciary recommend three persons each.

(b) The Foundation for the Broadcast Culture (FFBC) is the major stockholder of MBC. FFBC, established under the Foundation for Broadcast Culture Promotion Act, is a special corporation. The Executive Board of FFBC is composed of 10 members of whom the National Assembly and the Broadcast Committee recommend 4 or 6 persons respectively. The FFBC elects the president of MBC. The neutrality of MBC in political and social matters is fully guaranteed.

Restrictions on freedom of expression

244. Since freedom of expression is regarded as the cornerstone of democracy, it is fully guaranteed in the Republic of Korea. However, it is subject to restrictions in limited cases. As provided for in paragraph 3 of article 19 of the Covenant, freedom of expression is subject to restrictions in accordance with the general principle of restrictions on fundamental rights referred to in Article 37(2) of the Constitution. The restrictions on the right by law may be imposed only when necessary for national security, the maintenance of law and order or public welfare and even when such restrictions are imposed, no essential aspect of the right shall be violated. If an emergency order is issued by the President under Article 76 of the Constitution, freedom of speech and press may be restricted. Under martial law (Constitution Art. 77(3)), the martial law commander may take special measures concerning freedom of speech and the press. (Martial Law Act, Art. 9(1)).

National security law and freedom of expression

245. The National Security Law is a special law to cope with the special situation facing the Korean peninsula. The Korean people suffered a horrifying war for three years (1950 to 1953) started by the North Korean attack on the South. Therefore, most South Koreans are fearful of the North's aggression and are prepared to cope with the special situation of the divided nation. Under these circumstances, the Korean Government promulgated the National Security Law and has applied it to check anti-State activities that threaten the security and democratic system of the Republic of Korea.

246. Article 7(1) of the National Security Law provides that any person, who aids an anti-State organization by praising or encouraging the activities of the anti-State organization, shall be punished. Article 7(5) of the Law provides that any person, who produces or distributes documents, drawings or any other materials for the benefit of an anti-State organization, shall be punished. The Constitution Court has held that Article 7(1) and (5) of the National Security Law is not inconsistent with the Constitution because these provisions are applied when the security or safety of the State is in danger

or when the offences undermine the basic order of democracy (2 April 1990, 89-HUNGA-113). In accordance with the spirit of the decision, the Government has done its utmost in interpreting and applying these provisions so that the rights and freedoms of the people are fully protected.

247. On 10 May 1991, the National Assembly passed a series of amendments to the National Security Law in order to reduce the scope of its application. In particular, Article 7(1) and (5) of the Act was amended to eliminate the possibility of infringement of human rights by adding "with the knowledge that it will endanger national security or survivial, or the free and democratic order" to the previous provisions. The amended National Security Law was promulgated on 31 May 1991.

The convicts right to information

248. Under the Korean penal administration system, convicts are guaranteed the right to gather information, which comprises subscribing to newspapers, reading books, writing and receiving letters, meeting their relatives, listening to radio and watching television. Explanations have already been provided in paragraphs 168 to 170.

Right to know

249. With respect to the right to know, the Constitution Court has held: "It is in violation of the right to know of the claimant, and thus unconstitutional, that the provincial governor of Ichon-kun refused the claimant's numerous requests to obtain and review a copy of the Certificate of the Real Estate Registration." (4 September 1989, 88-HUNMA-22).

Article 20

250. The preamble of the Constitution states, "... to contribute to lasting world peace and the common prosperity of mankind ..." and Article 5(1) of the Constitution also provides "the Republic of Korea shall endeavour to maintain international peace and shall renounce all aggressive wars". On account of the absolute character of the above-mentioned provisions, no further legislation is required and the above-mentioned provisions are consistent with article 20, paragraph 1 of the Covenant. Under Article 112 of the Criminal Code, a person who violates an order to stay neutral in a war between foreign countries shall be punished by imprisonment or a fine.

251. As has been previously stated in this report, all citizens shall be equally assured of human worth and dignity without discrimination. In light of this principle, instigation of national, racial or religious hatred towards others is subject to punishment. Under the Criminal Code, a person, who, in conspiracy with a foreign country, instigates or propagates the crime of commencing hostilities or fighting against the Republic of Korea, or who instigates or propagates another person to act as a spy for an enemy country, shall be punished. (Art. 101(2)). A person who wages a private war against a foreign country shall also be punished (Art. 111). The Republic of Korea has acceded to the International Covention on the Elimination of All Forms of Racial Discrimination. The explanations thereof have been provided in article 2 of the Covenant (see para. 44).

Article 21

252. Article 21(1) and (2) of the Constitution provides that "All citizens shall enjoy freedom of assembly and association and licensing of assembly and association shall not be recognized.". Both juristic persons and natural persons are assured of freedom of assembly. It is also guaranteed to foreigners in the Republic of Korea.

253. Freedom of assembly shall not be violated by any of the State agencies. The violation of that freedom by a private person is also strictly prohibited. Article 3(1) of the Act Concerning Assembly and Demonstration provides that no person may disturb a peaceful assembly or demonstration by means of violence, intimidation or any other means and Article 3(3) also provides that the sponsor of an assembly or demonstration may, upon finding that there is a possibility of interference with the peaceful assembly or demonstration, notify the police and request protection.

254. The right of assembly is subject to certain restrictions when it conflicts with legal interests or fundamental rights of others, because the exercise of the right has a great impact on public order. First of all, an assembly or a demonstration should be peaceful and it should be carried out without violating Constitutional order, the rights of others and the morals of society. While the former Act Concerning Assembly and Demonstration prohibited assembly or demonstration which might have caused substantial social instability, the amended Act has narowed the scope of restriction and prohibits an assembly or a demonstration designed to achieve the purpose of a political party dissolved by the decision of the Constitution Court, or an assembly or a demonstration which would apparently cause a direct threat to the public peace due to its violent nature.

Restriction on freedom of assembly

255. Article 21(2) of the Constitution prohibits any requirement of a licence for the exercise of freedom of assembly. However, requiring notification of an assembly or demonstration for administrative purposes does not violate the said provision. In addition, the notification of an assembly or demonstration is considered as inevitable requirement in order to minimize the inconvenience of the general public and protect public facilities and avoid disruption caused by multiple assemblies occurring in one place.

Notification of outdoor assembly or demonstration

256. Any person who intends to sponsor an outdoor assembly or demonstration shall submit a written notice to the chief of the district police station 48 hours prior to the outdoor assembly or demonstration, describing therein its purpose, date, time, place and estimated number of participants, etc. (Act Concerning Assembly and Demonstration, Art. 6(1)):

(a) In case a planned outdoor assembly or demonstration violates the restrictions on time or places, or the notice thereof does not contain the required supplementary information, the chief of police station who has received the notice may notify the sponsor within 48 hours after receipt of the notice that the assembly or demonstration is prohibited (Act Concerning Assembly and Demonstration, Art. 8(1)).

(b) A sponsor of an assembly or a demonstration may, within 72 hours after the receipt of the notice of prohibition, file an objection thereto to the mayor of Seoul City, mayor of a major city or governor of the province who has jurisdiction over the police district that issued the prohibition notice. The mayor or governor shall rule on such objection within 24 hours after receipt of the objection. A petitioner who contests the ruling may file an administrative lawsuit to the High Court which has jurisdiction over the ruling administrative agency (Act Concerning Assembly and Demonstration, Art. 9).

Prohibited time and places for outdoor assembly and demonstration

257. No person may hold an outdoor assembly or demonstration before sunrise or after sunset unless the sponsor has designated a caretaker of the assembly or demonstration to maintain order and has notified the relevant authorities of the assembly or demonstration (Act Concerning Assembly and Demonstration, Art. 10). When it is deemed necessary for regulating the traffic, an assembly or a demonstration, which is to be held on main streets of major cities may be prohibited. Prohibition is not allowed if the sponsor of an assembly or a demonstration has designated a caretaker who will march with the participants to maintain order (Act Concerning Assembly and Demonstration, Art. 12).

258. There shall be no restrictions on assembling relating to academic research and study, arts, sports events, religious services, rituals, fraternization, entertainment, marriages, funerals, ancestral worship, and national celebrations (Act Concerning Assembly and Demonstration, Art. 13).

Prohibition of assembly or demonstration to protect public health

259. A mayor or governor may restrict or prohibit an assembly or demonstration when it is necessary for the prevention of first-class communicable diseases (Communicable Disease Prevention Act, Art. 39(1-2)). The above-mentioned restrictions on assembly are required for public safety, public order and the protection of rights and freedoms of the citizens. Thus, these restrictions are not inconsistent with article 21 of the Covenant.

Article 22

Paragraph 1

260. The Constitution guarantees freedom of association in Article 21 (all citizens shall enjoy freedom of association), Article 8 (political parties) Article 20 (religious groups) Article 22 (academic and art associations) and Article 33 (labour unions).

261. Freedom of association is guaranteed to all persons, i.e. citizens, foreigners and legal corporations.

262. Freedom of association includes freedom to form, participate in and to withdraw from an association.

0297

Restriction on freedom of association

263. Article 21(2) of the Constitution prohibits any requirement of a licence for the exercise of freedom of association. However, freedom of association may be subject to restrictions in accordance with the general principle of restrictions on fundamental rights provided for in Article 37(2) of the Constitution. In the case that the President issues an emergency order (Constitution, Art. 76) or martial law is declared (Martial Law Act, Art. 9(1)), restrictions may be imposed by the emergency order or the special measures taken by the martial law commander.

264. Although freedom of association should be guaranteed to the full extent without any regard to the purpose of associations, illegal associations such as anti-State organizations (National Security Law, Arts. 2, 3, 7(3)) and criminal organizations (Criminal Code, Art. 114) are prohibited.

Labour union of public officials

265. (a) Article 8 of the Labour Union Act guarantees that employees (who live on wages, salaries and/or other income) may freely organize or join labour unions. However, the employers (the owner or the manager of a business or the person who acts for the owner on matters related to the employees) or persons who always act for the benefit of the employer cannot organize or join labour unions (Labour Union Act, Art. 3(1)).

     (b) Article 33(2) of the constitution provides that only those public officials who are designated by law shall have the right to association, collective bargaining and collective action. In accordance with this provision, the Labour Union Act and the Public Officials Law place restrictions on the exercise of labour union-related rights by public officials. Public officials and teachers or professors of public and private schools, colleges and universities are prohibited from organizing or joining labour unions (Public Officials Law, Art. 66, Local Public Officials Law, Art. 58, Private School Act, Art. 55). However, public officials who perform physical labour, such as postmen, labourers in the railroad service and other labourers in the Ministry of Communication, the Office of National Railroads and the National Medical Centre may organize or join labour unions. The main reasons for these restrictions are that public officials have a special duty to serve the entire people, that they are responsible for the management of the State and that their collective actions affect all citizens. Therefore, the Korean Government is of the view that labour rights of public officials should be reviewed in the context of the benefit of all citizens and the development of the State.

     (c) Due to the reasons mentioned in paragraph 265(b), the Korean Government has made a reservation with respect to article 22 of the Covenant.

     (d) In addition, public officials such as members of the armed forces, policemen, prison officers and fire fighters are not entitled to enjoy labour rights. (Members of the Armed Service Rules, Art. 38, Police Officer's Service Rules, Art. 12, Public Officials Law, Art. 66, Public Officials Service Rules, Art. 28).

0298

(e) Article 33(3) of the Constitution also provides that the right to collective action of workers employed by important defence industries may be either restricted or denied under the conditions prescribed by law. These restrictions are imposed in order to protect the interests of the nation against individual interests and thus these limitations are not in violation of paragraph 2 of article 22 of the Covenant.

Privileges of a political party

266. Political parties are vested with various privileges. Under the Constitution, a political party shall be dissolved in accordance with the decision of the Constitution Court only when the purposes or activities of the political party are contrary to the fundamental democratic order (Art. 8(4)). Political parties may be provided with operational funds by the State (Art. 8(3)). In this connection, the Political Funds Act has been legislated in order to contribute to the development of democracy by guaranteeing a sufficient supply of political funds to the parties, and by making the receipt and disbursement of political funds open to public scrutiny (Arts. 4, 5-10, 11, 17-21). These privileges of the political parties are guaranteed in order to protect their inherent political function.

267. The Republic of Korea is not a Member of the International Labour Organisation (ILO). However, the Korean Government has continued to make efforts to join the Organisation and has, since 1982, been participating, as an observer State, in the works of ILO. The Korean Government believes that it will join ILO in the near future.

Dissolution of labour union

268. A labour union shall be dissolved for one of the following reasons only:

(a) Occurrence of an event which dissolves the labour union as set forth in its by-laws;

(b) Extinction due to a merger or a division;

(c) A resolution for dissolution adopted at a general meeting or a council of delegates by the affirmative vote of two thirds or more of the union members or delegates present at the meeting or council where two thirds or more of the entire union members or delegates are present;

(d) In the case where the labour union has no officer and has not carried out any activity for more than two years.

Major reasons for the dissolution of a labour union in Korea are the closure of the company and the resolution of dissolution.

Restriction on labour disputes

269. The provisions of labour laws in most countries, particularly those relating to collective activities are simple in spite of their complicated contents. Therefore, recourse has often been made to opinions of scholars and decisions of the court in order to determine whether or not the activities of a labour union are justified.

0299

270. In the Republic of Korea, where the history of the labour movement is relatively short and decisions by the court on the activities of labour unions are rare, opinions of scholars have usually been referred to in the settlement of conflict arising out of differences in the interpretation of labour laws. However, the settlement of disputes is sometimes impossible because both parties insist on adopting the interpretation favourable to them.

271. Thus, the Korean Government (Ministry of Labour) has published and distributed a booklet entitled "A Guide for Better Understanding of Labour Rights" in January 1990. The book provides detailed explanations on the object and scope of collective bargaining and the restrictions on labour disputes.

272. The Korean Government is making every effort to enhance public awareness of the rights and responsibilities of labour unions and their members.

Ex officio arbitration under the Labour Dispute Adjustment Act

273. If settlement of labour disputes, which are closely related to the national economy and the daily life of citizens, were entrusted entirely to the parties to the disputes, damage and inconveniences could affect not only the parties themselves, but also all citizens, and such labour disputes could also undermine the development of the national economy and threaten public interests.

274. Under the Labour Dispute Adjustment Act, the arbitration of a labour dispute in the public service sector shall be conducted if the labour committee decides to refer a dispute to arbitration ex officio or upon request of an administrative agency. Any act of dispute shall be prohibited for 15 days from the date of referral. Since the purpose of the arbitration is to prevent the abuse of labour rights by the parties in the public service sector, the Labour Dispute Adjustment Act does not violate the provisions relating to labour rights in the Constitution.

275. The applicability of ex officio arbitration has been greatly narrowed due to two amendments to the Act (31 September 1986 and 28 November 1987) which excluded Government invested enterprises, research projects sponsored by the Government, coal mining, industrial fuel business and securities transaction business from the public service sector.

276. On 16 March 1989, a lawsuit requesting the adjudication of the constitutionality of the ex officio arbitration system was brought to the Supreme Court in connection with the strike by subway workers. The Supreme Court decided that the labour dispute acts of the employees in the public service sector are subject to inherent restrictions. Since Article 31 of the Labour Dispute Adjustment Act legislates these inherent restrictions and does not violate the labour rights provided for in the Constitution, it was held to be constitutional (Supreme Court Decision of 15 May 1990, 90-KA-33).

Article 23

Protection of the family

Paragraph 1

277. In order to guarantee a democratic marriage and family system, Article 36(1) of the Constitution provides that marriage and family life shall be entered into and maintained on the basis of individual dignity and equality of the sexes and that the State shall do its utmost to achieve these goals.

278. Since Article 36(1) of the Constitution binds all State agencies without any further legislation, remedies may be obtained under this provision in the case that the State interferes with a person's marriage and family life.

279. Furthermore, the Civil Code was amended so as to abolish the patriarchal family system, to enforce the principle of individual dignity and equality of the sexes guaranteed by the Constitution and to guarantee the welfare of the family (proclaimed on 13 January 1990 and enforced from 1 January 1991).

280. In 1988, the Government planned to establish the "mother-child self-support facilities" to accommodate families headed by a mother who did not achieve economic independence after being discharged from the mother-child health care facilities. According to this plan and after a public discussion held in June 1988, the Mother-Child Welfare Act was legislated in April 1989 in order to support families headed by married or unmarried mothers. The Act became effective in July 1989.

Age requirement for marriage

Paragraph 2

281. Under the Civil Code, any adult may freely enter into a matrimonial engagement (Art. 800) and a man over 18 years of age and woman over 16 years of age may enter into matrimony (Art. 807). A minor shall obtain the consent of his parents in order to enter into matrimony (Art. 808).

Marriage System

Paragraph 3

282. The Korean marriage system guarantees monogamy based on the free will of each party and prohobits concubinage and bigamy. According to Article 815 of the Civil Code, a marriage shall be based on the free will of each party and any marriage without the consent of the parties shall be null and void. In addition, an annulment of a marriage may be sought if the declaration of intention to enter into a marriage was induced by fraud or duress (Civil Code, Art. 816).

0301

Rights of spouses

Paragraph 4

283. At the time of accession to the Covenant, the Republic of Korea made a reservation with respect to paragraph 4 of article 23 of the Covenant, since the Civil Code prescribes the rights and responsibilities of spouses in favour of the husband during marriage and after its dissolution. However, as the discriminatory provisions were revised by the amendments to the Civil Code, which entered into force on 1 January 1991, the reservation was withdrawn on 15 March 1991.

284. The amendments to the Civl Code provide for equal rights and duties of spouses during marriage and after its dissolution:

(a) Rights and duties during marriage

The amendments guarantee the quality of spouses during marriage through the following Articles: Duty to Cooperate (Art. 826), Joint Liability for Obligations with respect to Household Matters (Art. 832), Joint Responsibility for Living Expenses (Art. 833) and Joint Exercise of Parental Authority with respect to a Minor Child (Art. 909).

(b) Rights and duties after the dissolution of marriage

   (i) In the case of divorce, the parties shall determine, by an agreement, all matters concerning their children. If the parties are unable to reach an agreement, the Family Court may, upon request by a party, decide all matters relating to the children (Civil Code, Art. 837).

   (ii) Under the amendments to the Civil Code, parents who do not raise their children may visit, call and write to their children (Civil Code, Art. 837-2).

   (iii) In the case of divorce, a party may seek the division of joint property according to the party's contribution to the joint property (Civil Code, Art. 839-2).

Article 24

Prohibition of discrimination against children

Paragraph 1

285. Article 11(1) of the Constitution prohibits any discrimination against children by providing that no citizen shall be discrimated against in political, economic, social or cultural life on account of sex, religion or social status.

286. The term "child" means a person under 18 years of age under the Child Welfare Act and the Convention on the Rights of the Child. However, a minor under the Civil Code is a person under 20 years of age.

287. The population under 18 years of age was 14,620,000 in 1990 and constitutes 34 per cent of the entire population of Korea. The number of children is declining due to the Government's policy on population and family planning.

(Unit: thousand children)

1980	1990	2000
15 621 (40.7%)	14 620 (34.1%)	12 870 (27.5%)

* The number in the bracket is the population percentage of children in the entire population.

Institutional framework for the protection of children

288. The Korean Government has implemented the following policies for the protection of children:

(a) The Child Welfare Act was enacted in order to guarantee the welfare of children so that they are born safely and are brought up in good health (Art. 1).

(b) Article 18 of the Child Welfare Act provides that no person shall hurt, mistreat or exploit a child or have a child perform or mediate an obscene act. Any person who violates this provision shall be punished (Art. 34).

(c) 5 May has been designated as "Children's Day" a legal holiday, in an effort to enhance the nationwide affection for children (Art. 4).

(d) The Children's Charter of the Republic of Korea was legislated in 1957 (and amended in 1988) and the Charter prescribes the requisites for the welfare of children.

State agencies concerned with the welfare of children

289. The Child Welfare Bureau of the Ministry of Health and Social Affairs and the Family Welfare Bureau of local governments are responsible for implementing the policies on the welfare of children.

Protective measures for children who require protection

290. Articles 2 and 3 of the Child Welfare Act provide that the term "child to be protected" means a child to be protected under this Act if the child is lost, abandoned or separated from his guardian, the guardian is unsuitable for or incapable of bringing up the child, or in other cases prescribed by law. Protective measures under the above provisions are as follows:

0303

(a) In order to prevent the separation of children from their parents, 51 child guidance clinics with 380 professional counsellors were established in the cities, provinces and factory areas. Child guidance clinics accommodate children previously living in poor conditions in welfare centres or aid them through programmes of an adoption or job guidance. Furthermore, 5,400 Child Welfare Committee members are counselling children at each level of towns and villages.

(b) Children, who are separated from their parents on account of divorce or industrial accidents, are adopted, placed in foster care or accommodated in welfare centres, and the State and local governments subsidizes the costs of medical treatment, education, and raising the children (Child Welfare Act, Art. 27). As of 1990, 23,450 children were accommodated at 278 protection centres.

(c) In order to find missing children, there are child finding centres and 182 telephone lines were set up for notification of missing children.

291. The Government subsidizes the expenses needed for a normal life, including medical treatment and education for those children who head a family due to illness, death or other difficulties of their parents. At the end of 1990, the Government was supporting 13,778 such children.

Education of Children

292. In accordance with Article 31(2) of the Constitution, Article 8 of the Education Act provides "all citizens shall have a right to receive six years of primary education and three years of secondary education (para. 1), and citizens who have children under their protection have a duty to educate them in accordance with Paragraph 1 (para. 2), and the State shall enforce compulsory education as provided for in Paragraph 2 and shall take all necessary measures to secure the facilities therefor (para. 3)". In addition, Article 913 of the Civil Code provides that parents or legal guardians must protect, educate and raise their children.

Criminal responsibility

293. Under Article 9 of the Criminal Code, a person under 14 years of age shall not be punished for his act. The age of a criminal is a critical factor in determining punishment (Criminal Code, Art. 51) and if a minor has not committed a felony, "protective disposition" under the Juvenile Act is usually ordered rather than a sentence of penal punishment.

Protection of working children

294. Article 32(5) of the Constitution provides that special protection shall be accorded to working children. In accordance with this provision, the Labour Standards Act and the Child Welfare Act set forth special measures to protect working children:

(a) A person who has not reached 13 years of age shall not be employed (Labour Standards Act, Art. 50).

0304

(b) No minor under 18 years of age shall be authorized to engage in any work which is morally detrimental or harmful to health (Labour Standards Act, Art. 51).

(c) Working hours for minors between 13 and 18 years of age shall not exceed 7 hours a day and 42 hours a week. (In the case of an adult, it shall be 8 hours a day and 44 hours a week) (Labour Standards Act, Art. 55).

(d) No minor under 18 years of age shall be authorized to work between the hours of 22:00 and 6:00 or on holidays (Labour Standards Act, Art. 56).

(e) An employer shall not employ a minor under 18 years of age to work inside a pit (Labour Standards Act, Art. 58).

(f) A person who regularly employs more than 30 minors under 18 years of age shall establish an education facility (Labour Standards Act, Art. 63).

(g) A person shall not have a child under 14 years of age perform acrobatics to entertain an audience and shall not employ a child under 14 years of age in a bar or in other entertainment business (Child Welfare Act, Art. 18, items 3 and 4).

Legal status of illegitimate children

295. Illegitimate children were accorded unfavourable treatment due to the traditions of Korean society where monogamy and legal marriage were respected. However, the Korean Government has tried to eliminate discriminatory treatment toward illegitimate children with respect to their legal status and property rights. The Civil Code does not distinguish an illegitimate child from a legitimate one except in the succession order of the family headship (Arts. 985, 989).

Adoption of a minor

296. In order to adopt a minor, who has neither a parent nor any other lineal ascendants, it was sufficient that the person who wishes to adopt the minor obtain the consent of the minor's guardian under the old Civil Code. However, the amended Civil Code requires the approval of the Family Court with regard to the consent of guardian in order to prohibit the exploitation of the adopted minor (Civil Code, Art. 871). A guardian shall obtain the permission of the Family Court, if he adopts his ward (Civil Code, Art. 872).

Guardian of a minor

297. If there is no person with parental authority over a minor or if a person in parental authority is unable to exercise the right of representation with respect to the juristic acts or the right of management of the property of a minor, a guardian shall be appointed for the minor. The qualification is set forth in Article 937 of the Civil Code. Under the Civil Code, the guardian of a minor shall have the same rights and duties as a person who has parental authority with respect to protection, fostering and education of a minor (Art. 945).

0305

298. In order to participate fully in the efforts of the United Nations to protect children, the Republic of Korea signed the Convention on the Rights of the Child on 25 September 1990 and the Korean Government will ratify it in the near future.

Paragraph 2

299. Article 49 of the Family Registration Act provides that a birth report containing the name, date and place of birth of a new born child shall be filed within one month from the date of birth.

300. For abandoned infants, the chief of district shall determine the child's name and the permanent domicile with the permission of the Court and shall record them in the Family Register (Family Registration Act, Art. 57).

Nationality of a child

Paragraph 3

301. Under Article 2 of the Nationality Act, every child including an illegitimate child, an abandoned child and a child of a person without nationality shall acquire Korean nationality if born in the Republic of Korea.

Article 25

The sovereignty of the Republic of Korea

302. Article 1(2) of the Constitution states that the sovereignty of the Republic of Korea shall reside in the people and all state authority shall emanate from the people.

Right to vote

303. Article 24 of the Constitution provides that all citizens shall have the right to vote under the conditions prescribed by law. The Constitution provides for the right to vote for the President (Art. 67(1)), the members of the National Assembly (Art. 41(1)) and the members of local councils (Art. 118(2)). Article 8 of the Presidential Election Act provides that citizens who are 20 years of age or older shall have the right to vote.

304. The political rights, such as the right to vote, the right to be elected, and the right to hold a public office are accorded only to Korean nationals in accordance with the principle of sovereignty of the Korean people.

Right to hold a public office

305. Article 25 of the Constitution states that all citizens shall have the right to hold a public office under the conditions prescribed by law. The right to hold a public office includes the right to perform public duty as a member of the executive, the legislature, the judiciary and the local governments. In this regard, the right to hold a public office is broader than the right to be elected. However, in order to hold certain public offices, citizens must be qualified for the office as prescribed by law. This practice is in conformity with article 25, subparagraph (c) of the Covenant.

306. The National Assembly Members Election Act (Art. 9) and the Local Council Members Election Act (Art. 9) stipulate that citizens who are 25 years of age or more, shall have the right to be elected. However, a person who has been declared incompetent does not have the right to be elected to the National Assembly or the local council (Arts. 11, 12 of the said Acts). The Presidential Election Act provides that citizens, who are 40 years of age or more, shall be eligible to be elected as the President (Art. 9). However, a person who is declared incompetent shall not have the right to be elected to the Presidency (Arts. 11, 12).

Universal, equal, direct and secret voting

307. With respect to the voting system, the Constitution upholds the principal of universal, equal, direct and secret voting (Art. 41(1), Art. 67(1)). Under the constitutional principle, the election acts stipulate that the vote shall be cast directly or by mail, that there shall be one vote per person and that the name of the voter shall not be indicated on the vote (Presidential Election Act, Art. 94, National Assembly Members Election Act, Art. 100, Local Council Members Election Act, Art. 97). In addition, the secrecy of the ballot shall be guaranteed (Presidential Election Act, Art. 111, National Assembly Members Election Act, Art. 117, Local Council Members Election Act, Art. 114).

Restrictions on political rights

308. Under Article 13(2) of the Constitution, no restriction shall be imposed upon the political rights of any citizens by means of retroactive legislation. The Political Party Act provides that citizens under 20 years of age, public officials, certain teachers and journalists are prohibited from becoming founders or members of a political party (Arts. 6, 17). Under Article 42 of the Political Party Act, when a political party is dissolved by a decision of the Constitution Court, any representative or executive member of the dissolved party shall not establish a political party with the same or similar party platform (or basic policy) as that of the dissolved party.

Article 26

309. All citizens shall be guaranteed human worth and dignity and shall be equal before the law (Constitution, Art. 11(1)). All citizens shall have the right to pursue happiness and it shall be the duty of the State to confirm and guarantee the fundamental and inviolable human rights of individuals (Constitution, Art. 10). In connection with these provisions, Article 31 of the Constitution provides that the citizens shall have the right to receive an education corresponding to their abilities and a compulsory education, which is free of charge. Under Articles 32 and 33 of the Constitution, the right to work is guaranteed.

310. In accordance with the above-mentioned provisions of the Constitution, the Korean Government has been doing its utmost to ensure equal and effective protection of all citizens by improving social security and the social welfare system. In particular, as has been explained in this report in the description of article 2 of the Covenant, the Korean Government has been concentrating its efforts on persons who are in socially weak positions, such as persons with disabilities, children and the aged (see para. 32).

0307

311. The constitutional principle of equality before the law and the principle of equal protection of the law — referred to several times in this report — reflect the general precepts of article 26 of the Covenant.

Article 27

312. In Korea, no person is denied the right to enjoy his own culture, to profess and practice his own religion or to use his own language. However, ethnic, religious, linguistic or cultural minorities do not exist in the Republic of Korea.

0308

	분류번호	보존기간

발 신 전 보

WGV-1619   911116 1220 DQ

번   호 :   종별 :   WUN -3963

수   신 : 주   제네바   대사. 총영사   (사본 : 주 유엔대사)

발   신 : 장 관 (연이)
                  조약

제   목 : 아국 인권보고서 관련 보도

대 : GVW-2274

1. 91.11.16자 한겨레신문 보도에 의하면, 아국의 B규약 보고서에 (이제출한) 대해 국내 재야단체(한교협, 민변, 민가협등)가 동보고서가 국내 인권 상황을 충분히 반영하지 못하고 있다고 하면서 유엔인권위원들에게 반대 보고서를 제출할 것이라고 한바, 대호관련 업무에 참고바람.

2. 이후러 인천이사회의 각국 보고서 심의시 전향과 같이 반대 보고서가 제출되는 경우 심의 과정상 특별한 전과가 있는지등 관련사항 타약 보고바람.

3. 동 기사사본과 아울러 대한변협이 최근 발간한 인권보고서 (90년도 제5집)를 11.18자 파편송부 예정임.

4. 아국의 인권보고서 관련 인권사무국 문서(CCPR/C/68/Add.1)를 3부정도 추가 송부바람. 끝.

(국제기구국장   문동석)

일반문서로 재분류 (1991 .12.31.)

	보 안 통 제	

앙고재	9/ 년 // 월 /6 일	기안자 성명		과 장	심의관	국 장		차 관	장 관	
	연이과	애								

외신과통제

정부인권보고서 관련 한겨레신문 보도

91. 11. 17.
국제기구국

1. 재야인권단체의 인권보고서 입수경위

가. 관련기사내용

○ "정부는 130쪽에 이르는 최초 보고서를 내놓았다."

나. 인권보고서 국회제출

○ 정부의 인권보고서는 국문 130쪽, 영문 148쪽으로 구성되어 있으며 91.9. 정기국회전 국회요청에 따라 국문은 법무부에서, 영문은 외무부에서 국회에 제출함.

○ 따라서 재야인권단체는 국회를 통하여 국문보고서를 입수한 것으로 추측됨. (영문도 입수하였을 것으로 추측)

2. 보고서 전반에 관한 재야단체의 주장 내용

가. 관련기사내용

○ "보고서 내용이 국내인권 현실과는 거리가 먼 추상적 법률의 나열에 불과"

나. 인권보고서 작성 지침

○ 이는 인권보고서 작성 지침을 잘 모르고 하는 주장인 바, 인권보고서는 인권규약내의 각각의 권리와 관련하여 시행되는 사법적, 행정적 또는 기타 조치를 법령 또는 관행에

0310

근거하여 기술토록 되어 있음. 따라서 정부보고서는 우리의
사법적, 행정적 인권보장장치를 상세히 기술함으로써 보고서
작성 취지에 정확히 부합함.

3. 재야단체의 반박보고서 작성방향

가. 관련기사내용

① 국가보안법이나 집시법등 국내법조항 자체가 국내 인권규약에
   어긋난다는 내용

② 법과는 상관없이 행해지는 인권유린 실태 고발

③ 문제법령에 대한 인권위의 주위환기를 통하여 정부에 법률개정
   압력 행사

나. 반박보고서 작성방향의 적합성

○ 상기 ①-③ 모두 재야단체로서 제기 가능한 사항이며, 이에대해
   정부는 인권이사회의 보고서 심의시 질문에 답변할 의무가 있음.

○ 그러나 ②의 경우 법령을 위반한 인권유린이 있다면, 이는 범법
   행위에 해당하므로 재야단체는 우선 국내적인 시정조치를 먼저
   취하여야 할 것임.

4. 인권보고서 심의

가. 관련기사내용

① 반대보고서를 기초로 인권위는 정부대표에게 이에대한 추가설명
   요구 가능

0311

② 경우에 따라서 추가보고서 요구 가능

③ 심의시기는 내년 하반기로 예상

나. 심의절차

    ㅇ 인권위의 우리보고서 심의시 인권이사회 위원들은 보고서의 내용에 대해 정부대표에 질문을 하게되며 동 질문시 재야단체의 보고서 참고가능

    ㅇ 인권이사회는 우리정부대표의 답변이 불충분할때 추가 설명서 제출을 요청할 수 있으나 추가보고서 요구는 가능성 매우 희박

다. 심의시기

    ㅇ 92.3월말로 결정됨. (당초에는 92년 하반기로 예상하였음.)

    ※ 기사에 따르면 민가협은 금년말까지, 한교협·민변쪽은 92.3-4월까지 반대보고서를 낸다고 하는 바, 인권이사회는 민가협보고서만 참고할 수 있을 것으로 예상됨.

5. 기 타

    ㅇ 유엔인권사무국은 우리나라 인권보고서를 유엔문서(91.9.28자)로 배포함. (11.12.접수)

0312

유엔제출 정부 '인권보고서'문제점

재야인권단체들이 최근 정부의 '인권보고서'에 대한 반대보고서를 유엔 인권위원회에 내기로 한 것은 외교적 성과를 바탕으로 "더이상 남한에 정치범은 없다"는 식으로 자신감을 보이는 정부의 주장을 검증하고, 국제인권규약을 활용해 '합법적'으로 국내 인권상황을 선진국 수준으로 개선해보려는 구체적 노력이라는 측면에서 큰 뜻이 있다고 할 수 있다.

이는 물론 직접적으로는 정부가 지난해 국제인권규약에 가입함에 따라 가능하게 된 것이지만 그 이면에는 이제까지와 같은 정부 '도덕성'에 대한

정부 보고서에 대해 재야인권단체들은 일단 국제인권규약 조항과 관련한 국내 법조항들을 상당히 충실히 정리했다는 점은 인정하고 있다.

그러나 그 내용이 국내 인권현실과는 거리가 먼 '추상적 법률의 나열'에만 그쳐 아직도 열악한 인권문제를 호도할 가능성이 크다고 지적한다.

현재 재야인권단체들이 반대보고서에 담으려는 내용은 국가보안법이나 집회 및 시위에 관한 법률 등 국내법 조항 자체가 국제인권규약에 어긋난다는 취지의 내용과, 법과는 상관없이 행해지는 인권유린실태를

권위의 주의를 환기시켜 정부에 대해 법률 개정의 '압력'효과를 얻자는 게 인권단체들의 목적인 셈이다.

재야인권단체들이 제출하는 반대보고서는 원칙적으로 유엔 인권위에 정식접수될 수는 없지만 인권위 전문위원들에게 배포되는 것이 관례화돼 해당국가의 보고서 검토회 때 '참고자료'로 활용된다. 반대보고서를 읽은 인권위 전문위원들은 이 사실을 토대로 정부보고서 검토회 때 정부 대표에게 이에 대한 추가설명을 요구할 수 있으며, 경우에 따라선 추가보고서를 요구할 수도 있다.

추상적 법률나열 일관
열악한 한국현실 호도
재야 '진실'알리려 반대보고서 서둘러

공격 형식의 인권운동만으로는 더이상 국민의 관심을 끌 수 없다는 자체판단도 크게 작용한 것으로 보인다.

한국기독교교회협의회(KNCC) 인권위 신승민 목사는 이와 관련해 "6공 출범 뒤 다소 개선됐던 인권상황이 89년의 공안정국 이후에는 다시 크게 악화되고 있다"면서 "최근에는 국가보안법 등 반민주악법의 개폐가 완전히 무산됐는데도 이에 대한 국민들의 관심은 눈에 띄게 무뎌지고 있는 게 사실"이라고 말했다.

정부는 지난해 국제인권규약에 가입하고 올해 7월 1백30쪽에 이르는, 상당히 방대한 분량의 '최초보고서'를 내놓았다.

고발하는 것이다. 전자의 대표적 예로 인권단체들은 국제인권규약중 B규약 제21조(집회의 권리)에 대해 정부보고서가 설명한 부분을 들고 있다.

정부보고서대로라면 "집회 또는 시위에 관하여 당국의 사전허가를 받게 되는 허가제는 헌법 제21조 제2항에 따라 폐지된다. 다만 행정상의 참고를 위한 신고제는 무방하다"면서 집회신고 절차를 상세히 설명해 마치 집회의 자유가 보장된 것처럼 기술하고 있지만 실상은 집회신고절차의 불합리성 때문에 B규약 제21조가 규정한 "평화로운 집회권리보장"에 위배되는 부분이라는 것이다.

이런 부분들에 대한 국제인

88년 7월에 열린 일본 정부보고서 검토회가 반대보고서의 효력을 과시한 대표적 경우로 손꼽힌다.

당시 일본의 사회당·조총련·자유인권협회 등 14개 비정부기구(NGO)가 대용감방문제, 소수민족문제 등에 관한 반대보고서를 내자 인권위 위원들이 일본정부 대표에게 이 부분에 대한 자세한 설명을 요구해 일본 국내에서도 인권상황에 대해 큰 논란이 벌어지기도 했다. 정부보고서 검토회는 보고서 제출 뒤 보통 1∼2년 사이에 행해지므로 우리나라 보고서에 대한 검토회는 내년 하반기쯤 열릴 것으로 예상되고 있다. 〈박찬수 기자〉

0313

유엔 인권규약 정부 보고서에 반발

재야, 별도 보고서 작성 착수

KNCC인권위·민변·민가협

정부가 지난해 4월 국제인권규약에 가입하면서 그에 따른 의무조항으로 지난 7월 유엔에 제출한 '시민적 및 정치적 권리에 관한 국제규약 제40조에 따른 최초 보고서'(흔히 '인권보고서')에 대해 재야 인권단체들이 국내의 인권상황을 제대로 담아내지 못했다고 주장하며 유엔 인권위원회에 반대보고서를 낼 움직임을 보여 주목된다. 〈관련기사 3면〉

한국기독교교회협의회(한교협) 인권위원회와 민주사회를 위한 변호사 모임(민변)은 최근 반대보고서를 공동작성하기로 하고 작성팀을 구성하는 등 준비작업에 들어갔다. 또 민주화실천가족운동협의회(민가협)도 정부의 인권보고서를 입수해 내용을 검토하고 있으며, 다음주부터 본격적인 반대보고서 작성작업을 벌일 계획이다.

민가협은 반대보고서를 올해 안으로 완성한다는 계획이며, 한교협·민변쪽은 늦어도 내년 3·4월까지 보고서를 낼 방침이다.

재야 인권단체들은 국제인권규약의 정신에 비춰볼 때 정부의 인권보고서에는 △인권규약이 정하고 있는 권리가 헌법 또는 법률에 의해 어떻게 보호되고 있는가 하는 점뿐 아니라 △그 권리들을 누리는 데에 법률, 관행 또는 다른 방법에 의해 어떤 제한이나 한계가 있지는 않은지 여부 △인권규약 조항을 실현하기 위해 구체적으로 어떤 조처가 취해져 왔는가 하는 점 등의 사항이 담겨져야 하는데도 정부보고서는 단지 '추상적인 법률의 나열'에만 그치고 있다고 지적하고 있다.

이에 따라 한교협 인권위와 민변은 반대보고서에서 집시법의 금지통고에 대한 불복절차의 불합리성, 국가보안법의 죄형법정주의 위반 문제, 피고인의 교통

권이 사실상 제한되고 있는 점 등을 집중적으로 다룰 예정이다.

인권위는 이와 별도로 내년 1월 공청회를 열 계획을 세워놓고 있다.

민가협도 반대보고서에서 인권규약 조항들이 국내 법규정과는 달리 실제로 지켜지지 않은 사례들을 제시할 예정이다. 인권규약에 따르면 민간단체들이 유엔에 정식으로 보고서를 제출할 수는 없지만, 관례적으로 정부보고서에 대한 반대보고서를 인권위 전문위원들에게 배포하는 것을 인정해왔다.

이에 대해 법무부 관계자는 "정부보고서는 유엔이 정한 바에 따라 구체적 사실이 아닌 일반적인 인권보호장치를 충실히 담고 있다"면서 "정부의 보고서는 전혀 문제될 게 없다"고 밝혔다.

0314

주 제 네 바 대 표 부

제네(정) 2031-1017   1991. 11. 20.

수신 : 장관

참조 : 국제기구국장

제목 : 아국 인권 보고서 송부

연 :

   연호 아국 인권보고서를 별첨 송부합니다.

첨부 : 상기 보고서 35부.   끝.

주 제 네 바 대 사

0315

관리
번호 91 -122

원 본

외 무 부

종 별 :

번 호 : GVW-2387

일 시 : 91 1120 1900

수 신 : 장관(연이) 사본:주유엔대사중계필

발 신 : 주 제네바 대사

제 목 : 아국 인권 보고서 관련 보도

대: WGV-1619

1. 대호 재야 단체의 보고서 관련, 유엔 인권 사무국 KLEIN 담당관과 면담 (이성주 참사관, 위성락 서기관)한 결과를 아래 보고함.

가. 소위 반대보고서 처리 절차

0 인권 규약 보고서는 정부가 제출하는 것으로서 동 보고서 이외 재야 단체NGO 등이 작성하는 보고서 (이른바 COUNTER REPORT)는 인권 이사회에서 다루어지지 않음.

- 인권 사무국이나 인권 이사회는 여사한 보고서에 대한 처리 권한이나 의무 없음.

0 다만 동 단체들이 스스로 작성한 COUNTER REPORT 를 인권위원에게 개인적으로 제공할수 있으며, 인권위원은 이를 참고, 자신의 판단에 따라 필요시 자신의 의견 형식으로 제기하는 경우도 있음.

나. 소위 반대 보고서가 인권 사무국으로 전달되어올 경우, 사무국의 대응

0 이를 위원 개인에게 가는 우편물에 준하여 처리하는바, 이를 위원들에게 전달함.(실제로 NGO 들이 위원앞으로 가는 여사한 문건을 봉부에 봉하여 사무국에 보내오는 사례가 있으며, 사무국은 이를 해당위원에게 전달하고 있다함.)

다. 향후 협조 관계

0 우리의 인권 보고서 심의시까지 제기될수 있는 상황에 대응함에 있어서 상호 긴밀히 연락하기로 합의함.

2. 아국 인권 보고서 책자 35 부 파편 송부함.(대사 박수길-국장)

예고 91.12.31. 까지

일반문서로 재분류 (1991. 12 31

| 국기국 | 장관 | 차관 | 1차보 | 외정실 | 분석관 | 청와대 | 안기부 | 중계 |

PAGE 1

91.11.21   07:23

외신 2과 통제관 BD

0316

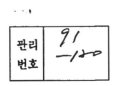

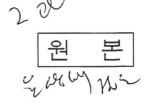

외　무　부

종　별 :

번　호 : GVW-2393 　　　　　　　　　　　일　시 : 91 1121 1500

수　신 : 장관(연이, 법무부)

발　신 : 주 제네바 대사

제　목 : 아국인권 보고서 심의

　　　연: GVW-2274

　　　연호 표제심의에 대비한 준비 관련 유엔인권사무국 KLEIN 규약 담당관과 면담(이성주 참사과, 위성락 서기관)한 결과를 아래 보고함.

　　　1. 대표단 구성

　　　0 사례 1: 국내 인권업무 주무부서의 국장이상급을 수석대표로 하고, 관계부처, 현지공관 관계관을 참여시켜 4-5 인으로 구성

　　　- 폴란드의 경우 법무성의 차관보급이 수석

　　　- 에콰도르는 공공행정성 차관이 수석

　　　0 사례 2: 인권 관련 주무 재외공관의장을 수석대표로 하고 법무성, 내무성등의 관계관 참여

　　　- 호주, 모로코등은 주 제네바 대사가 수석

　　　0 사례 3: 수상실등 관계부처중 총괄적 위치에 있는 부서의 국장급이 수석대표로 관계부처, 현지 공관의 관계관 참여

　　　- 오지리는 수상실 국장이 수석

　　　2. 심의 일정 및 절차

　　　0 아국의 경우 상금 일자는 미정이나, 인권이사회가 92.3.23. 개최되므로 익일인 3.24. 부터 심의케 될 가능성

　　　연호 니제, 알제리의 최초 보고서 이외에도 벨지움, 콜롬비아등 3-4 개국의 정기 보고서가 심의 대상인바, 최초 보고서를 첫주에 심의, 최초 보고서의 경우, 아래 절차에 따라 진행

　　　- 대체로 첫날 오전 10 시 개회

　　　0 해당국 수석대표 및 1 인 의장석(HEAD TABLE)에 착석

국기국	장관	차관	1차보	외정실	분석관	청와대	안기부	법무부

ㅇ 수석대표 서두 발언(15 분가량 제안 설명하는바, 특별히 강조할 사항 및 보고서 제출이후 변화 사항등 언급 가능)

인권위별로 번갈아 질문(실제 의장은 질문하지 않으므로 17 인이 질문)

ㅇ 오후 1 시경 종료(다만 질의가 길어질 경우 오후 3 시부터 심의 속개도 가능)

- 둘째날은 답변 준비를 위해 휴회하며 셋째날 오전 10 시 속개

ㅇ 수석대표 답변

ㅇ 추가 질의 및 답변

ㅇ 인권위원별로 견해 표명(CONCLUDING OBSERVATON 으로서 개선 방안 제시, 총평등 포함 가능)

ㅇ 수석대표 언급(최종소감, 기타 코멘트)

ㅇ 대체로 오후 1 시경 종료(다만 상황에 따라 연장도 가능)

3. 인권위원

ㅇ 현위원 명단 및 의장단은 아국 보고서 심의시까지 불변(동 명단 별첨 FAX편 송부)

4. 질문 내용

ㅇ 최초 보고서의 경우를 정형화된 질문 목록없이(2 차 보고서 심의부터는여사한 리스트가 있음) 인권위원이 보고서 전반을 대상으로 질문(항목별 질문이 아님)

5. 타국, 여사유엔기구 NGO, 기타 인권단체의 참여

ㅇ 누구나 방청은 가능하나(옵서버 제도는 없음) 질문등 심의에 참여는 불가

ㅇ ILO, FAO 등 일부 유엔전문기구는 이사회 결정에 의거, 사실관계 문건(NOTES)를 사무국에 제시할 수 있으며, 사무국은 이를 위원에게 전달

- 동 전문기구는 상기 내용을 해당국에는 불제공

ㅇ 여타 단체들은 위원에게 개인적으로 자료 제공 가능

- AI 등은 동자료를 해당국에도 제공하나, 그리하지 아니하는 단체가 대다수

6. 기타 준비자료

ㅇ 헌법을 위원들에게 배포하며, 사무국에도 약간량을 제출요

ㅇ 기타자료(예컨대 관계 국내법령)는 해당국 판단에 따라 배포하여도 무방

7. 통역

ㅇ 영, 불, 서, 러시아, 아랍어 이외의 언어에 대한 통역이 필요한 경우, 해당국 대표단이 대동 가능

PAGE 2

0318

- 실제 폴란드의 경우 폴란드- 서반어 봉역을 대동한바, 유엔 봉역들은 폴란드 봉역의 서반어를 듣고 봉역하였으며, 폴란드 봉역은 유엔봉역의 서반아어를 듣고 봉역

0 심의가 장기간 계속되므로 봉역 대동시 최소 2 인 가량 필요

첨부: 인권위원 명단

(GVW(F)-0521). 끝

(대사 박수길-국장)

예고:91.12.31. 까지

GVW(항)- 0521   II/가 /5:00

"첨부"

Membership of the Human Rights Committee

1991-1992

Name of Member	Country of Nationality
Mr. Francisco José AGUILAR URBINA (부의장)	Costa Rica
Mr. Nisuke ANDO (라포터)	Japan
Miss Christine CHANET	France
Mr. Vojin DIMITRIJEVIC (부의장)	Yugoslavia
Mr. Omran EL SHAFEI	Egypt
Mr. János FODOR	Hungary
Mr. Kurt HERNDL	Austria
Mrs. Rosalyn HIGGINS	United Kingdom of Great Britain and Northern Ireland
Mr. Rajsoomer LALLAH	Mauritius
Mr. Andreas V. MAVROMMATIS	Cyprus
Mr. Rein Avovich MYULLERSON	Union of Soviet Socialist Republics
Mr. Birame NDIAYE	Senegal
Mr. Fausto POCAR (의장)	Italy
Mr. Julio PRADO VALLEJO	Ecuador
Mr. Waleed SADI	Jordan
Mr. Alejandro SERRANO CALDERA	Nicaragua
Mr. S. Amos WAKO (부의장)	Kenya
Mr. Bertil WENNERGREN	Sweden

3323Q

| ― |

0320

외 무 부

110-760 서울 종로구 세종로 77번지 / (02) 723-8934 / (02) 723-3505

59431

문서번호 연이 20314-

시행일자 1991.11.30.

(경유)

수신 법무부장관

참조

취급		장 관
보존		ん
국 장	전결	
심의관	乙	
과 장	六	
기안	김종훈	협조

제목 아국의 인권규약(B) 최초보고서

　　아국이 91.7월 제출한 인권규약(B) 최초보고서가 유엔문서로 배포되었기에
이를 별첨 송부합니다.

첨부 : 아국 보고서(CCPR/C/68/Add.1) 5부.

0321

주 제 네 바 대 표 부

제네(정) 2031-1083   1991. 12. 19.

수신 : 장관

참조 : 국제기구국장

제목 : 아국 인권 보고서 심의

        연 : GVW-2727

인호 유엔사무총장의 표제관련 공한 사본을 별첨 송부합니다.

첨부 : 상기 공한 사본 1부.   끝.

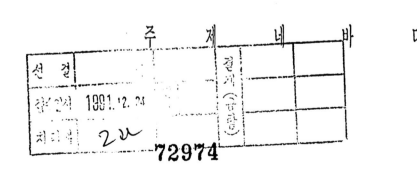

72974   0322

OFFICE DES NATIONS UNIES A GENÈVE

CENTRE POUR LES DROITS DE L'HOMME

Télégrammes : UNATIONS, GENÈVE
Télex : 28 96 96
Téléphone : 34 60 11   31 02 11
RÉF. N°: G/SO 221/922 (3)
(à rappeler dans la réponse)

The Secretary-General of the United Nations presents his compliments to the Minister for Foreign Affairs of the Republic of Korea and has the honour to refer to the initial report of His Excellency's Government, submitted in accordance with article 40, paragraph 1 (a) of the International Covenant on Civil and Political Rights for transmission to the Human Rights Committee.

At its forty-third session, the Committee decided to consider the initial report of the Republic of Korea at its forty-fourth session, which will be held at United Nations Headquarters New York from 23 March to 10 April 1992. Under the timetable for consideration of reports of States parties at the forty-fourth session of the Committee, the initial report of the Republic of Korea (contained in document CCPR/C/68/Add.1) is scheduled for consideration on Tuesday (afternoon) and Thursday, 24 and 26 March 1992.

In this connection, the Secretary-General wishes to indicate that members of the Committee need to have before them, well in advance of the consideration of States reports, copies of the Constitution and other relevant legal documents.

Furthermore, the Committee considers it important that the representatives of the States parties present at the meetings of the Committee when their reports are examined have such status and experience as will permit them to respond to questions asked and comments made by members of the Committee and to give up-to-date information on the situation of human rights in the country concerned.

The Secretary-General would appreciate being informed, as soon as possible, of the name(s) and title(s) of the representative(s) whom the Government of the Republic of Korea wishes to designate for the above-mentioned purpose.

12 December 1991

0323

OFFICE DES NATIONS UNI█ GENÈVE

UNIT █TIONS OFFICE AT GENEVA

CENTRE POUR LES DROITS DE L'HOMME

CENTRE FOR HUMAN RIGHTS

Télégrammes : UNATIONS, GENÈVE
Télex : 28 96 96
Téléphone : 34 60 11   31 02 11
RÉF. N°: G/SO 221/922 (3)
(à rappeler dans la réponse)

Palais des Nations
CH - 1211 GENÈVE 10

COPY

0143

The Secretary-General of the United Nations presents his compliments to the Minister for Foreign Affairs of the Republic of Korea and has the honour to refer to the initial report of His Excellency's Government, submitted in accordance with article 40, paragraph 1 (a) of the International Covenant on Civil and Political Rights for transmission to the Human Rights Committee.

At its forty-third session, the Committee decided to consider the initial report of the Republic of Korea at its forty-fourth session, which will be held at United Nations Headquarters New York from 23 March to 10 April, 1992. Under the timetable for consideration of reports of States parties at the forty-fourth session of the Committee, the initial report of the Republic of Korea (contained in document CCPR/C/68/Add.1) is scheduled for consideration on Tuesday (afternoon) and Thursday, 24 and 26 March 1992.

In this connection, the Secretary-General wishes to indicate that members of the Committee need to have before them, well in advance of the consideration of States reports, copies of the Constitution and other relevant legal documents.

Furthermore, the Committee considers it important that the representatives of the States parties present at the meetings of the Committee when their reports are examined have such status and experience as will permit them to respond to questions asked and comments made by members of the Committee and to give up-to-date information on the situation of human rights in the country concerned.

The Secretary-General would appreciate being informed, as soon as possible, of the name(s) and title(s) of the representative(s) whom the Government of the Republic of Korea wishes to designate for the above-mentioned purpose.

12 December 1991

0324

외 무 부

종 별 :

번 호 : GVW-2727
일 시 : 91 1219 1530

수 신 : 장 관(연이) 사본: 주유엔 대사(직송필)

발 신 : 주 제네바 대사

제 목 : 아국 인권 보고서 심의

1. 당관은 유엔 사무총장이 장관께 보내는 아국인권보고서 심의관련 공한 사본을접수한바, 요지아래 보고함.

가. 심의 일정: 92.3.24(화) 오후 및 3.26(목)

나. 준비사항: 충분한 시간 여유를 두고 헌법 및 기타적절한 법률 관계자료를 인권위원에게 제출

다. 요망사항: 가능한 한 조속히 아국 대표 명단 통보

2. 상기 사본 파편 송부함.

(대사 박수길-국장)

국기국   미주국

국제인권규약(B) 아국 최초보고서 심의

1991.12.20.
국제연합 2과

1. 일시 및 장소

   O 92.3.24-26(3일간), 뉴욕(유엔본부)

   - 제44차 인권이사회(Human Rights Committee) 기간중(92.3.24-4.10)

   - 아국 보고서는 91.11월 유엔문서로 배포

   O 동 인권이사회 기간중 아국, 니제, 알제리의 최초보고서 및 벨지움,
     콜롬비아등 3-4개국의 정기보고서 심의예정

2. 심의절차

   O 보고서 심의는 공개회의로 진행되며, 인권이사회 위원 18명(의장 :
     이태리) 및 당해국 정부대표단이 참가

   - NGO 방청가능

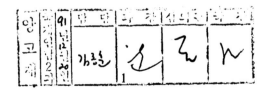

0326

ㅇ 심의일정

　1) 제1일(3.24. 오후)

　　- 수석대표의 제안설명(약 15분)

　　- 위원별 질의

　　　. 보고서 전반을 대상으로 자유로이 질문

　2) 제2일(3.25)

　　- 답변준비를 위해 휴회

　3) 제3일(3.26)

　　- 수석대표 답변

　　- 추가질의 및 답변

　　- 위원별 견해표명(concluding observation)

　　- 수석대표 최종발언

3. 향후 조치사항

가. 대표단 구성

1) 고려사항

○ 수석대표 역할

- 보고서 제안설명 및 최종발언, 위원들의 본질의 및 추가질의에 대한 답변을 주관하므로, 헌법등 법률지식과 인권관계 국제법 및 국내법에 대한 지식이 요구됨.

○ 각국의 수석대표 임명사례

- 뉴욕 개최시

ⅰ) 검찰총장(인도, 파나마, 스리랑카)

ⅱ) 외무부 및 국무부 국장급이상(스웨덴, 영국)

- 제네바 개최시

ⅰ) 주제네바 대사(카나다, 스페인, 모로코, 마다가스칼)

ⅱ) 외무부, 법무부, 내무부 국장급 인사(핀란드, 우크라이나, 수단, 요르단, 이라크)

3

0328

* 법무부 입장(비공식 타진)

    - 부내실정상 인권과장 및 인권과 검사 1명 참석 고려중

2) 대표단 구성(안)

    ㅇ 법무부측이 수석대표로 적절한 인사를 추천할수 없다면 주유엔 또는

       주제네바 대사를 수석대표로 외무부, 법무부 담당관 및 유엔 또는

       제네바대표부 관계관등 5명내외 대표로 구성

      - 사전준비등을 고려, 92.2월초까지 확정 필요

나. 심의관련 준비자료 작성

    ㅇ 위원들의 예상질의 및 답변자료, 수석대표 제안설명문등을 법무부와

       협의, 사전준비

      - 최근 재야단체의 별도 보고서(counter report) 작성 움직임도

        감안

다. 인권이사회 위원 사전접촉

    ㅇ 필요한 경우 3-4명의 인권이사회 위원을 사전접촉, 아국보고서에

       대한 평가 및 미비점 협의   - 끝 -

4

외교문서 비밀해제: 한국 인권문제 6

한국 인권문제 시민적 · 정치적 권리 국제규약 인권보고서 1

초판인쇄 2024년 03월 15일
초판발행 2024년 03월 15일

지은이 한국학술정보(주)
펴낸이 채종준
펴낸곳 한국학술정보(주)
주 소 경기도 파주시 회동길 230(문발동)
전 화 031-908-3181(대표)
팩 스 031-908-3189
홈페이지 http://ebook.kstudy.com
E-mail 출판사업부 publish@kstudy.com
등 록 제일산-115호(2000. 6. 19)

ISBN 979-11-7217-060-8 94340
      979-11-7217-054-7 94340 (set)